SPORTING HEROES
OF THE NORTH

SPORTING HEROES OF THE NORTH: SPORT, RELIGION AND CULTURE

Edited by
Stephen Wagg *and* Dave Russell

northumbria | press

Published by Northumbria Press
Trinity Building, Newcastle upon Tyne NE1 8ST, UK

First published 2010
© Northumbria Press

A catalogue record for this work is available from the British Library.

ISBN: 978 1 904794 29 5

Designed by Northumbria Graphics, Northumbria University
Printed by Short Run Press Ltd, Exeter, UK

Contents

List of Illustrations

Illustrations are reproduced by permission of named organisations and individuals.

Fred Trueman, Raymond Illingworth, Geoffrey Boycott, Joe Brown, Dorothy Hyman, Jane Tomlinson, Brian Statham, Clive Lloyd, Andrew Flintoff, Ellery Hanley, all Getty Images. Alf Tupper, D.C. Thomson & Co, Ltd; Anita Lonsbrough, Rex Features/Daily Mail; Rebecca Adlington, Rex Features/Sipa Press; William Sudell, Lancashire County Library and Information Service; Jackie Milburn, Rex Features/Daily Mail; John Conteh, Rex Features/Daily Mail; Beryl Burton, William Bellhouse and Horace Skinner all Dave Russell.

Introduction

Stephen Wagg *and* Dave Russell

There is an abiding, and a growing, interest in the north of England, and especially in its culture, modes of self-expression and oft-claimed difference from 'the South'. This interest is expressed first of all in the academy, where research centres and archives dedicated to northern culture are beginning to spring up.[1] Similarly, an increasing body of scholarly literature rooted mainly, although by no means exclusively, within the fields of cultural history and historical geography, has emerged, adding significantly both to our knowledge and to the range of debates.[2] However, the issue of the North and its identity also has the capacity to engage powerfully with popular interest. 'The Myth of the North' exhibition at Salford's Lowry Museum in 2007, for example, gained high levels of media interest and attracted and engaged large audiences.[3]

Sport has enjoyed a place within this widening discussion, not least due to the pioneering set of essays contained in Jeff Hill and Jack Williams' edited volume, *Sport and Identity in the North of England*, published in 1996. Both Hill and Williams have contributed to this volume as has Richard Holt, whose essay in their book, 'Heroes of the North: sport and the shaping of regional identity', provided much of the initial stimulus behind this project.[4] Given the centrality of sport to the articulation and construction of territorial identities, however, the sporting North can bear a great deal more analysis than has thus far been the case. This book seeks to demonstrate that fact. Intended to satisfy a broad constituency of readers, it arose out of a successful one-day conference organised by Professor Tony Collins of Leeds Metropolitan University's Institute of Northern Studies and held, appropriately, at Headingley Stadium, Leeds in February 2007. It aims to provide a rounded account of sporting heroism in the North, rather than a string of biographies of famous sports people. Certainly, some of the chapters will be more concerned than others with aspects of the life of iconic sport figures who happen to be northern, rather than with explicit considerations of northern heroism. But the book's central purpose is to place a range of individuals within the contexts of the social classes, communities and gender groups which spawned them and to deal imaginatively and critically with ideas of the social world(s) that historically have constituted 'up North'.

Locating the North

Where exactly, however, is that 'North' to be found? Just how far 'up' must we go? The contributors to this book are ultimately concerned with what might be termed 'cultural regions', imagined spaces, which, while often rooted in objective realities such as landscape, built environment, economy and dialect, are constructed, refined and articulated by a set of discursive relationships between local populations and a whole range of cultural forms. The territorial identities thereby generated are effectively personal and/or collective narratives forged by engagement with, and exposure to, these discourses. For simplicity's sake we are often forced to map cultural regions on to physical or politico-administrative ones, but that is rarely an adequate way of capturing structures that are dynamic, ever shifting and 'as much a state of mind as a place'.[5] Placing the southern boundary of the North has proved especially problematic. It could (perhaps generously) be seen as congruent with the 53rd line of latitude that formed, in the Yorkshire writer Phyllis Bentley's humorous but far from flippant 1930s construction:

> a distinct social boundary within England. North of that flourishes high teas, industrialisation, choral societies and speaking one's mind; south of it comes agriculture, the Oxford accent and the desire to be polite.[6]

Alternatively, it might be drawn along the southern boundaries of Cheshire, Lancashire and Yorkshire, or yet again, it might be placed somewhere further north. While someone born in Cheshire might regard themselves as a northerner, such a claim might excite derision in the north-east of England. This personal element, this relative angle of vision, is crucial. Defining the English North becomes, then, to a substantial degree a matter of individual perspective, decided (if at all) according to family tradition, place of occupation, location of leisure activities and much else. The North has also been defined in innumerable ways according to period, context and subject matter. The latter is especially relevant in a sporting context. Where does the Peak District, beloved of climbers and walkers, sit upon our northern mental map? A similar point might be made about Nottingham. In Victorian and Edwardian cricketing culture, Nottingham and its wider county could be regarded as northern, with its batsman George Parr (1826–91), widely known as 'the Lion of the North'.[7]

In the light of these complexities, no attempt has been made to impose a single, controlling definition of 'the North' upon the authors here.[8] Most have actually chosen subjects associated with Yorkshire or Lancashire, the two counties that tend to dominate writing about the North generally (perhaps unhelpfully so at times) and northern sport more specifically. (Their centrality in this collection in no sense reflects any assumption that they enjoy some form of northern sporting superiority; studies of Geordie rowers and Cumberland hunters and wrestlers would have been welcome.) What readers can expect, then, is a search not so much for a definable North as for the display by various sporting heroes and their fans of the languages, expressions and forms of behaviour that people from many different parts of the nation might acknowledge as 'northern', or associate with something they call 'the North'. This does not remove the definitional problem, however. The next section of this chapter discusses the nature of 'northern' sports and how can this be done without reference to a broadly agreed territory? Purely for the sake of the simplicity and convenience noted above, that section takes the North to be the area contained within the pre-1974 counties of Northumberland, Durham, Westmorland, Cumberland, Yorkshire, Lancashire and Cheshire.

Sports of the North

No matter how the North is defined, it is a highly complex place, cut across by numerous differences of physical geography, economic experience, linguistic expression and cultural habit. On the largest scale, many have posited a basic division between a 'far' and 'near' North.[9] Purely in terms of county-based definition, Durham, Northumberland, Cumberland and Westmorland are the clearest components of the 'far North', tending to share a harsher climate than some of their southern counterparts and obviously experiencing a much more acute sense of distance from the capital. Counties can in some cases serve as specific sub-regions within the wider North as can such configurations as the 'North-East' or 'North-West', although these are often highly problematic and fragile constructions.[10] Yet again there are numerous differences and rivalries between neighbouring towns and cities – sport has had an especially important role in maintaining and shaping these – that can give the North a remarkably fractured appearance.

It is hardly surprising that these many variations have both been reflected in, and have helped to define, patterns of sporting diffusion, development and allegiance. This was especially the case in the late nineteenth and early twentieth centuries, when patterns of sporting preference were still being established. Until the late 1890s, for example, association football was the popular code in the Sheffield and district but was virtually unknown elsewhere in the West Riding where rugby clearly dominated. In Lancashire conversely, the 'dribbling code' had swiftly superseded rugby in the east and centre by this date but had made poor progress elsewhere.[11] Although cricket had strong roots throughout the North, the Victorian county game only emerged in Lancashire and Yorkshire with Durham graduating to the County Championship as recently as 1992. The lower status accorded to the first-class game in the 'far' North has been attributed to both the thinner population base and the less hospitable climate, but this issue would repay greater investigation.[12] Even Rugby League has only really established itself in south-west Lancashire, west Cumbria, 'textile' West Yorkshire and Humberside. Indeed, a 1994 survey showed that 60 per cent of those regularly attending rugby league matches came from 'just four postal districts in the M62 corridor'.[13] Generalisations about 'northern' sporting culture must always be made with care.

One that can be offered is that the English North has few claims as originator of the nation's major sports. Horse racing, athletics, boxing and rowing (early and mid-Victorian Newcastle was a particularly vigorous centre) were very much part of its culture without being in any significant sense distinctive to it.[14] Similarly, many team sports had, if not exclusively southern roots, then certainly strong southern influences; cricket's growth from the later eighteenth century was certainly concentrated most notably in Kent, Hampshire and London. As the recent work of historians including Adrian Harvey and Peter Swain has suggested, the industrial North may have played a larger part in the emergence of football in the second and third quarters of the nineteenth century than had previously been appreciated. The extent of the region's 'popular', often public-house based, football culture of that period is now better understood, as is the role and significance of the Sheffield Football Association (1867), effectively the governing body for clubs playing a kicking game within a considerable area on the eastern side of the North and Midlands until about 1880.[15] Nevertheless, both Association and Rugby Football were codified in London by, respectively, the Football Association in 1863 and the Rugby Football Union in 1871 and these organisations rapidly became the accepted national bodies. Moreover, between 1860 and 1880 both games emerged at many points beyond the North and most leading sides were initially rooted in London and the Home Counties.

This is not to deny that there are sports that, due to origin and/or association, can be seen as essentially 'northern'. Popular versions of northern culture would undoubtedly claim whippet and pigeon racing to fit that category especially well. However, while both have become signifiers *par excellence* of northern working-class male culture – a process worthy of future exploration – neither can be seen as distinctive to the region. Pigeon racing certainly had many adherents in the North but it is far better conceived as a pastime of working-class industrial Britain (and London) rather more generally.[16] As so often, class and region have become too easily elided, with the North's imagined place as 'the land of the working class' obscuring the complexities of actual lived experience. The relationship between northern and class identities will be encountered many times in this book. One sport that undoubtedly does meet the criteria of both origin and association is Rugby League, known until 1922 as Northern Union and originating in battles over 'broken-time' payments to working-class players.[17] An interesting cross-class alliance between the players and many of those members of the industrial and commercial middle classes who generally ran northern clubs and supported payment met fierce opposition from the London-based Rugby Football Union and their northern sympathisers, often drawn from the professional middle classes and wedded to a strict amateur ethos. After several years of conflict over this and other issues, representatives of twenty Yorkshire and Lancashire sides (two others soon followed) established the Northern Rugby Football Union at the George Hotel, Huddersfield on 29 August 1895. From the early 1900s, and particularly 1906 when sides were reduced from 15 to 13 players, Northern Union began to emerge as a separate sporting code. The dramatic growth of association football from the 1890s prevented the game from breaking out of its northern confines, although it has periodically tried to do so. However, as will be seen, in its heartlands it has become a northern signifier of real potency.

A similar case can be argued for crown green bowling. Although existing as far south as Worcestershire, the greater majority of the almost 3,000 clubs affiliated to its governing body are situated between the River Trent and North Yorkshire.[18] Both its major tournaments, the Talbot (begun in 1873) and the Waterloo (1907), originated on the greens of the eponymous Blackpool hotels and it was also in Lancashire that a modestly sized but popular form of professional bowling emerged in 1908 under the auspices of Lancashire Professional Bowling Association, more commonly termed 'The Panel'. Originally rooted in a core territory between Bolton and Chorley, the Panel's reach has expanded 'to take in venues at many points between two west–east lines drawn from Manchester to Warrington and Burnley to Blackpool'.[19] The list of northern sports can be further extended by reference to a number of activities that have tended to be associated with very specific regions within the North. Knur and spell, a game between two individuals involving the striking of a small wooden or porcelain ball (the knur) fired from a trap (the spell) with a stick or mallet, had a strong popular following in South and West Yorkshire and East Lancashire from the early nineteenth century until at least the 1930s.[20] Other sports more or less falling into this category include potshare bowling, the subject of intense interest amongst Northumberland miners at least until the early twentieth century; Cumberland wrestling; hunting (on foot) with beagle packs, a popular activity in the industrial villages of south-west Yorkshire and, as Pete Bramham demonstrates in this volume, fell running.[21] Finally, there are also a number of sports that, while in no way restricted to the North, have been strongly associated with it at certain times. Baseball enjoyed a number of brief moments of popularity in Yorkshire and Lancashire, not least in the 1930s; Manchester and district water polo teams were nationally prominent in the late Victorian and Edwardian periods and numerous male lacrosse teams emerged in and around the same city following the visit of two Canadian touring teams in 1876. Given that the Canadians also visited other British locations 'it is one of the least explicable quirks of the local sporting scene that lacrosse should have become more popular in and around Manchester than in any other part of Britain'.[22]

While a basic mapping of northern sport produces only a small body of objectively 'northern' sports, it is nevertheless the case that the English North has made a highly distinctive contribution to the national sporting culture. Tony Mason has argued that while association football 'as a game was not invented in the North ... football as a spectator sport certainly was' and it is in this role as an engine of commercialisation and professionalisation that the region has made its most characteristic contribution.[23] As sport emerged as a mass, increasingly commercial phenomenon from the mid-nineteenth century and especially in its last quarter, it was above all the urban North that nourished and sustained that process. The histories of association football and cricket, the chosen examples here, certainly demonstrate this extremely clearly, although a similar case might be made for athletics or 'pedestrianism' as it was initially termed.[24] From the later 1870s, particularly in the textile towns of Lancashire where higher than average family incomes combined potently with the relatively widespread availability of the Saturday half-holiday, the willingness of a growing body of spectators to pay at the 'gate' led to the swift development of professional football. By 1888, the professional game was strong enough to demand the establishment of a properly regulated and financially viable competition in order to progress; Lancashire provided no fewer than six of the twelve founder members of the resultant Football League. The seven-county North provided at least 50 per cent of Football League clubs at all times before 1920 and usually 40–45 per cent from that point until the later 1970s when the figure fell to about 35 per cent, where it currently remains. Equally important, northern clubs have also consistently competed successfully at the game's highest levels.[25]

Although cricket's growth across the country was far more uniform, northern and near-northern counties were again heavily involved in its emergence as a commercial spectator sport, with, as noted, the 'border' city of Nottingham an important early centre. In 1838, William Clarke, landlord of the Trentbridge Inn, laid out a cricket ground on adjacent land which was to become a leading cricketing venue and from where, in 1846, Clarke organised the All-England XI whose tours were crucial in helping establish professional cricket in England. Yorkshire, and especially in the 1820s and 1830s, Sheffield, was also a major forcing ground and eventually the place where the professional game reached its apotheosis. As Rob Light's research has shown, it was the sheer strength of Yorkshire's professional cricketing community that led to the county side, founding members of the County Championship in 1873 along with Lancashire and Nottinghamshire, being so strongly infused by professional values and culture.[26] Yorkshire's exceptional playing record, winning twenty-one of the forty-six championships between 1890 and 1939 and another nine titles between 1946 and 1968, owes much to this. Finally, league cricket, a Saturday afternoon variant that involved a degree of professionalism and was designed to fit the work patterns of the industrial working and lower-middle classes, although not peculiar to the North – the first League was founded in Birmingham in 1888 – was most highly developed there, especially in Lancashire and the West Riding, and provided further distinctive flavour to northern sporting geography.[27]

Being northern

One of the most striking features of northern sport and the discourses surrounding it has been its capacity, far greater than that found in any other English region, to articulate the supposed values, aspiration and character of the North and its inhabitants. The extent of professionalism and the wider commercial sporting environment has undoubtedly played a major role in this. It is the professional or semi-professional sports, especially team sports, that have been most heavily implicated in the construction and performance of 'northern-ness'. Critically, the values associated with playing for money – competitiveness, seriousness of purpose, determination and so forth – accord well with a set of wider cultural characteristics long seen as being distinctively northern. These might not be shared exactly across all the territorial sub-cultures within the region – local and sub-regional differences abound – but they would broadly recognised and agreed upon. While it is not possible to trace here the interconnections between the North as imagined in sport and in a fuller setting, this congruence has given particular weight to the myths of northern distinctiveness.

From at least the late nineteenth-century, therefore, but probably from much earlier, its inhabitants (and, in fact, many outsiders) have deemed northern sport to be infused with a particular set of characteristics and values. Indeed, northerners have often been seen as inherently interested in sporting affairs and blessed with particular knowledge or expertise. This has perhaps been most markedly an internal conceit as when a northern magazine claimed in 1903 that there was 'no more devoted sporting city in the north than Sheffield', but external validation has also been plentiful.[28] Similarly, the idea that northern sport is especially competitive has become a modern cliché, but that only underscores the longevity and power of the idea within the region's narratives of identity. The litany of quotations relating to Yorkshire cricket, most notably that usually attributed to Wilfred Rhodes to the effect that 'we doan't play cricket in Yorkshire for foon', are the best known here but similar ideas can be found expressed about many other sports.[29] Closely allied to this is the notion that northern sport placed a premium on physical hardness and bravery, a cultural expression of the economic realities that many faced in their daily occupation. Understandably, Rugby League is arguably the game most closely associated with this particular trope although non-contact sports, including cricket, have been embraced within it. In 1932, for example, during a game (significantly) against Surrey in which Yorkshire fast bowler Bill Bowes was booed by the Surrey crowd for his persistent short-pitched bowling, the *Yorkshire Post* chose to dismiss the cries of 'ruthlessness' uttered in some southern papers and celebrate his determination and stamina. 'Bowes, an heroic figure, bowled 28 overs ... on a day when it was a trial for the man in the street to move about.'[30] Yet again, northern sportsmen have been expected to adhere to the notions of 'ordinariness' and lack of show that are deemed central characteristics.

These apparently distinctive and intrinsically superior approaches to sport were at their most powerful when set against the culture of a helpfully ill-defined South. Historically, southern sport was believed to have been taken less seriously and played with less physical commitment and effort, and to have been too much in the hands of dilettante amateurs and of national bodies anxious to challenge and retard northern sporting ambition and to deny northern sportsmen national representative honours.[31] As sociologist Brian Jackson noted of rugby league and crown green bowling in his 1968 study of northern working-class life, northern sport is invariably at some time set against a southern 'other', albeit one overladen as so often with class tensions.

> There is an awareness of a middle-class or south-country sport which is not quite what they want. Rugby Union or Flat Green bowls is not quite what they want. Both are regarded as snooty (though working men may play bowls in the South and Welsh rugby is known to be different). Both are considered to be less skilled. The northern games ... are very concerned with the spectator ... activities within a strong communal setting.[32]

Sport, heroism and the north of England

We turn now to the notion of sporting heroism. In the thoughtful introduction to their collection of essays on European sport heroes, Richard Holt and J.A. Mangan observe that 'heroes epitomise the qualities their society esteems'.[33] Holt and Mangan quote a number of key writers on the matter of heroism in sport and popular culture and beyond. They cite, for example, both the American professor of literature Michael Oriard's assertion that, in the United States, the athlete hero represents the rags-to-riches openness and democratic ideals of that society[34] and the American academic Wiley Lee Umphlett's argument that 'spectators, in identifying with their sport heroes, are really spectators of themselves'.[35] Sport heroes are also acknowledged sources of collective identity, status and pride, be it in national, supra-national[36] or, as in this paper, regional or local contexts. And, as Marshall Fishwick, a founding father of the study of popular culture, observed, heroes reflect the age: in the eighteenth century they were 'enlightened gentlemen', in the nineteenth self-made men – 'In our own time we are seeing the common man become heroic'.[37]

In his eloquent introduction to a book-form gallery of British sporting heroes Richard Holt suggests a periodisation of British sport heroism: firstly, the early champions – pugilists, jockeys and the like – who were under the patronage of the eighteenth century nobility; then, the public school amateurs of the imperial age; the rise of the modest, often professional 'ordinary man' (Jack Hobbs, Stan Matthews…) in the twentieth century; and finally the sport hero as celebrity. And while the turn-of-the-century gentlemen amateurs such as C.B. Fry and Prince Ranjitsinhji were 'heroes of the classes, not the masses' nevertheless, regardless of the period, sporting heroes, unlike great artists or inventors, are 'more like us'.[38] Holt then reflects on the transition, in recent times, from the third period to the fourth. Here society moves from the pantheon of sporting heroism that encompassed the cricketer Jack Hobbs, whom Holt describes as 'a respectable, kindly and ordinary man' and innumerable 'local civic heroes' – to the postmodern sporting landscape inhabited by figures who, although in media commentary and among admirers they may attract the designation 'hero', can really only be understood as celebrities.

There are several, interrelated reasons for this transition from the third period defined by Holt to the fourth, during which sport culture has moved into an age which Hughson, Inglis and Free call 'post-hero'.[39] For one thing, sport is now primarily understood through the mass media and the media have the simple power to make people famous.[40] This defines celebrities: they are, in the familiar phrase, famous for being famous. Moreover, as one of us has written, acknowledging the work of the sociologist Chris Rojek, 'celebrities do not ascend, spontaneously from among the common people; on the contrary, they are, to a degree, a "cultural fabrication", fashioned by an array of PR, fashion and other impression management professionals'.[41] The now-pervasive media and the phenomenon of the celebrity are fundaments of postmodern culture which, in turn, disdains judgements of morality or cultural value. Sportspeople therefore appear before their public primarily as texts and, as befits an age of consumer sovereignty, the public makes of them what they will. Paul Gascoigne springs to mind here. The son of a hod carrier who grew up on council estates in Gateshead in the north-east of England, Gascoigne was widely seen as the most gifted British footballer of his generation. He has also lived a chaotic existence characterised by extravagant spending, alcoholism, drunken pranks, domestic violence and periodic mental distress – much of it played out, via mass communication, in public view. While its subject might be seen by some as a working-class hero, this reality TV show of a life could never be reduced to a simple, benign word like 'heroism'; Giulianotti and Gerrard refer wittily to the 'mediated meaninglessness' of Gascoigne's persona.[42]

Another important factor here is the ideology of the open society, initially exemplified by the 'American Dream' and increasingly globalised since the Second World War. While Oriard's suggestion that those who go, via sport, from rags to riches may become heroes to those who stay in rags, equally, in a society of ostensibly equal chances, those who 'make it' are often an implicit indictment (and diminution) of those who don't – something brought home recently in a piquant observation to journalist Robert Chalmers by the Hollywood screenwriter Budd Schulberg:

> As a young man, Schulberg tells me, he was once in a limousine, travelling to a Hollywood premiere.

> 'These girls crowded round the car. They kept screaming: "Who are you? Who are you?" I said: "I am nobody." As they backed off, I heard one of them say: "Hear that? He's a nobody. Just like us." '[43]

This means that the relationship between sporting notables and their public will be far more various and volatile than in the era of, say, Brian Statham, Jackie Milburn, Beryl Burton or many of the others described in these pages. Today outstandingly successful players can no longer rely on the unequivocal admiration even of their own constituency: Manchester United's Cristiano Ronaldo, for instance, FIFA World Player of the Year in 2008 and, on the face of it, a northern sporting hero, was described soon afterward in the United fanzine *Red Issue* as a 'preening, perma-tanned, posturing, petulant prick'.[44]

Ronaldo, of course, is Portuguese and resided in the north of England for only six years (2003–9). Most of the sportspeople described in this book were native to the north of England and were close in social status to the people that admired them; indeed, in some cases, as we will see, they were largely indistinguishable from their public. The book explores the relationship between sport and identity in the north of England through an examination of the careers of a number of eminent northern sportspeople. In doing so, it ranges across most of the principal regions which, as we have observed, ordinarily constitute the north of England and across an array of sports – cricket, association football, rugby league, climbing, fell running, boxing, swimming, cycling and speedway – that have been historically embedded in northern culture. Within this, there are essays which discuss regional sporting identity in relation to social class, gender and ethnicity and many of these essays also analyse either the transition from the sporting heroism of Holt's ordinary folk to postmodern sport celebrity or, perhaps, the refusal to make that transition.

The first chapter in the book, by Stephen Wagg, is a detailed historical exploration of 'Yorkshireness' in relation to its principal flagship in British culture – the Yorkshire County Cricket Club. This is a chapter about the complex historical relationship between social class and gender which seeks to explain the 'muck or nettles' philosophy that was for so long associated both with the team and with the wider county. It also raises the question of whether the apparently egalitarian Yorkshire ethic of never getting above oneself militated against the whole idea of heroism. This latter notion is more deeply examined by Peter Bramham in his chapter on the definitively northern sport of fell running. A fell runner himself, he describes a sport culture in which, although certain performers are celebrated for their skill and endurance and are, perhaps honoured by having a specific run named after them, they are not accorded, and do not seek, any elevated status. All the runners are heroes, and none. A similarly egalitarian spirit defined the philosophy of Joe Brown, seen as the best British rock climber of his generation, whose career is described by Carol Osborne in Chapter 3. This chapter has a strong theme of social class. Brown was born in Ardwick, in working-class Manchester, became part of a tendency in the rock climbing fraternity (represented by the working-class Rock and Ice Club) which not only matched the achievements of the gentlemanly Alpine Club, but did so on their own terms. They climbed principally for fun and fellowship. Pursuing the theme of social class, Jeffrey Hill contributes an elegant essay on the legendary Alf Tupper, 'Tough of the Track' – a comic strip hero of the late 1940s. This is a study in how the sporting conflict between ordinary working-class bloke (usually from the North) and the socially advantaged toff (invariably from the South) was played out in popular comic fiction. Tupper was never explicitly located in the North but almost certainly had his greatest resonance there.

Chapter 5, by Dave Russell, is a reminder that, when they were given the opportunity, women too could express these mythic northern qualities of grit and physical toughness and that the opportunities afforded by the strength of popular acceptance of those regional qualities could, in turn, allow for the significant expansion of women's 'traditional' sporting roles. His chapter is a portrait of the extraordinary Beryl Burton, a working-class cyclist from Leeds, who during the 1960s, left all female and some male opposition in her wake. Probably the most accomplished and celebrated British cyclist of all time, Burton never left Yorkshire and, throughout the period of her athletic achievements was doing an ordinary day job. So were Yorkshire Olympians Anita Lonsbrough and Dorothy Hyman, two young women who competed for England in the Olympics of 1960 in Rome. Chapter 6, by Stephen Wagg, discusses the contrasting experiences of Lonsbrough and Hyman and two northern sports women of more recent vintage – the late Jane Tomlinson and Rebecca Adlington, the first English woman to win an Olympic gold medal for swimming since Lonsbrough. This chapter reveals key changes in the sense of community and the civic prevailing in the contemporary North. The culture of this 'North', it is argued, has been shorn of much of its vital structural support – heavy 'smokestack' industries, the pits, stable working-class communities and a more central role for local government – and the place of sports and sports people in the new, postmodern North is greatly changed as a result.

Chapter 7, by Neil Carter, is also essentially about sport celebrity. The chapter describes the career of William Sudell. Sudell was arguably the first football manager of note, largely because he managed the first League football team to be identified as great – his Preston North End team of the 1880s was known as 'The Invincibles'. Although perhaps ultimately a local hero, his assertiveness and willingness to challenge association football's southern-based ruling body made him a potent representative of a confident late-Victorian industrial North. As Richard Holt points out in Chapter 8, the heroic status of Newcastle United and England footballer Jackie Milburn (1924–88) seemed to grow after his retirement. Milburn, who left Newcastle in 1957, became 'Wor Jackie' to the football public of the north-east of England and, in Holt's judgment, 'the most complete example of the professional footballer as a regional hero and symbol of community'. This escalating reverence for Milburn as he grew older may have had something to do with the decline of the communities that spawned him and men like him. Milburn was a hero in, and to, a community trying to preserve the notions of heroism and community; his successors – Paul Gascoigne and Alan Shearer (born in Gosforth, Newcastle in 1970) among them, were celebrities in a social world that was, as we observed, largely post-hero and post-community. The essay by Jack Williams that is Chapter 9 is about Lancashire cricket and traces the idea of hero through three generations. The fast bowler Brian 'George' Statham (1930–2000) was, like Jackie Milburn, a close approximation to Holt's ordinary-bloke-as-hero, while Clive Lloyd, who captained Lancashire between 1981 and 1983, and again in 1986, is an interesting choice. Lloyd was born in Guyana and is a reminder of the longstanding interplay between the local and the global in northern cricket: Lloyd first came to the north west of England to play for Haslingden in 1967. The chapter closes with an analysis of Andrew 'Freddie' Flintoff, whom Jack Williams identifies as a 'flawed' (arguably today all heroes are flawed) hero of Lancashire cricket, even though, because of his 'central contract' with the national team, he rarely plays for them.

Williams having nominated a black Caribbean man as a sporting hero of the north of England is an apt cue for discussion of 'race' and ethnicity as a factor in the history of northern sport. Chapter 10, by Karl Spracklen, examines rugby league, another definitively northern sport and one shrouded in an historically white, masculine mystique. Ellery Hanley, born into a Caribbean family in Leeds in 1961, made his debut for Bradford Northern in 1978 and went on to become one of rugby league's most respected figures. Known as 'The Black Pearl' he three times won the game's 'Man of Steel' award (begun in 1977), was capped thirty-four times for Great Britain and in 2007 was voted British rugby league's greatest ever player. For a long time, however, as Spracklen shows, Hanley's status as working-class hero in this most northern of sports was threatened by the enduring 'whiteness' of a game which only now is beginning to confront the realities of globalisation and a multi-ethnic world. Ellery Hanley belatedly made the transition from hero to celebrity in his mid-forties and spent 2009 competing in ITV's *Dancing on Ice*.

'Race', social class and celebrity are also themes of Chapter 11, in which the Liverpool-born academic John Sugden describes the fluctuating career of *scouse* sporting hero John Conteh, one of Britain's best ever boxers. Sugden suggests, echoing the arguments of historians such as John Belchem,[45] that Liverpool is a special place – a western facing once flourishing port with its own identity, distinct to a great extent from mainstream English 'northern-ness'. Conteh came from the city's African community, the son of a sailor from Sierra Leone, and his skill in the ring, coupled with his quick wit and good looks, gave him what many Liverpudlians were looking for in the 1960s and 1970s – a means of escape from a city whose prosperous life as a port was over. Conteh swapped the hard life of Kirby, a desert of tower blocks on Liverpool's periphery, for the celebrity high life of London's West End – the path of unrestrained consumption trodden concurrently by George Best and subsequently by Paul Gascoigne. Conteh, Best, Gascoigne and others were able, through sporting success, to fulfil the working-class quest for excitement but, as the book's final chapter by Vanessa Toulmin shows, this quest would not necessarily end with drink, drugs or sex (although 'the freedom and excitement of life on the wall' that one female rider refers to was almost certainly intended to hint at reasonable quantities of the latter for those who sought it). The speedway riders, who began to ply their trade in the north of England in the late 1920s, brought the excitement of velocity and danger to the expectant masses of Manchester and Sheffield. Through two case studies of northern riders, Toulmin charts this development and explains how these heroes of the track made an early transition to the Globes and Walls of Death on Britain's fairgrounds.

Part of the pleasure of any research project is in highlighting the scope for further work; future opportunities are certainly plentiful in this context. As this book is undoubtedly focused on the twentieth century, the identification and study of northern sporting heroes from earlier periods would make a valuable contribution to our understanding of sport and regional identity. Again, while not all the individuals studied here can be defined as working class, the essays do concentrate largely on individuals from that social grouping and it is essential that we consider the upper- or middle-class sporting hero and, indeed, what sporting 'heroism' might actually mean when applied to the Yorkshire cricketer Lord Hawke or aristocratic sporting grandees such as Lancashire's Earls of Derby. Crucially, we really do need to know more about sport, heroism and territorial identities in places other than the North. N.A. Phelps's work on Portsmouth Football Club, which suggests that northern 'hardness' is a construct as much of class as of region, might prove a useful *entrée* to a set of comparative studies comparing and contrasting the role and meaning of individual careers across a range of national (and international) locations.[46] Many other possibilities will be raised by the essays in this collection. Editing it has been an enjoyable and educative experience, largely because of the commitment of the contributors and the quality of their work. We thank them warmly.

1   From 2000–2005, for example, the Arts and Humanities Research Council
    funded the Centre for North East England History, rooted in the Universities of
    Durham, Northumbria and Sunderland, while the Institute of Northern Studies
    was founded at Leeds Metropolitan University in 2006.

2   Taking 1990 as a somewhat arbitrary starting point, key works – not all of
    which are exclusively 'northern' – include, P. Joyce, *Visions of the People.
    Industrial England and the Question of Class, 1848–1914* (Cambridge, 1991);
    R. Colls and B. Lancaster (eds), *Geordies: Roots of Regionalism* (Edinburgh,
    1992); H. Jewell, *The North–South Divide. The Origins of Northern
    Consciousness in England*, (Manchester, 1994); J. Hill and J. Williams,
    'Introduction" to their, *Sport and Identity in the North of England* (Keele, 1996);
    E. Royle (ed.), *Issues of Regional Identity* (Manchester, 1998); M. Saler, 'Making
    it new: Visual Modernism and the "Myth of the North" in Interwar England',
    Journal of British Studies 37, 4 (1998), pp. 419–60; N. Kirk (ed.) *Northern
    Identities. Historical Interpretations of 'The North' and 'Northernness'* (Aldershot,
    2000); John Belchem, *Merseypride* (Liverpool, 2000); Dave Russell, *Looking
    North: Northern England and the National Imagination* (Manchester, 2004);
    A. Baker and M. Billinge (eds), *Geographies of England. The North–South
    Divide, Material and Imagined* (Cambridge, 2004); P. Davidson, *The Idea of
    North* (London, 2005); A. Green and A.J. Pollard, *Regional Identities in North-
    East England, 1300–2000* (Woodbridge, Suffolk, 2007); B. Lancaster, D.
    Newton and N. Vall (eds), *An Agenda for Regional History* (Newcastle, 2007).
    Two essential works from a slightly earlier date are G. Turner, *The North
    Country* (London, 1967) and C. Dellheim, 'Imagining England: Victorian views
    of the North', *Northern History*, xxii (1986), pp. 216–30.

3   It may well have contributed to the 50 per cent increase in the Lowry's visitor
    numbers in 2007. services.salford.gov.uk/scripts/.../25-final-minutes-
    17.7.07.doc (accessed 15 January 2009).

4   See also D. Russell, 'Sport and identity: the case of Yorkshire County Cricket
    Club, 1890–1939', *20th Century British History*, 7, 2 (1996), pp. 206–30 and
    Looking North, pp. 236–66; T. Collins, *Rugby's Great Split. Class, Culture and
    the Origins of Rugby League Football* (London, 1998); M. Huggins, 'Sport and
    the construction of identity in north-east England, 1800–1914', in Kirk,
    Northern Identities, pp. 132–62.

5   Hill and Williams, 'Introduction', *Sport and Identity*, p. 6. The 'North' as a
    Standard Government Region has never comprised more than the historic
    counties of Northumberland, Durham, Cumberland, Westmorland and the
    North Riding of Yorkshire.

6   *Yorkshire Post*, 15 May 1935.

7   Melanie Tebbutt, '"In the Midlands but not of them": Derbyshire's Dark Peak –
    an imagined northern landscape', in Kirk, *Northern Identities*, pp. 163–94;
    R. Holt, 'Sporting heroes', in Hill and Williams, *Sport and Identity*, p. 144.

8   Or, it must be said, to a regularised spelling of the 'northern-ness' that many
    find within it.

[9] These terms are certainly London-centric, with the capital the point of reference here. 'Upper' and 'lower' might be more usefully neutral terms.

[10] See the essays in Green and Pollard, *Regional Identities in North-East*; J.K. Walton, 'Imagining regions in comparative perspective: the strange birth of North-West England', in Lancaster *et al, An agenda*, pp. 289–302.

[11] D. Russell, '"Sporadic and curious". The development of rugby and soccer zones in Lancashire and Yorkshire, c.1860–1914', *International Journal of the History of Sport*, 5, 5 (1988), pp. 185–205.

[12] M. Huggins, 'Sport and the construction of identity', p. 135.

[13] S. Kelner, *To Jerusalem and Back* (London, 1996), p. 99.

[14] Huggins 'Sport and the construction of identity', pp. 141–46.

[15] A. Harvey, 'Football in Sheffield and the creation of modern soccer and rugby', *International Journal of the History of Sport*, 18, 4 (2001), pp. 53–87 and *Football. The First 100 Years: The Untold Story* (London, 2005); P. Swain, 'Cultural continuity and football in nineteenth-century Lancashire', *Sport in History*, 28, 4 (2008), pp. 566–82.

[16] Martin Johnes, 'Pigeon racing and working-class culture in Britain, c1870–1950', *Cultural and Social History*, 4, 3 (2007), pp. 361–83.

[17] See T. Collins, *Rugby's Great Split*.

[18] Hugh Hornby, 'Bowling for a living. A century on the Panel', *Manchester Region History Review*, 20, (2009), pp. 91–110. The relative rarity of the game in the North-East where its flat green equivalent prevails, might to seen as indicative of the broad cultural division between 'far and 'near' Norths.

[19] Ibid., p 91.

[20] J. Arlott, ed., *The Oxford Companion to Sports and Games* (Oxford, 1975), pp. 578–81; Alan Tomlinson, 'Shifting patterns of working-class leisure – the case of knur and spell', *Sociology of Sport Journal*, 9, 2, (1992), pp. 192–206.

[21] A. Metcalfe, 'Resistance to change: potshare bowling in the mining communities of East Northumberland, 1800–1914', in Holt, *Sport and the Working Class*, pp. 29–44 and 'Sport and the community: a case study of the mining villages of East Northumberland, 1800–1914', in Hill and Williams, *Sport and Identity*, pp. 221–2, 27–9; See also his *Leisure and Recreation in a Victorian Mining Community* (London, 2006); M. Huggins, 'Cumberland and Westmorland Wrestling c. 1800–2000', *The Sports Historian*, 21, 2 (2001), pp.35–55; 'A Fine Hunting Day: Songs of the Holme Valley Beagles', Leader Records, Lee 4056, accompanying booklet.

[22] Daniel Bloyce, 'John Moores and the "professional" baseball leagues in 1930s England', *Sport in History*, 27, 1 (2007), pp. 64–87; Simon Inglis, *Played in Manchester* (London, 2004), p. 19.

[23] T. Mason, 'Football, sport of the north?', in Hill and Williams, *Sport and Identity*, p. 45.

[24] For example, Huggins, 'Sport and the construction of identity', p. 145; D. Russell, 'Sporting Manchester, from c1800 to the present: an introduction', *Manchester Region History Review*, 20, (2009), p. 4.

25 Russell, *Looking North*, p. 237.

26 Robert F. Light, 'Cricket's Forgotten Past: A Social and Cultural History of the Game in the West Riding of Yorkshire 1820–1870', unpublished Ph.D. thesis De Montfort University, 2008; Russell, 'Sport and Identity'.

27 J. Hill, 'League cricket in the North and Midlands', in R. Holt (ed.), *Sport and the Working Class in Modern Britain* (Manchester, 1990); R. Light, 'The other face of cricket', unpublished MA thesis, De Montfort University, 2002.

28 *County Monthly*, April 1903, p. 212.

29 Quoted in Holt, 'Heroes', p. 147. The dialect does not entirely convince.

30 *Yorkshire Post*, 22 August 1932.

31 Russell, *Looking North*, pp. 240–59.

32 Brian Jackson, *Working Class Community* (Harmondsworth, 1972, ed.), p. 116.

33 Richard Holt and J.A. Mangan 'Prologue: heroes of a European past', in Richard Holt, J.A. Mangan and Pierre Lanfranchi (eds) *European Heroes: Myth, Identity, Sport* (London, 1996), p. 2.

34 Michael Oriard, *Dreaming of Heroes: American Sports Fiction 1868–1980* (Chicago, 1982), p.26, quoted in Holt and Mangan 'Prologue', p.3.

35 Wiley Lee Umphlett *The Sporting Myth and the American Experience* (London, 1975), p.170, quoted in Holt and Mangan 'Prologue', p. 2.

36 Holt and Mangan 'Prologue', p. 3.

37 Marshall W. Fishwick, *American Heroes: Myth and Reality* (Westport, 1954), p.225, quoted in Holt and Mangan 'Prologue', pp. 4–5.

38 Richard Holt 'Champions, heroes and celebrities: sporting greatness and the British public', in *The Book of British Sporting Heroes* (London, National Portrait Gallery Publications, 1998), pp. 13, 18.

39 John Hughson, David Inglis and Marcus Free, *The Uses of Sport: A Critical Study* (London, 2005), p.108.

40 Daniel Boorstin, *The Image* (Harmondsworth, 1963), p. 55

41 Stephen Wagg 'Angels of us all? Football management, globalization and the politics of celebrity', *Soccer and Society*, 8, 4 (2007), p. 443. See also Chris Rojek, Celebrity (London, 2001), p.10.

42 Quoted in Hughson, Inglis and Free, *The Uses of Sport*, p.109.

43 Robert Chalmers, 'Marlon and me: Budd Schulberg tells his amazing life story', *Independent on Sunday*, 'The New Review', 15 February 2009, p.10.

44 Andy Mitten '"Better than Best" but memories fade', *Independent on Sunday*, Sport Section, 14 June 2009, p.15.

45 John Belchem, *Merseypride: Essays in Liverpool Exceptionalism* (Liverpool, 2006, Second Edition).

46 N. A. Phelps, 'The southern football hero and the shaping of regional and local identity in the south of England', *Soccer and Society*, 2, 3 (2001), pp. 44–57.

CHAPTER 1

Muck or Nettles: Men, Masculinity and Myth in Yorkshire Cricket[1]

Stephen Wagg

Yorkshire is an idea, not a place.

Roy Hattersley, *Goodbye to Yorkshire*[2]

He plays the part of the blunt-spoken Yorkshireman rather well … he is rugged, energetic, versatile and in a way professional; that is, everything that comes his way will be material.

Raymond Chandler, after meeting J.B. Priestley in 1951[3]

The mystique that has surrounded the county of Yorkshire has had no parallel in English culture. For no other shire has it been so relentlessly claimed that people born within its boundaries were people of a certain stamp. Wiltshire people, Suffolk people, Middlesex people, are, on the whole, not held to be intrinsically this or that. Even in the context of popular ideas about 'up North', the people of this fabled county somehow stand apart. It's said they are blunt, fractious and unsentimental. They are competitive, commercially acute – seeking immediately to accumulate brass whenever muck has been found – and dislike anything fancy. They have craggy surnames like Ackroyd and Earnshaw and the names of the mill and moorland towns that they inhabit are similarly evocative. From time to time in the late twentieth century writers have had affectionate fun with these myths: 'The very name of Stradhoughton', a local columnist in Keith Waterhouse's novel *Billy Liar* observes, 'conjures up sturdy buildings of honest native stone, gleaming cobbled streets and that brackish air…'[4] However, like all myths, they carry enough credibility to make them viable when measured against human experience. They are also, in large part, myths of men and

1

it's hard to think of a social world in which these male myths have received a greater currency than the world of Yorkshire cricket. This chapter examines these myths of the Yorkshire cricketer and looks, in particular, at how these myths have been played out in the fifty and more years that followed the Second World War. It tries, therefore, to understand a succession of Yorkshire cricket heroes – Len Hutton, Brian Close, Fred Trueman, Raymond Illingworth, Geoffrey Boycott and others – *as men* and as the embodiment of regional myths of adult maleness. But it considers the 'Yorkie' masculinity expressed by these leading cricketers in relation to time, place and social class. As the Australian academic Bob Connell has argued, 'to understand gender … we must constantly go beyond gender …'[5] and so often, when one examines one or other of the acrimonious male confrontations that have informed the history of the Yorkshire County Cricket Club, one finds oneself talking not of masculinity, but of *class*.

The Yorkshire man

The history of English popular culture is littered with images of the Yorkshire man. There was, of course, Emily Brontë's untamed Heathcliff, whom readers first encountered in 1847. Popular fiction in the last fifty years has steadily mined the rich seam of brooding Yorkshire maleness. In the 1960s and 1970s there were the novels of David Storey and Stan Barstow. During the same period there was a regular diet of TV drama on the 'trouble at mill' theme and this genre was eventually parodied in Granada's situation comedy *Brass* (1983-4). In recent times the most popular and visible version of the Yorkshire male stereotype has probably been provided by the vet novels of James Herriot and by their television adaptations. Time and again, Herriot arrives at a remote farm in the Yorkshire dales, ready to deliver a calf or attend to a sick sheep dog, and finds himself dealing with an emotionally stunted male farmer in a cloth cap, who offers mostly grunts for conversation. Similarly, many people still recall Harvey Smith, the no-nonsense Yorkshire show jumper who, from the saddle, celebrated winning the Showjumping Derby of 1971 with a defiant V sign, and was disqualified. Michael Parkinson's column in *The Sunday Times* during the 1970s featured a whole gallery of grizzling, muck-or-nettles Yorkshire sportsmen. And so on.

By contrast, little, save for the occasional monologue by Alan Bennett, has been said about Yorkshire females. Still less has been said *by* women about the cult of the Yorkshire male and, in this regard, a book published in 1986 by the feminist writer Nicole Ward Jouve is extraordinary. The book is about the 'Yorkshire Ripper' murders carried out in the county between 1975 and 1981 and its title, *The Streetcleaner*, derives from the killer's own perception of his behaviour. Jouve related the killings to the culture of masculinity in which the killer, Peter Sutcliffe, had grown up – a male code in which, to quote Sutcliffe's brother and his mates, women are strictly 'for frying bacon and for screwing'.[6] In this world, there is an assumed fear of the feminine: accounts of the Ripper's life, notes Jouve, show him perceived by his father and brothers as unmanly and striving to counter such perceptions with ever more aggressive, masculine gestures – body-building, motor bikes, casual disparagement of women, and so on. In his progressively more gruesome behaviour, Sutcliffe, Jouve suggests, sought to obliterate the feminine in himself. Yorkshire men of legend are 'hard'. Extending Jouve's argument, what counted as 'soft' in the prevailing masculine ideology of post-war Yorkshire society was bound to vary, but was likely to include expressions of emotion and/or undue concern for others, such as ethnic minorities or even workmates. But these notions of male behaviour appropriate to the region were well entrenched, both in Yorkshire cricket culture and the wider life of the county well before the Second World War, as I will try to show in the following section.

Yorkshire cricket and the politics of ee-bah-gummery

The special configuration of class and masculinity in the county's cricket culture is rooted in important cultural developments during the nineteenth century. One such development was the emergence, from the mid-1800s, of regional identities in the north of England. Common to all of these identities was an anti-metropolitan animus, wherein the privileged people of London and the South were seen as living off the honest toil of their unacknowledged northern compatriots. 'The stress on the workers' contribution to regional and national advance is strong', writes Patrick Joyce. 'But it is balanced by the inclusion of those outside the ranks of workers who also make industrial Britain great. They too may suffer the condescension of the South'.[7] Indeed, entrepreneurs in the North could more easily be assimilated to this northern chauvinism because often they had much in common, culturally, with the common people. The writer Derrick Boothroyd, for example, remarks, perhaps fancifully, that many mill owners in the town of Batley, made rich by military contracts in the Crimean and Franco-Prussian wars, far from becoming 'posh' remained unable to read or write and signed their cheques with a cross.[8] In Yorkshire these notions helped to fashion the discourse of 'the Tyke', which was popularised by the regional press and which appeared, as Dave Russell has shown, to dissolve class differences into local singularity.[9]

From the late nineteenth century, metropolitan culture grew in importance, inspiring heightened resentment in the still prosperous North. Moreover, in the 1920s and 30s when depression began to afflict the heavy industries of the North, counties such as Yorkshire began to experience a decline in population figures.[10] During this period, roughly 1890 to 1939, Yorkshire County Cricket Club (founded in 1863) was 'arguably the major vehicle for the construction and negotiation of key elements of the county's identity'.[11] During this time, the Yorkshire team, unlike most other county sides, was composed largely of professional cricketers and was captained on

3

many occasions by the eleven's solitary amateur. (No professional captained the side between 1883 and 1959.) For much of this time Yorkshire cricket was dominated by Lord Hawke, a paternalist and autocrat who typified the popular submergence of class relationships in the language of the 'Tyke'. Although he called for an end to the practice of making the county's professional cricketers enter the field of play by a separate gate (disbanded in 1902) and was prepared to grant the occasional financial concession to the professionals at the club, Hawke nevertheless devoutly upheld the amateur–professional distinction. He once famously declared that he hoped never to see the day when a professional captained England. Yorkshire cricket culture, then, had real class relationships that were, if anything, more rigid than those prevailing in the much despised southern counties. This contradiction seems to have been contained within popular local expressions of masculinity – of what it meant to be a man, playing for Yorkshire. Yorkshire cricketers of this era might grumble from time to time, but they accepted orders and reserved their spleen for the 'softies' of the South, all of whom were presumed to have been born with the inevitable silver spoon in their mouths. Not to have accepted their lot would have been a breach of Yorkshire manhood as it was conventionally perceived. For example, the story is often told of Edmund Peate, a Yorkshire cricketer sacked by Hawke for drunkenness in 1887; Peate, Hawke reflected, 'bore no grudge'. Ten years later Yorkshire pro' Bobby Peel was dismissed in similar circumstances. Moreover, and more importantly, every Yorkshire professional knew that the county would discard him as soon as his usefulness was over. Many ended up back on the shop floor where they had begun; one such was England international Percy Holmes, who, finished by the county when he developed a bad knee in 1933, worked in a mill in old age.[12] Before the Second World War, Yorkshire didn't offer contracts and there was no guarantee of regular money until a player received his county cap.[13]

Hostility which might otherwise be directed at their employer tended among Yorkshire players to be suppressed, perhaps manifesting itself in a dourness that was inevitably rendered as typically 'Yorkshire'. Chroniclers of the life of the county club delighted in stories of the grudging, muck-or-nettles demeanour of Yorkshire professionals. Arthur Mitchell, for example, a Yorkshire batsman between 1922 and 1939, and later the club's coach, is said never to have uttered a word of praise.[14] Similarly, in a match against Nottinghamshire in 1932, George Macaulay refused to assist fellow Yorkshire bowler Hedley Verity, who had taken nine wickets, in taking the remaining one: 'If he's good enough to get nine,' team mates remember Macaulay saying, 'let him earn the tenth. I shall get it if I can.'[15] As Russell points out, leading cricket writers such as Neville Cardus assimilated these incidents and personalities to ongoing myths of the county and its people.[16]

Of course, much Yorkshire cricket culture didn't fit the convention and this led to open confusion in the literature of cricketing Yorkshireness. For example, within a few pages Derrick Boothroyd, a leading writer on the subject, implies, first of all, that people who didn't conform to the popular stereotype were simply exceptions. Edgar Oldroyd, for instance, was styled as 'a more typical Yorkshireman' than either Percy Holmes or one of the county's most famous cricketing sons, Herbert Sutcliffe. Holmes, it's said, was 'too cheerful' and Sutcliffe too 'lah di dah'.[17] Later, though, the same writer identifies Oldroyd as but *one* type of Yorkshireman:

> If Edgar Oldroyd typified the cautious, shrewd, calculating, lugubrious, money-conscious Yorkshireman mercilessly caricatured by southerners, Maurice Leyland represented the warm, genial, magnanimous, happy-go-lucky type of Yorkshireman who is just as typical of the county although less eagerly publicised.[18]

Beyond a certain point, this insistence on fixed breed(s) of Yorkshire male are absurd and the diversity of masculinities in the Yorkshire dressing room can be explained in other ways. Sutcliffe, in particular, points up the contradictions in the notion of an egalitarian Yorkshireness better than any pre-war player. Although he was a Yorkshire patriot, who wrote of his 'jealous love' of the county, Sutcliffe is nevertheless described by his biographer as a man whose 'cultivated manner was motivated by a wish to make himself socially acceptable'.[19] He might even rebuke his wife for 'lapsing' into a Yorkshire accent.[20] Sutcliffe, a former checkweighman at a Yorkshire colliery, set up a sports outfitters' business in Leeds in 1924. By the mid-1930s he was driving a limousine. He had bought a mill owner's house outside Pudsey, put his children in private schools and acquired a clipped accent 'redolent of a country gentleman'.[21] Sutcliffe, then, perfectly evokes the manifest denial, but tacit acceptance, of social class in the constructed Yorkshireness of the pre-war county cricket club. His gentrified masculinity drew smiles and resentment by turns among the other pro's but his subaltern mentality was not unique there. Len Hutton, who came into the Yorkshire side in 1934, was socially ambitious and Hedley Verity (1930-9), another Yorkshire patriot, was commissioned as a captain in the British Army at the outbreak of the Second World War. Verity's quiet demeanour met all the cultural expectations of the pre-war Yorkshire dressing room. To the aspirants he had gentlemanly decorum; to the others he was phlegmatic, as men of the county should be. Bill Bowes wrote: 'Verity never altered his expression or his attitude to life and cricket, from the first ball he bowled to the last'.[22] 'I missed people like Hedley after war,' said Hutton later.

This, then, was the (wholly expectable) range of masculinities among the professional cricketers of Yorkshire at the end of the 1930s. The socially aspiring, petit bourgeois (Sutcliffe, Hutton, Verity) rubbed shoulders with the workers, be they cheerily deferential (Leyland, Holmes) or stern and grudging (Mitchell, Macaulay). These personalities were not, in all probability, much different from the clutch of male psyches to be found in any other county dressing room but they were, as they remain, steeped in regional mythology. In the period after the Second World War this mythology began to assume the status of a northern and in time a national, melodrama.

You can go, and any bugger else: class, manhood and modernity in Yorkshire cricket

During the post-war period the class relationships that had previously prevailed in the Yorkshire County Cricket Club steadily became unviable. However, because notions of gender and place loomed so large in the discourse of the club, this unviability was seldom recognised. Yorkshire cricket controversies, which were frequent, were therefore rendered and played out as clashes of personality and as issues of manhood and local character.

In the years immediately following the Second World War the Yorkshire eleven was captained by Brian Sellers. Sellers, an amateur like all Yorkshire captains of the twentieth century hitherto and an old boy of St Peters School York, had led the side since 1933. Sellers is portrayed in all the (considerable) post-1945 literature about the club as a 'disciplinarian'. For England bowler Bill Bowes, for example, he was at times 'a martinet' who nevertheless 'did a grand job'.[24] He seems to have possessed the sternness of Hawke, while lacking Hawke's paternalism. Yorkshire players under Sellers did as they were told. Although there were other 'Captain Blighs' around the county circuit in the 1940s, Sellers, while provoking the inevitable disgruntlement, was generally rendered as culturally specific: a no-nonsense, muck-or-nettles, dyed-in-the-wool Yorkshireman.

On Sellers' retirement in 1947 the captaincy passed to Norman Yardley. Yardley was another former pupil of St Peters, York. While he expressed himself, like most of his Yorkshire compatriots, as proud to have been born in the county, his social world was some way removed from that of the gruff, working class pro's he would be leading. At Cambridge University in the 1930s he had played the elite games of hockey and squash and stayed on an extra year in order to captain the university at cricket. Photographs taken of him at the time he assumed the captaincy give him the aura of a fighter pilot in the Battle of Britain. As he himself notes in an early autobiography, the position of the club had changed materially by the time he took over: they had fallen to eighth position in the championship.[25] Just as all relevant literature depicts Sellers as a firm-but-fair disciplinarian, all the writing on this period agrees that Yardley was 'too nice'. Accounts of life in the Yorkshire dressing room during the 1950s describe season after season of recurrent strife. One talks of 'a terrifying machismo [which] gripped the Yorkshire dressing room like a pestilent plant in the turbulent 1950s'.[26] Certainly, Hutton, the county's best and most prestigious player, was less at home there than during the 1930s.[27]

The implication of this seems clear. Yardley was credible as a cricketer – a growing issue in the post-war years – but he wasn't credible as a Yorkshire authority figure.[28] The pattern for dealing with Yorkshire pro's had been established during the first half of the century by Hawke and Sellers. The players, ordinarily, would be treated with some severity; they would, at some level, resent this but their anger would be turned inward. Peremptoriness met grumbling deference and both were rendered as 'typically Yorkshire'. Open defiance was met with sanction. Percy Holmes, for instance, once recalled an altercation with Hawke: "'E said to me one day, "Olmes." And I said, "Yes, 'Awke. Wot?" And that's why I nivver went to Australia [with the England team]'.[29] Men used to such visible and punitive policing were likely to become more fractious once it was removed. While some players were happy enough under Yardley's regime – 'We were Yorkshiremen, that was enough,' said off spinner Bob Appleyard. 'We had learned our cricket the hard way in the leagues' – others felt the absence of a necessary toughness.[30] But there were clearly other factors than this in the apparent unravelling of the team's authority relations.

For one thing, Yorkshire's domination of county cricket ceased in the 1950s. It was an axiom of Yorkshire cricket culture that cricket in the South was played by 'fancy caps' and privileged amateurs, ignorant of life's hardships. The Yorkshire players had often feuded with Middlesex between the wars, for example.[31] Now Surrey became the team of the 1950s. They won the county championship every year from 1952 to 1958, with a solitary win for Yorkshire to close the decade. As in the 1920s, for many observers, viewing English cricket outside the refractions of regional prejudice, it was the southern side, privileged or not, who played the more efficient, professional 'muck-or-nettles' cricket. Predictably, though, the imagined Yorkshire, perpetual victim of southern shenanigans, was invoked in the face of this new threat. When Yorkshire played Surrey during the 1950s, slow bowler Johnny Wardle would summon team mates to watch Tony Lock, his rival for an England place, whom he believed to have an illegal action. 'Come on, lads,' he'd call. 'Just watch that bastard throwing it out there.'[32] Similarly Sellers, now on the club's committee, responded to the crisis with Yorkshire hubris. When Wardle became the fourth England player to be dismissed by Yorkshire within 12 months over 1957-8 Sellers stated that to be good enough to play for England was not necessarily to be good enough to play for Yorkshire.[33]

Yardley retired in 1955 and was succeeded by Billy Sutcliffe, son of Herbert. As with Yardley, Sutcliffe is described in the annals of Yorkshire cricket as a likeable man, but in 1957, apparently trying to offset the departure of the England player Willie Watson, a number of players got up a petition demanding his resignation. Sutcliffe's father, now a member of the Yorkshire committee, insisted that he submit it.[34] Ronnie Burnett, captain of the Yorkshire Second XI now stepped up. Burnett's appointment furnished another bone of contention. He was widely acknowledged to be a player of below county standard and had plainly been appointed for his amateur status. In other clubs where argument was less constrained by regional identity, the arbitrary imposition of an amateur captain of mediocre playing ability bred open discord. At Yorkshire it brought more tantrums. Burnett and the committee dealt summarily with some of these. Burnett stood for no backchat. Fred Trueman, the latest in a long line of stormy petrels in the Yorkshire team, was impressed when Burnett insisted to dissident players like Appleyard and Brian Close that his instructions be carried out. 'It was then that I thought Burnett would do for me and I supported him right from the start,' he wrote later, 'although I knew we would have to do a bit of carrying.'[35] The committee also dismissed Johnny Wardle, the senior professional, following a long series of altercations with Burnett, culminating in the publication of newspaper articles critical of the club and bearing Wardle's name.

The Wardle episode captures perfectly the double bind in which Yorkshire cricketing masculinity had often been trapped. In the imagined Yorkshire, tradition dictated that they be proud, independent-minded, blunt spoken craftsmen who nevertheless did as they were told without demur. As the sociologist Paul Willis wrote later of a bunch of working-class schoolboys in the West Midlands, they were 'exhorted to behave in precisely those ways of which they are supposedly incapable of behaving'.[36] The truculence of Wardle, 'at his happiest amid the bonhomie of … solid, forthright pitmen' was trumped by class power. Friends said his sacking left him 'grief-stricken'. Later he appeared before the Duke of Norfolk to be told of his removal from the MCC party to tour Australia. According to his biographer, Wardle 'stood erectly to attention' when given the news.[37]

There were, in any event, now reservations among the players themselves about the accustomed expression of grumpy Yorkshire manhood. Younger cricketers such as Raymond Illingworth and Bob Platt felt that older members of the team could be more supportive and less reproving. In his first autobiography, for instance, Illingworth describes how he questioned the long established practice at Yorkshire of bawling out fielders who dropped catches and the boorishness of the side's senior 'hard men'. Conversely, he praises Yardley for encouraging him to express himself in his play – to 'go for his shots'.[38]

This, in time, pointed up two further factors that were soon introduced into this apparent flux of masculine values and which dogged the Yorkshire dressing room through the 1960s. Again they struck right at the heart of regional male identity. Firstly, there was the growing lobby for 'brighter cricket' and the consequent introduction into the county game both of one-day tournaments and (linked to these) commercial sponsorship; secondly, there was a threat to their traditional (and outmoded) employment practices. Both issues clearly revealed once again the double binds inherent in Yorkshire cricket culture.

In 1968, Raymond Illingworth, now 36, asked Yorkshire for a three-year contract. In doing so he was, inevitably, challenging the club's long-entrenched employment policy. He was offered only a one-year contract, which he declined. Illingworth recalls

Sellers' response: 'I could go, and any other bugger who wanted to go could go with me'.[39] Illingworth left the county. Then, in November of 1970, Yorkshire dismissed their captain, Brian Close, a professional and the most conspicuous heir to the county's 'hard man' tradition. In Close's autobiography he recalls his dismissal: 'by God, whatever was happening to me now was hurting. It was really hurting'. He remembers stopping his car on the way home to weep and to vomit. Of course, this does not mean that, in baring his emotions, Close was departing from the code of masculine Yorkshireness. He, and his ghostwriter, were, unwittingly perhaps, simply pointing up its contradictions. As Close himself said: 'It was my Yorkshire as much as the committee's'.[40]

Buy the book: Tykes in white flannels

These contradictions were made more public, in the county and beyond, by a series of books and articles bearing the names of Yorkshire players. The paradigm for these books was based on the same tension that had seemingly always contoured the county's cricket culture – a love of the Yorkshire jostling with an increasingly explicit resentment of some Yorkshiremen by others. Many of the books were written by the journalist Don Mosey.

In the period since 1945 no one did more to perpetuate popular notions of the vexed, put-upon masculinity of Yorkshire cricket than the late Don Mosey. Mosey, who died in 1999, was the chief purveyor of Yorkshire cricket myths in the 1980s and 1990s. Mosey was one of the first to see the commercial possibilities of these myths and the men who represented them. There was now a market, both for sport biography and for Yorkshireness – especially the fractious dealings of the county's cricketing sons. As a sports reporter and, latterly, as a BBC producer in the 1950s and 1960s, Mosey befriended many of the Yorkshire players of the time. He wrote biographies of them, or for them, and for many years was a curmudgeonly presence in the BBC's Test Match Special commentary box. Through Mosey, a number of Yorkshire cricketers became popular cultural figures in their own right, known for their association with the game, but also as carriers of a blunt, no-nonsense, yet troubled northern masculinity.

The books Mosey 'ghosted' for Yorkshire players (Brian Close, Fred Trueman and Ray Illingworth among them) all invoke the specialness of the county and of 'we Yorkies'. But the ethos of difference is most explicitly set out in We Don't Play It For Fun, his history of Yorkshire cricket, published in 1988. Here Mosey revels in the idea of the Yorkshireman's separateness, calling his book 'by no means a formal history of Yorkshire cricket … more an exploration of our native character as seen through the careers of some of our cricketing giants.'[41] The sheer perversity of this 'native character' was meat and drink to Mosey. For instance, he celebrated the very notion of a row, as a fundament of regional culture: 'I love 'em. There is something about the passion, the grandeur, the sheer majesty of a Yorkshire cricket row which transcends just about everything except the outbreak of war.'[42] Later, in a chapter entitled 'Archetypal Yorkies', he lovingly recounts how once the crowd at a Bradford League game in Keighley in the early 1900s left early so as to avoid contributing to a collection for local player Emmott Robinson.[43] But, saturated though he is in the cult of Yorkshireness, Mosey is sensible enough to acknowledge that, in the history of English cricket, 'Yorkshire' is often a metaphor for class. Yorkshire captains weren't born with the tendency to have arguments or set defensive fields. These traits had their roots in the working-class culture of the county. Country house cricket, as Mosey notes, never made much impact in the county: 'the strength of Yorkshire cricket has always rested firmly in its leagues, and our attitudes to the game as well as each other in North and South have progressed accordingly'.[44]

True man: the legend of Fiery Fred

Mosey freezes history at this point. The working classes made the cricket leagues. They played to win and were better at the game than the effete southern gentlemen. The gentlemen continued to disdain them, however, to pick them for England only when absolutely necessary and to punish them for minor breaches of etiquette. Thus, among the dalesmen of Yorkshire cricket, grievance piled upon grievance and they became characters in an ongoing melodrama – tough, wronged men, glowering at the hyphenated silver spoons of the South. 'There has always been a "them",' wrote Mosey, 'and they never liked "us".'[45] This reasoning always suited Fred Trueman, a close friend of Mosey, arguably England's greatest fast bowler and for fifteen years a leading player in the Yorkshire melodrama. This status as leading player has been amplified by, among other things, a steady stream of biographical material, including three autobiographies published in 1961, 1965 and 1976 respectively. Much of this material was written by Mosey and through it, and subsequent radio broadcasts, Trueman became a leading signifier of Yorkshireness in national popular culture.

Trueman was born in the Yorkshire village of Stainton. (Interestingly, when Trueman reported for trials at Headingley in 1948, the Yorkshire coach George Hirst had not heard of Stainton and a map had to be consulted to verify that it was within the county boundary. Stainton was found to lie barely within the border with Nottinghamshire and it may be that, beneath Trueman's aggressive espousal of muck or nettles Yorkshire patriotism lay an anxiety at having come from the county's geographical margin.) His father was a miner, but Stainton was not apparently a mining village and lacked the proletarian traditions of such a place. Trueman prefers to describe his family as country people, pointing out that his grandfather was a horse dealer. In his various 'ghosted' memoirs, two things, principally, inscribe Trueman's life as a man of Yorkshire cricket: his relationship with his father and his capacity to engage

10

in Mosey's most celebrated Yorkshire cricket activity: the row.

Trueman's relationship with his father is steeped in notions of Yorkshire and rugged masculinity. 'He was a hard man, my Dad ... a real stickler for discipline,' Trueman said in *Ball of Fire*, his third autobiography. His father was 'the only man I suppose I was ever afraid of' but, if Trueman was treated harshly as a boy, he never said so.[46] While rowing at some stage with most of the other authority figures in his life, he revered his father and would talk things over with him on the frequent occasions when Fred was in trouble with county or national cricket authorities. For Trueman, authority figures, especially if they were from the South, might represent privilege, but he probably despised them more if they showed weakness. Three of his early county captains, the amateurs Norman Yardley and Billy Sutcliffe and the professional Vic Wilson, he perceived as weak and therefore, as Jouve would see it, feminine. But Ronnie Burnett, who led the side as an amateur in 1958 and 1959, Trueman according to *Fast Fury*, an earlier autobiography, saw as 'a man of iron' prepared to face down the senior players and their tantrums.[47] The man whose own brushes with authority were legendary across the cricket world throughout the 1950s and 1960s nevertheless still responded to a strong paternal discipline.

It is possible that the tradition of tough Yorkshire masculinity made Trueman feel guilty at escaping the world of physical toil inhabited by working-class men like his father. Having hoped to be a bricklayer, Trueman instead earned his living from playing cricket and from words (he was a journalist, a broadcaster and, briefly, a stand-up comedian). This may explain Trueman's persistent talk of grievance and persecution – a soft life masquerading, perhaps, as hard times. And it may also account for Trueman's known aggressiveness toward autograph hunters. Deep down he may have felt unworthy of their request: they should be asking real men, like his father. Trueman, who as a boy had taken up cricket to please his father, a cricket lover, gave his county cap (awarded in 1951) to his father and, when his father died, it was placed in his coffin. Trueman cloaks this gesture in regional mystique: 'Only a Yorkshireman will understand' he reflects in *Ball of Fire*.[48]

Fred Trueman made his first appearance for Yorkshire in the spring of 1949 and, fittingly for a man who railed so frequently at the gentleman class in English cricket, this was against Cambridge University. Maybe, once again, there is an echo of guilt in his resentment of 'posh sods who had come straight from university into a county side and never done a real day's work in their lives'.[49] Trueman confronted individual members of the game's elite on many occasions. In Australia on tour with England during the winter of 1962-3 he flatly told the Duke of Norfolk that he would be addressed as 'Fred' or as 'Mr Trueman', but not by his surname alone. And when the Rev. David Sheppard dropped a catch off his bowling he suggested acidly that Sheppard pretend it was Sunday and keep his hands together. There were numerous altercations at cocktail parties and receptions. But the essence of Trueman's philosophy was that Jack was as Good as his Master; he never questioned the system itself. Better, perhaps, than any sportsman of the modern era, Trueman embodied the paradox of a Yorkshireness in which class frustrations were imprisoned by gender. He confronted authority, but wanted to be governed by an iron fist. He angrily demanded to be put in his place. As Willis observed in 1977, the 'them and us' philosophy necessarily involves an acceptance of prior authority relations.[50] Trueman, moreover, was disdainful of organised labour, which had no place in the imagined Yorkshire of county cricket club mythology. Mosey, in a later biography of Fred, tells on the very first page of his subject's loathing for Arthur Scargill, the leader of the National Union of Mineworkers, whose power base was in the South Yorkshire coalfields.[51] Indeed, beyond the immediate world of masters and men, Trueman recognised a higher, traditional eminence – 'I refused to call anybody "sir",' he reflected in 1976, 'except the Duke of Edinburgh.'[52] Needless to say, Trueman always voted Conservative.[53]

There were thousands of Fred Truemans to be found on the building sites and in the factories of England in the 1950s and 1960s. They gave the foreman some lip. Sometimes they maybe took a swing at him. But they did a hard day's work, as their masculinity dictated; this distinguished them from posh sods and wet nellies. They accepted existing class relations, but not the condescension that went with them. In this, Trueman made a striking contrast with his England fast bowling partner, Lancashire's Brian Statham. Statham, placid and unassuming, liked to curl up after a game with a couple of pints and a packet of fags. Trueman, a natural populist with a withering tongue, more accurately caught the mood of post-war professional cricketers and their growing opposition to amateur dominance. Indeed, so confident was his populism that in 1969, the year after he retired from first class cricket, he worked briefly as a comedian on the northern club circuit. Here Trueman's repertoire reminded his audiences that the imagined Yorkshire of the county cricket club not only has little place for women or femininity, but that it was white. 'The jokes,' observed Mosey coyly in his biography of Trueman,

> 'were mostly of the variety known in polite company as 'risqué', liberally sprinkled with racial overtones. It is doubtful, for instance, if Fred would ever be invited to read the lesson (or whatever the equivalent is) in one of the mosques of Bradford.[54]

Later, regional media began to avail themselves of Trueman's populist touch. In the 1970s for example, Yorkshire Television employed him as anchorman of a sports programme called *Indoor League*. His purportedly dialect catchphrase, 'Reight? Ah'll sithee', drew on the same imagined 'Tyke' Yorkshire of earlier eras and illustrated the expanding local media market for demotic 'Yorkshireness'.[55]

Fair do's?: Raymond Illingworth

However, as I suggested earlier, if Trueman was but the latest in a long line of brooding, recalcitrant professionals at the cricket club, the masculine traditions of Yorkshire dressing room did not go uncontested. The challenge to these traditions, such as it was, seems to have come principally from Ray Illingworth.

Raymond Illingworth first played for Yorkshire in 1951 and made his England debut against New Zealand in 1958. He played first class cricket for over thirty years. Under his captaincy, England won a series on Australian soil and Leicestershire the county championship for the first time in their (generally undistinguished) history. He also captained his native Yorkshire when he was over fifty. Widely acknowledged as the shrewdest cricket brain of his time, on retiring as a player he was appointed manager of Yorkshire CCC before becoming successively Chairman of England selectors and manager of the England team. For much of the 1980s and early 1990s he was a broadcaster on cricket for BBC radio and television. Unlike Trueman or Geoffrey Boycott, Illingworth in his public cricket career seemed a largely benevolent figure, conducting himself both as captain and pundit rather like a TV gardener advising viewers on how best to protect their chrysanthemums from the frost. On the other hand, like Trueman and Boycott, Illingworth did have some history of public altercation, but, unlike the others, Illingworth's disputes as a player had an acknowledged class rationality. Often styled as a barrack room lawyer, he sought to negotiate on issues of employment relations and not to have them dissolve into angry displays of regional masculinity.[56] In this he was perhaps the early, authentic face of a coming modernity among the Yorkshire players.

Like Trueman, Illingworth has put his name to three autobiographies. In them he makes two clear departures from the expected dourness of conventional regional manhood. He admits that he hoped for happiness – not something that was part of the lexicon of the tradition Yorkshire pro' – and laments publicly that he failed to find it in Yorkshire cricket. His first memoir *Yorkshire and Back* (written for him by Mosey) gives him the 'Yorkshire' credential of emotional diffidence. A chapter is given over to Illingworth's wife in which she recalls that he never, for example, found the courage to ask his wife to marry him – something that she rendered as 'Yorkshire practicality'.[57] But, Illingworth insisted that rowing – something that Mosey would later claim was a defining characteristic of the true Yorkshireman-in-Flannels – was not a necessary part of local cricket culture. Indeed, he modifies Wilfred Rhodes' famous dictum – 'We don't play it for fun' – by adding 'but we do play it for pleasure'.[58] And in his second autobiography, *The Tempestuous Years*, he implies regretfully that the happiest ten years of his cricket life were spent, not with his native Yorkshire, but with Leicestershire.[59] He condemned the bullying of the younger Yorkshire players in the 1950s and the strife that attended Yorkshire cricket in the early 1980s. He relished neither, nor saw them as inescapably 'Yorkshire'. Indeed he saw the ructions of the early 1980s as a betrayal of the county's traditions: 'it was the skulduggery, the scheming and the downright dishonesty that sickened me most. We Yorkies have always been proud of our honesty and integrity.'

In his time as a player Ray Illingworth was often prepared to confront authority. But while Trueman contented himself with rows and one-liners, Illingworth challenged the substance of English hierarchical practices. Young Yorkshire players of the 1950s were publicly scolded for dropping a catch, but never praised for taking one. As I observed earlier, Illingworth, in an (almost certainly unintentional) echo of Dr Spock, questioned the rationality of this, stressing that open approval of things done well would achieve more, in the long run, than the punishment of mistakes. Later, on England's tour of Australia in 1962-3, he remonstrated with gentleman amateur vice-captain Colin Cowdrey for being an hour late for net practice. This was a challenge to existing class relations in cricket and an assertion that pro's and amateurs alike should put in a decent day's work. It's reputed to have cost him £50 of his 'good behaviour' bonus for the tour. Moreover, when in Australia in 1971 an extra test match was added to the itinerary, Illingworth, as England captain, insisted on extra payment for the players.[60] In his writing he refers often to the need for fair shares, square deals and good spirit among the lads:

> My point was that when I first went into the Yorkshire side I was paid (on being capped) the same as Len Hutton, who was the greatest batsman in the world at the time. Similarly, young players now came in without one-tenth of Brian [Close]'s or Fred [Trueman]'s or my experience, and they were paid the same as us. In short, it evened itself out over the years, and it was by far the best thing for team spirit to have all capped players on the same amount.[61]

So far as I know Raymond Illingworth never embraced the left, but the values he often expressed and pursued as a cricketer were labourist and egalitarian and, thus, close to those of many shop stewards in British industry during the period. They recall the 'dressing room socialism' of the British football world of the 1960s, best exemplified by the club managers Jock Stein and Bill Shankly. And they set Illingworth a little apart from the other main exemplars of cricketing Yorkshireness, who buried class relations in maleness and regional mythology.

This is my press conference: Geoffrey Boycott and a different drummer

Geoffrey Boycott, by contrast with most previous exemplars of Yorkshire cricketing masculinity, is an established figure in global, postmodern cricket culture. While both Trueman and Illingworth have worked extensively for the media, one senses they did so as 'themselves', giving the same opinions that they might express privately over a drink. Boycott, though, sells more than his opinions; beyond his expertise, he sells Geoffrey Boycott-ness – an on-tap abrasiveness and plain-speaking demeanour, in which 'Yorkshire' is subsumed. This is variously purchased in different sectors of the cricket media market (BBC, Channel Four, BSkyB, Talk Radio) and, extensively, by advertisers. For many people around the world – especially on the Indian subcontinent – the only thing they know of Yorkshire is that Geoffrey Boycott is from there. Whereas Illingworth, in particular, worked from a Take-Me-or-Leave-Me sense of himself, Boycott can *do* Take-Me-or-Leave-Me, if that's what the employer requires. He *performs* 'Geoffrey Boycott'. As a television floor manager told Boycott's most recent biographer: 'He is the most insecure man I have ever met. When we started together, he would go on the air and always come out at the end of it and say, "Was that all right? Was that OK? What did I do right? Did I do anything wrong?"'[62]

Boycott, like Trueman and Illingworth (whose father was a self-employed craftsman, in and out of work), was born into a family of comparatively slender means; the son of a miner, he grew up in the Yorkshire pit village of Fitzwilliam, near Wakefield. He first played for Yorkshire in 1962 and for England two years later. His last England cap was on England's winter tour of India in 1981–2 and he finished as a first class player in 1987. Significantly, Boycott was dropped on occasion by both club and country for slow scoring and made himself unavailable for England between 1974 and 1977.

Once he was an established first class cricketer controversy followed Boycott wherever he went. In these controversies the interests of the individual (Boycott) were invariably pitted against those of the collectivity (his team mates, the club). There was, inevitably, an interesting class element to this. Historically, the bowlers of the first class game had been drawn principally from the working classes. Since the nineteenth century, many of the stroke-making batsmen had, according to convention, been middle-class toffs, carefree and chancing their arm. The slower scoring bats were often working-class men, who, while pedestrian and unglamorous by comparison with the amateurs, nevertheless, in holding up an end, did a good job for the side. What made Boycott extraordinary was that he emerged in the mid-1960s as a working-class batsman apparently demanding the right to score slowly *on his own account*. (Boycott *compiled* himself. Like so many people in the postmodern era, he is his CV: his best-selling autobiography, published in 1987, closes with no fewer than eighteen pages of statistics on his cricket achievements.)

Reprimanded for slow progress by both Yorkshire and England and deprived of the Yorkshire captaincy, in the winter of 1983-4 Boycott challenged the leadership of the county club. In doing so he appeared to mobilise a regiment of disgruntled police sergeants, self-employed businessmen and others across Yorkshire, which succeeded for a while in dislodging the county committee.

An account of this campaign to take over the club covers two chapters and over fifty pages of Boycott's autobiography, but these pages do not disclose a coherent political project.[63] Instead, the contention between the club and the Reform Group – Boycott's supporters, whom he styles in his autobiography as 'rank and file' – appears to have been an extended and well-organised version of what Mosey had, as we've seen, claimed as a defining Yorkshire trait – the row. In this row, Boycott himself was the lightning rod and, thus, the issue: you were either for him or against him. I discussed this with an experienced Yorkshire cricket writer, formerly with the *Yorkshire Post*.

SW: 'In the Boycott Affair, did the two sides – the Reform Group and their opponents – represent any wider groupings in Yorkshire society?

Writer: 'Yes. In a word, class. The Reform Group were mainly, say, working class ...'

SW: 'And perhaps lower middle class? The police sergeants, and so on?'

Writer: 'Yes, people like Reg Kirk [a police officer], whereas the anti-Boycott faction were men like Desmond Bailey [a landowner, maintaining in civilian life the rank of captain, whose address was given as Aldborough Hall in the North Riding]. The Reform Group were very efficient. They called press conferences in a hotel in Wakefield. They had microphones. They had clear, prepared statements. They spoke well. It was all over in hour because that's how long they'd booked the room for. The other group met in a village pub near Harrogate and we drank all day ...'

SW: 'But those people represented traditional authority in the county. In a way they were saying that theirs was the way things had always been done.'

Writer: 'Yes.'

SW: 'Did the Reform Group have a political project?'

Writer: 'No, not really. Mainly their campaign was about the one individual. And quite a few of those elected to club committees turned out not to know that much about cricket.'

SW: 'So, it was a sort of phantom revolution?'

Writer: 'Yes.'

Boycott's detractors saw him as awkward and selfish. He preferred to see his separateness as heroic and at the beginning of his autobiography he implies that, like the eighteenth century American philosopher Henry David Thoreau, he simply 'hears a different drummer'. But he also caught the mood of the lower middle classes in Yorkshire in the late 1970s and early 1980s. He stood for individualism, profit and self-advancement. His support for cricket links with white South Africa was unwavering and he helped organise the first 'rebel tour' there in 1981. He was an archetypal Thatcherite who, updating the traditional 'muck and brass' ethic, turned his own notoriety into a small business, whose every action carried marketing possibilities. In 1969, he had signed for the US-based International Financial Management group, which represented sportspeople with an international profile.[64] Jackie Hampshire, Boycott's last captain at Yorkshire, was once told that he could only meet Geoffrey if Boycott's ghostwriter were present.[65] In the regional row, of which he was the focal point, Boycott brought the undercurrents of class and status, so often inherent in Yorkshire cricket disputes, closer to the surface. In his rhetoric, the silver spoon came north: it was right here, in Yorkshire. Boycott identified his principal adversary among the players as Richard Hutton, son of Len:

> Richard went to Repton, a good public school, where he learned the value of contacts and the rudiments of snobbery that come to some people with an expensive if not expansive education. He clearly resented me as some sort of country bumpkin, totally without social graces.[66]

All this helped, until the late 1990s, to make Boycott's own personal masculinity less obtrusive. In most of the disputes involving Boycott that have been made public, he himself has been the issue. His ploughing of a lonely furrow, which made him a pariah in the dressing room and a hero to the political right, rendered him less a man alone than a withdrawn adolescent, in a permanent mode of self-exculpation. This may relate in part to his upbringing. As observers have noted, he had a legendary closeness to his mother, who indulged him. 'Even when he was an international sporting star in the seventies, she still washed and ironed all his laundry. "I owe it all to Mum", Boycott has often said,' notes Boycott's most recent biographer.[67] This, it is suggested, may have diminished his sense of independent identity. He remains, so to speak, primarily 'the child' and is perhaps distant in other relationships.

From Boycott's apparent solitariness and closeness to his mother, some people might have assumed that he was gay. Such thoughts, as Jouve notes, are of course incompatible with traditional Yorkshire manhood, but they were in any case dispelled in 1998 when Boycott was convicted in a French courtroom of assaulting Margaret Moore. Moore, it turned out, was one of an apparently large number of commercially-minded women of middle age with whom Boycott had been intimate since the 1960s. One was the mother of his daughter. His latest biographer describes a Boycott, confident of his own attractiveness, striding through life with a condom in his wallet.

Boycott's reaction to his conviction, which he appealed unsuccessfully, necessarily involved a more complex presentation of self than would have been the case for an ex-Yorkshire cricketer of the 1950s. Boycott was more than a man on trial; he was also a widely consumed media text – a brand, with custom to safeguard. He was publicly indignant with his accuser and with some journalists – 'Shut up,' he told one, 'this is my [press] conference, not yours' – but he was noticeably reticent when the *Sun* newspaper, for which he himself wrote a column, attacked him.[68] He knew that in the postmodern world of publicity, the matter of whether he had actually struck the woman in question was of less concern than whether his commercial credibility would be damaged. Could the brand image of Straight-Talking Yorkshireman Geoffrey Boycott be salvaged? Thus, when Boycott arrived in France in 1999 to appeal his case, he was accompanied by a support team of thirteen people. This team included several of his platoon of apparently adoring businesswomen, anxious to attest to his caring nature, along with a consultant psychiatrist, prepared to state that Miss Moore was suffering from a 'personality disorder', and the publicist Max Clifford. Boycott's conviction was confirmed, but Moore was widely discredited and Boycott, the brand, survived. Soon afterward Boycott signed to the commercial station Talk Radio, as commentator on England's forthcoming tour of South Africa.[69]

Boycott the Brand is essentially an unintended pastiche of the blunt, muck-or-nettles Yorkshire male stereotype. Fellow commentator Henry Blofeld said recently: 'He calls all Pakistani waiters George and says, "George, you've got the brains of a bloody chocolate mousse." And it's not said in a friendly manner.'[70] Nevertheless, he has established a huge media presence on the Asian sub-continent, where he is in heavy demand as a TV personality and endorser of products (Genesis Rare Old Premium whisky, Honda motor bikes).

'They call him "Sir" Geoffrey wherever he goes in India, even in the print and electronic media. ... Thanks to the reach of TV in India, today he is one of the most recognised faces and voices and he is mobbed at every [cricket] ground,' observed one journalist.[71] 'Now you have people who imitate the way Boycott talks and it's wonderful, you know,' said Radio DJ Kushal Bishash in 2001, '"Eeeess not a baad baatsman". We find it greatly amusing. I find it very attractive, this kind of English, but a lot of people would not associate an Englishmen with this kind of English.' [72] 'The key to his popularity,' according to the Indian writer Tunku Varadarajan, 'lies in his pithy approach. Indian viewers, accustomed to stilted commentators, whose language veers between the ornate and the long-winded, enjoy his devil-may-care independence.'[73] Moreover, the novelist Shashi Tharoor recently pointed out that by far the most popular English-language author in India is still P.G. Wodehouse, whose books are set among the English upper classes on the early 1900s. If the English males of popular Indian imagination are 'Wodehouse's decadent young Edwardian Men in

Spats',[74] the excitement generated on the subcontinent by Boycott's voice is not difficult to explain.

In February 2001, the Pakistan Cricket Board paid Boycott £30,000 for two weeks' coaching and consultancy. The deal was sponsored by McDonalds and Boycott made eight appearances in McDonalds restaurants in Lahore, signing bats and 'dressed in a bright yellow jacket and tie decorated with mini Ronald McDonalds'. His chosen mode for coaching the young Pakistani batsmen was precisely that which Raymond Illingworth had felt was outmoded at Yorkshire in the 1950s: this, of course, was based on reproof and the conspicuous withholding of approval. 'You've got to sharpen up. You've got two wooden legs, you have,' he told one. 'You move like an ugly crab,' another was informed.[75]

This is a clear case of cultural serendipity. Boycott is now seen as an effectively post-colonial figure, speaking for the former subject peoples – a globalised, self-made Mr No-Nonsense pitted against the traditional image of the plume-hatted colonial administrator, and against the anglophile political and media elites who came after him. Here, ironically, an identity rooted partly in white regional exclusiveness becomes a symbol of post-colonial emancipation, exportable to huge agglomerations of formerly subject peoples. Boycott has become used to playing himself in the Bollywood movie of his own life; he works hard at being natural. 'I've always tried to be myself,' he told Dileep Premachandran in 2000,

'never tried to put on airs and pretend to be someone I'm not. I'm quite proud of being born in Yorkshire and I wouldn't dream of trying to change my accent or the way I speak. I just cross my fingers and hope that the Indian public understands what I'm saying. I'm lucky that they took to me straight away. I've also tried to be honest and objective. If I think someone's playing badly, I won't hesitate to say that they're playing "roobish".'[76]

Here the unashamed Yorkshireness and its concomitant blunt speaking signifies a 'non-toff', who in some sense shares the struggles of ordinary folk. Though by now a millionaire several times over, Boycott is not slow to reiterate his working-class, unprivileged credentials: 'My father was a miner. He was badly injured in the mines in an accident in 1950. Never recovered, it destroyed his health … he was a broken man. He never wanted any of his children to go down the pits.'[77] Here, then, is an old set of popular fictional images – bluff Yorkshiremen, the mines, hard physical toil, wasted and broken lives, a route out of it all through sport – being consumed voraciously in surprising new markets. Boycott's life and identity have become myth – a cultural credit card to be flashed in a hundred TV studios and rotary clubs across the Asian subcontinent.

19

Tykes in the twenty-first century: Yorkshire cricket and postmodernity

Geoffrey Boycott lost his seat on the committee of Yorkshire County Cricket Club in 1993 and he moved his English habitat to the southern coastal county of Dorset in 1997. In his wake, the culture of the cricket club and the ideals of manhood and regional identity that it now embodies are perceptibly different from those typified by so many of the cricketers discussed in this chapter and popularised around the world by Boycott himself. In this closing section I'd like to suggest why and how.

Firstly, there is a sense that the traditional Yorkshire masculinity is now in decline, partly because the material life of the county has changed. The culture of smokestack industry, which in part bred and sustained this pattern of maleness, is disappearing. The local cricket writer I consulted said:

'You take a city like Leeds. It was a grimy industrial city in the 1960s. Now there's all the new technology and the new firms like First Direct and Vodaphone. People from the south come to Leeds for jobs and the town's full of wine bars and bistros. As someone once said, we're all middle class now.'

Some of the more perceptive of observers also argued that the Boycott Affair and preceding ructions likewise, had had an identifiable material basis. For example, David Bairstow, who was made captain of Yorkshire in 1984, wrote that same year:

It was Geoffrey Boycott's bad luck in 1971 to become captain of a team that would win nothing. But this was not merely because the team was not strong. The 1960s were the last years of the old county championship, again dominated by a Yorkshire led by Brian Close, and county cricket was about to be turned upside down.

Sponsors appeared for one, two, and finally three one-day competitions. Sponsors appeared for individual county clubs. No sponsor can afford to be associated with failure, so some strong and unusual pressures were exerted on Lord's.

County sides were placed on a more or less level footing by permitting the introduction of overseas players; Yorkshire insisted on their players being born inside the pre-1974 boundaries.[78]

Since the furore of the 1980s, therefore, the club has finally engaged in crucial modernisation. In 1992 Hawke's longstanding prohibition on players from outside the county's boundary was revoked and for the summer of 1993 Yorkshire engaged their first overseas player, the Indian batsman Sachin Tendulkar. This, by definition, began to undermine the notion of a link between the team and any fixed regional identity. The club also embraced sponsorship and for most of the 1990s wore the logo of Yorkshire Tea.

It goes without saying, of course, that commercial companies will not rush to associate themselves with a club prone to feuding and fractious particularism. They seek winners. Importantly, though, in their recent public pronouncements the county's cricketers have not necessarily identified the qualities required to achieve victory as inherently Yorkshire traits. In 1999, for instance, wicketkeeper Richard Blakey openly acknowledged that a winning formula might be generated in another county:

> Leicester are a side we have looked up to for a number of years. They have no real superstars but play well as a unit, work hard for one another and have deservedly picked up a couple of titles. We probably have a bit more quality these days but we still see them as a yardstick ...

A three-page tribute to the work done for the Yorkshire team by a Scottish sports psychologist is further testament to the decreased explanatory power of local character.[79] Similarly, in 2001, Yorkshire captain David Byas' comments on the will to win of the county's fast bowler Steve Kirby are instructive: 'He has a massive amount of aggression. He is right in a batsman's face, abusing them, swearing at them, brilliant! He is a breath of fresh air.'[80] This is an important observation. What Byas describes here is a simulated row, springing not from grievance, not from identity, not even from Yorkshire (Kirby was born in Lancashire and played previously for Leicestershire), but from *professionalism*. It represents, in effect, the rationalisation of the row, linking it to efficiency and the achievement of ends.

Moreover, by the end of the twentieth century, in global cricket culture and beyond, the imagined, muck-or-nettles Yorkshire of Mosey's and previous generations was perhaps more visibly contested than before. In the 1990s, for example, Boycott's chief rival as the world book trade's best known and most marketable Yorkshire cricket name was ex-Test umpire Harold 'Dickie' Bird. Bird, who played for Yorkshire between 1956 and 1959 is in no way a progressive figure, but neither does he conform to the austere Yorkshire male stereotype. As his biographer David Hopps observes, Boycott, Illingworth and Trueman

> present 'Yorkshireness' as dogmatic, inflexible and opinionated. 'So what's new?' many of those born outside those broad acres might ask. But there is another type of Yorkshireness, a guileless and straightforward way of life, in which friendships are valued and behaviour is sincere and unfeigned. It is those qualities that have exemplified by Dickie Bird.[81]

And, while a string of Yorkshire cricketers have been perceived as prickly, working-class men who confronted authority, Bird was an unassertive, unmarried working-class male who exercised it: 'Off the field, I'm a born worrier. But when I step across that boundary rope, I'm a different man. It's the only time I feel in total control.'[82]

Bird stood as a first-class umpire between 1970 and 1998 and as a test umpire between 1973 and 1996. Competent, though visibly fretful and eccentric, Bird's quirkiness and vulnerability made him an ideal authority figure at a time when international cricket became primarily a television show. He was voted 'Yorkshireman of the Year' in 1996 and his memoirs, published the following year, are said to be the best-selling sports autobiography ever. He is also, like Boycott, popular with advertisers on the Asian subcontinent. In this biography he emerges as a sentimental county and national patriot, who would have played for Yorkshire for nothing and whose MBE, which 'means more to me than life', was received in tears in 1986.[83] He is also, importantly, an apparently asexual icon, despite the aggressive masculinity of his county's cricket tradition and the increasingly sexualised nature of much contemporary popular culture. Having lived with his widowed mother until her death in 1980 and now looked after by his sister, he has said on many occasions that he could not take a wife because he was 'married to cricket'.[84] He's given no public hint of any sexual proclivity and in 1996 refused to be interviewed in bed by the transvestite comedian Lily Savage on Channel Four's *The Big Breakfast*.[85]

Elsewhere, Darren Gough, Yorkshire's best known and most accomplished current player at the turn of the twenty-first century, has tried to distance himself from some of the county's traditions of emotional restraint and inward-looking regional patriotism. 'I can walk into my folks' house and sit down and watch TV without saying a word,' he wrote recently.

> We are not ones for big greetings. Anna [his wife] could not believe it. She was used to the full works: hugs, kisses, the lot. And my folks couldn't believe it when that's what they got from Anna's family. We Yorkies don't show our feelings. In a way, that's sad.[86]

Similarly, in the context of cricket, Gough speaks confidently for modernity and against the county's traditions, as mediated by the many past Yorkshire players who now comment publicly on the club's affairs:

> The players thought we were living in the dark ages, though we appreciated that this was where some of the old-timers still wanted to live … 'Used to be' counts for nothing in sport. Yorkshire had stood still for more than a generation. The world and cricket had moved on. I have no doubt that the influence and the public moaning of old Yorkshire players had a seriously negative effect. When we have meetings with our psychologist now, he tells us: 'They are history. You have got to make your own history. You have got to forget these old players.' It's always been a problem at Headingley. Sometimes it's as if the likes of Illingworth, Close and Trueman have never left the place.[87]

Part of the critique of the club mounted by prominent ex-players and others had to do with perceived threats to Yorkshire tradition and identity. For example, globalisation, the escalating demands of international cricket and, in particular, the introduction of central contracts for England players in 2000, have led to a resurgence of the popular argument that the metropolis is stripping the North of its best talent. Gough, who moved house to Buckinghamshire in 2001, has been widely accused of neglecting his home county. Gough has countered that, not only does he retain a strong local pride but that there is no necessary contradiction between the local and the global here. Yorkshire CCC itself is, after all, now, like him, a global motif.

> A few clever-clogs thought it was funny to award Darren Gough the OBE: that's 'Only Bowls for England'. Those sort of remarks have gone the rounds, even before central contracts. My view has been that what I achieve for England brings credit to Yorkshire. Surely spectators must be proud that a Yorkshire fast bowler, born and bred, has led the England attack for several years. I still hear the odd 'But he never plays for Yorkshire' ... I play when I can and when I'm allowed to. Me in person, my name, my picture are always a prominent part of any Yorkshire marketing campaigns.[88]

In other words one global brand promotes another. Darren Gough may not physically often be in Yorkshire, but his image is married to the county's.

However, the tension inherent in developing an essentially postmodern view of Yorkshire County Cricket Club – that's to say, as a text – was probably best exemplified by the controversy which surrounded the opening in 2001of some gates at Headingley cricket ground, built in honour of Sir Leonard Hutton. In this controversy clear battle lines were drawn. Variously Gruff Yorkies (Trueman, Close, Illingworth, Boycott, Appleyard) claiming to defend cultural heritage, faced down the club's new commercially-minded administration, with the humble and emollient Bird interceding. The principal bones of contention were that a 'southerner' (John Major, former Prime Minister and current President of Surrey County Cricket Club) had been asked to open the gates and that the design of the gate included images of Asian women wearing saris. The latter could be read as an attempt by the club to present itself as more socially inclusive: here would be a symbolic departure from the brooding, white male ethos that had so frequently characterised it in the past. The club officially described the gates as representing Headingley 'yesterday, today and tomorrow'. The opposition sought to concentrate on yesterday, stressing literal historical accuracy and, thus, bulwarking an exclusive regional identity. In their argument, past discrimination and exclusion dissolved into cultural heritage. 'When Len played there were no Asian women in the crowd,' said Illingworth, 'and he never played in India'.[89] The opening went ahead in August 2001 but the old guard remained largely unreconciled.

> Fred Trueman was not present; Geoffrey Boycott was seen not applauding; Brian Close chuntered; and Bob Appleyard ... thought the gates were 'inappropriate' and 'a mismatch'. Only Dickie Bird wanted peace: 'All this

bickering! We've got to get behind the Yorkshire team. We're on the verge of winning the Championship'.[90]

Afterword 2009: The Headingley Experience

This chapter was first published in 2004 and, in re-presenting it here, I have amended it only slightly and then just to tinker with the language and punctuation. Yorkshire cricket, its leading exponents (past and present), its headquarters at Headingley in north Leeds and the broader question of Yorkshire identities have all moved on. So, as we observed in the introduction to this book, have notions of heroism.

Taking heroism first, it's doubtful, given the preceding arguments, that sport heroism, in the conventional sense, could ever have fully flourished in Yorkshire cricket culture. This is largely because the pattern of class relationships and concomitant emotional dynamics that prevailed in this culture were, largely by default, egalitarian: people were customarily 'cut down to size', discouraged from 'getting above themselves' and so on and praise was in short supply. Arguably, none of the leading Yorkshire cricketers mentioned above transcended controversy or factionalism in a way that might define a truly heroic figure: for example, Brian Statham, ably depicted as a Lancashire cricket hero in these pages by Jack Williams, would very likely not have achieved the same status on the other side of the Pennines.

In any event, as we have seen, Yorkshire – socially, culturally and politically – has experienced rapid change. Leeds, like so many other towns and cities in the county and across the north of England, has become more decisively postmodern – its centre now dominated by bars, bistros, nightclubs and shopping malls; its economy more rooted in the service sector and its public face more culturally diverse than when Fred Trueman ran in from the Kirkstall Lane End. Whatever purchase the baleful Yorkie masculinity of yore has on the life of contemporary Yorkshire, there is now little public acknowledgement of it. In an age of globalisation, cities like Leeds seek to attract employers and tourists to the area; they therefore address the outside world with a smile, and not a grunt or a frown. Recently a local professor of tourism stressed the importance of tourism to the regional economy and of the consequent need to regard Yorkshire as a text, adding that:

> Yorkshire is where the people have a strong sense of place, great pride in their locality, grit, and a swagger of self-confidence that says Yorkshire is better than anywhere else. Of course, in tourism terms, this is usually characterised as a *great Yorkshire welcome*!

> Just for the record – I *am* being ironic. There are many other ways of narrating Yorkshire and some are rather depressing.[91]

These changed priorities were illustrated when in 2009 the British television channel ITV announced the discontinuation of *Heartbeat*, its gentle and popular drama about friendly police in the Yorkshire dales during the 1950s, and a few weeks later Channel Four screened a dramatisation of *The Red Riding Quartet* – a series of novels mired in misogyny and police brutality in Yorkshire in the 1970s and 1980s by the locally born writer David Peace – one journalist commented that '[t]hey must have gone to the foot of their stairs at the Yorkshire Tourist Board'.[92] Indeed, if postmodern Yorkshire has thrown up any approximation to a sport hero, a case could be made for the short-lived Paul Hunter (1978-2006). Hunter was the antithesis of previous Yorkshire sporting notables: a 'Jack the Lad' figure and formidable snooker player from a council estate in Moortown, north Leeds, he represented unashamed and un-self-conscious working-class hedonism and *joie de vivre*, fitting his early snooker career around a life of clubbing, mates, dope-smoking and the ingestion of large amounts of vodka. Confidently androgynous, he often wore his long blonde hair pinned back by an Alice band and, conforming to the Victorian gentlemanly ideal, he accepted defeat with a smile and an embrace of his opponent. He married a local beauty therapist in a Caribbean ceremony at which both bride and groom wore white, having in February 2001 become famous, via a frenzy of tabloid lip-licking, for having sex with her in their hotel room between sessions of the Masters final. He'd declared this at his victory press conference, pronouncing it the ideal way to relax.[93] Clearly, while much of this defines the territory where contemporary working class postmodern sport hero and sport celebrity meet, none of it is traditionally 'Yorkshire'.

Hunter was Yorkshire's chief representative in a popular and globally televised sport. Indeed the Crucible Theatre in Sheffield had, through its hosting since 1977 of the televised World Snooker Championship, become a global sporting marker for Yorkshire itself. Cricket, by contrast is near-moribund at county level and Headingley Stadium, like all county grounds, receives sparse crowds for mainstream, four-day county matches. Moreover, again like all other county grounds, the club has sought alternative sources of income. In 1999, The Headingley Experience was inaugurated. This is an independent profit centre, owned by Leeds Rugby Club (who share the stadium), which offers facilities for conferences and corporate and social functions. The commemoration of Yorkshire players in these facilities is noticeably circumspect and to Darren Gough's insistence, cited earlier, that the club should not become shackled to its own history can be added the recognition that some of that often fractious history (the Boycott saga, for instance) serves no marketing purpose. As a representative of The Headingley Experience told me: 'We had to get the balance right with the commercial side. Former players are not always a recipe for success, on or off the field.'[94] References in the Experience's publicity material to the leading figures of Yorkshire cricket are certainly sparing: there is a 'Legends Suite' and a 'Hirst and Rhodes Suite', commemorating George Hirst and Wilfred Rhodes, who finished playing for Yorkshire in 1929 and 1930 respectively. Beyond that, there is little cricket specificity in the Experience's web publicity – merely an undertaking to 'cater for all types of events from private parties such as weddings, christenings and birthdays through to business functions including conferencing, networking events and business meetings'.[95] Only in Headingley Lodge, the hotel in the Stadium complex, are particular spaces designated to commemorate the chief architects of the county's cricket heritage: here Brian Sellers, Norman Yardley, Herbert Sutcliffe, Lord Hawke, Ronnie Burnett, Johnny Wardle, Geoffrey Boycott, Ray Illingworth, Fred Trueman, Len Hutton, Bob Appleyard and Brian Close – their differences symbolically settled – all, along with 24 others, have bedrooms named after them. The other twenty four includes Sachin Tendulkar, the first breach in the historic wall of indigenous and disputatious whiteness that was once the county team.

[1] This chapter was developed from a shorter article published in 2001 in *The New Ball*, edited by Rob Steen. I'm grateful to Rob for his encouragement. It then appeared, in elaborated form, in the journal *Sport in History*; I must thank the current editors of *Sport in History* – Matt Taylor, Paul Dimeo and Martin Johnes – for permitting me to republish it here. Shaun Callighan of 'The Headingley Experience' was a great help to me in my more recent research for the Afterword and so was Rhod Thomas in kindly supplying a copy of his inaugural lecture.

[2] Roy Hattersley, *Goodbye to Yorkshire* (London, 1991), p.15

[3] Raymond Chandler, after meeting J. B. Priestley in 1951. Quoted in Tom Hiney, *Raymond Chandler: A Biography* (London, 1998), p.195.

[4] Keith Waterhouse, *Billy Liar* (London, Penguin ed. 1962).

[5] R.W. Connell, *Masculinities* (Cambridge, 1995), p. 76.

[6] Nicole Ward Jouve, *The Streetcleaner* (London, 1986), p. 91.

[7] Patrick Joyce, *Visions of the People: Industrial England and the Question of Class 1848–1914* (Cambridge, 1991), p. 294.

[8] Derrick Boothroyd, *Nowt So Queer As Folk* (Bradford, 1976), pp. 3–4.

[9] Dave Russell, 'Sport and identity: the case of Yorkshire County Cricket Club, 1890–1939' *Twentieth Century British History*, 7, 2 (1996), pp. 206–230; Dave Russell, 'Amateurs, professionals and the construction of social identity' *The Sports Historian* 16 (1996), pp. 64–80.

[10] Donald Read, *The English Provinces c.1760–1960 A Study in Influence* (London, 1964), pp. 271–3.

[11] Russell, 'Sport and identity', p. 207.

[12] Derrick Boothroyd, *Half a Century of Yorkshire Cricket* (Keighley, 1981), pp.35, 67.

[13] Alan Hill, *Hedley Verity: Portrait of a Cricketer* (Edinburgh, 2000), p. 37.

[14] Ibid., pp. 50–2.

[15] Bill Bowes, *Express Deliveries* (London, 1949), p. 91.

[16] Russell, 'Sport and identity', p. 227.

17 Boothroyd, *Half a Century*, p. 67.

18 Ibid., p. 70.

19 Herbert Sutcliffe, *For England and Yorkshire* (London, 1935), p. 160.

20 Alan Hill, *Herbert Sutcliffe: Cricket Maestro* (London, 1991), pp. 84–5.

21 Ibid., p. 86.

22 Bowes, *Express Deliveries*, p. 64.

23 Hill, *Hedley Verity*, p. 110.

24 Bowes, *Express Deliveries*, pp. 148–9.

25 Norman Yardley, *Cricket Campaigns* (London, 1950), p. 157.

26 Alan Hill, *Johnny Wardle: Cricket Conjuror* (Newton Abbot, 1988).

27 Gerald Howat, *Len Hutton: The Biography* (London, 1999) p. 170.

28 Stephen Wagg, '"Time, gentlemen, please": the decline of amateur captaincy in English county cricket' in Adrian Smith and Dilwyn Porter (eds), *Amateurs and Professionals in Post-War British Sport* (London, 2000), pp. 31–59.

29 James P. Coldham, *Lord Hawke: A Cricketing Biography* (Ramsbury, Wiltshire, 1990), p. 187.

30 Hill, *Wardle*, p. 42.

31 Russell, 'Amateurs, professionals', p. 77.

32 Hill, *Wardle*, p. 52

33 Ibid., p. 106.

34 Ibid., p. 48.

35 Boothroyd, *Half a Century*, p. 125.

36 Paul Willis, *Learning to Labour: How Working Class Kids Get Working Class Jobs* (Farnborough, 1977), p. 81.

37 Hill, *Wardle*, pp. 18, 113, 115.

38 Ray Illingworth and Don Mosey, *Yorkshire and Back* (London, 1980), pp. 39–42.

39 Ibid., p. 104.

40 Brian Close, with Don Mosey, *I Don't Bruise Easily* (London, 1978), pp. 142–3, 145.

41 Don Mosey, *We Don't Play It For Fun: A Story of Yorkshire Cricket* (London, 1988), p. 7.

42 Ibid., p. 2.

43 Ibid., p. 44.

44 Ibid., pp. 4–5.

45 Ibid., p. 5

46 Fred Trueman, *Ball of Fire* (London, 1976), pp. 15, 111.

47 Freddie Trueman, *Fast Fury* (London, 1961), p. 146.

48 Trueman, *Ball of Fire*, pp. 39–40.

49 Ibid., p. 60.

50 Willis, *Learning to Labour*, p. 109.

51 Don Mosey, *Fred: Then and Now* (London, 1991), p. 3.

52 Trueman, *Ball of Fire*, p. 60.

53 Mosey, *Fred: Then and Now*, p. 149.

54 Ibid., pp.135-6.

55 Ibid., p. 142.

56 Boothroyd, *Half a Century*, p. 152.

57 Illingworth and Mosey, *Yorkshire and Back*, p. 84.

58 Ibid., p. 11.

59 Ray Illingworth and Steve Whiting, *The Tempestuous Years 1979–83* (London, 1987), p. 2.

60 Illingworth and Mosey, *Yorkshire and Back*, pp. 64, 78–9.

61 Ibid., p. 104.

62 Leo McKinstry, *Boycs: The True Story* (London, 2000), pp. 270–1.

63 Geoffrey Boycott, *Boycott: The Autobiography* (London, 1987). See also Peter Wynne-Thomas and Peter Arnold, *Cricket in Conflict* (Feltham, Middlesex, 1984), pp. 157–73.

64 Boycott, *The Autobiography*, p. 119.

65 Hampshire, 1983: 128–9.

66 Ibid., pp. 146-7.

67 McKinstry, *Boycs*, p. 10.

68 Ibid., p. 306.

69 Ibid., p. 308–12.

70 Ibid., p. 291.

71 Gulu Ezekiel, 'India falls for Boycott's charms', *Wisden Cricket Monthly*, January 2000, pp. 10–11.

72 *Guardian: The Editor* magazine, 22 September 2001.

73 McKinstry, *Boycs*, p. 290.

74 Shashi Tharoor, 'How the Woosters captured Delhi', *Guardian Review*, 20 July 2002, pp. 4–6.

75 Rory McCarthy, '£30,000. So what? Beckham wouldn't get out of bed for that', *Guardian*, 14 February 2001, p. 32.

76 Dileep Premachandran, 'I've always tried to be honest' (Interview with Geoffrey Boycott), *Cricket Talk*, 7 October 2000, pp. 9–11

77 Ibid.

78 David Bairstow, with Derek Hodgson, *A Yorkshire Diary: Year of Crisis* (London, 1984), pp. 4–5.

79 Richard Blakey, with Andrew Collomosse, *Taking It From Behind* (Edinburgh, 1999), pp. 98, 183–5.

80 *Mail on Sunday*, 19 August 2001.

81 David Hopps, *Free as a Bird: The Life and Times of Harold 'Dickie' Bird* (Basingstoke, 1997), p. 9.

82 Ibid., p. 19.

83 Dickie Bird, with Keith Lodge, *My Autobiography* (London, 1997), pp. 22, 181–2.

84 Ibid., p. 149.

85 Hopps, *Free as a Bird*, p. 199.

86 Darren Gough, with David Norrie, *Dazzler: The Autobiography* (London, 2001), p. 45.

87 Ibid., p. 38.

88 Ibid., pp. 284–5.

89 Vivek Chaudhary, 'Yorkshire ex-players erupt as "southerner" Major asked to unveil gates', *Guardian*, 4 August 2001, p. 6.

90 Matthew Engel, 'England stand at the gates of despair', *Guardian*, 16 August 2001.

91 Rhodri Thomas, 'Reflections on tourism policy and policy-making in Yorkshire' Inaugural Professorial Lecture, Leeds Metropolitan University, 22 May 2008.

92 Katy Guest, 'A writer on the wilder side of Yorkshire's psyche' (profile of David Peace), *Independent on Sunday*, 8 March 2009, p. 54.

93 Lindsey Hunter, *Unbreakable: My Life with Paul* (London, 2007); Clive Everton, Obituary of Paul Hunter, *Guardian*, 11 October 2006 http://www.guardian.co.uk/news/2006/oct/11/guardianobituaries.obituaries1 (accessed 18 March 2009); Trevor Baxter, Obituary of Paul Hunter, *Independent*, 11 October 2006, http://www.independent.co.uk/news/obituaries/paul-hunter-419492.html (accessed 18t March 2009).

94 Telephone interview, 9 March 2009.

95 http://www.headingleyexperience.co.uk/ (accessed 18 March 2009).

CHAPTER 2

Northern Heroes and Heroines?: Fell Running[1]

Peter Bramham

A hard place

THIS IS HOW DEATH MUST FEEL. Not the pain,
although I imagine most deaths must be painful, but the fear. Fear
of what? I hardly dare say.

Something has happened to me. For more hours than I can
remember, a storm has been screaming around me. For more hours
than I can remember, I have been running – or trying to run – in
the mountains. Now I am lost, utterly. Every muscle in my body is
shaking, both feet are blistered raw, every joint aches, and my last
reserves of warmth and strength are gushing away as a stream . . .

. . .

This, I should add, is what I do for fun

R. Askwith, *Feet in the Clouds*[2]

Why would anyone race up and down mountains in foul weather? There are some
things beyond the scope of comprehension – like quantum physics and mobile
phone tariffs. And then there's fell-running. How can anyone delight in something
that just looks horrible?

Tarquin Cooper, 'Fell-running'[3]

Introduction

On the last weekend in October, when the clocks go back to British Winter Time, the
Original Mountain Marathon (OMM), previously known after its original sponsor as
the Karrimor, is held somewhere in the UK. Pairs of competitors have to complete a

two-day course of approximately 50 miles in the hills, with various checkpoints to visit and a camp overnight. It is commonplace for at least a third of competitors in the various categories, elite, A, B, C and Score, not to get round the designated course within the time limits. In 2008 2,500 people participated in atrocious conditions in the OMM; eight severe weather warnings had been issued by the Environment Agency on that Saturday in Cumbria. Parts of Keswick had 65mm of rain in 24 hours on the day before the race – average monthly rainfall in the north-west in October is 80mm.[4] It became the first item of national news broadcasts that hundreds of runners had gone missing on the fells and had to be 'rescued'; an RAF helicopter from Anglesey was drafted into to winch some of those stranded and injured to safety. Authorities in the form of police and mountain rescue organisations heavily criticised race organisers for letting the event go ahead. Mass media voiced their disbelief that people would take gigantic risks in such adverse circumstances and the Cumbrian fells were described 'as a battleground with bodies everywhere'. Journalists offered interviews with individual competitors who had been frightened by the gales, flooding and poor visibility. Some competitors were forced to abandon the race and take shelter in Honiston slate mine museum or in farm buildings or, as expected, just camp out. However, despite the media frenzy, all competitors turned up safe the next day and all were accounted for. One interviewee suggested that people are invariably well equipped and experienced in such events and hardship. Many were angry that the second day of the event had been called off. It all fuels the view that people who run around in the hills are both eccentric and masochistic. In the words of the Fell Runners Association (FRA) secretary, Alan Bentall 'It's a Zen thing, you thrive on that pain. In the end, you get to love it.'[5]

On the nature of fell running

There is some debate as to what to call such outdoor exercise. The OMM demands a partner, a range of orienteering skills, survival expertise and a capacity for endurance running in the mountains as well as transport to get to and from the events, annually staged by the organisers in isolated locations. In contrast fell walking, as celebrated in Alfred Wainwright's insightful and delightfully illustrated books of the Lake District, is purely pleasurable recreation. Nevertheless, both cyclists and walkers often compete to complete Wainwright's Coast to Coast walk, 190 miles from St Bees Head to Robin Hood's Bay in the shortest time possible.[6] But, as philosophers assure us, naming is everything. As we shall see later, it is a constant irritant to the Fell Runners Association, the organising body for fell runners since 1970, that mainstream athletics never mention fell running as part of its policy documents and development plans. There are some who have suggested that it really should be named hill running or mountain running, so that Europeans can understand what is going on.[7] Mountain races in some countries are exclusively uphill challenges, some, such as the World Cup Trophy alternate between 'up' and 'up and down', with many mountain challenges held on specified routes, tracks or trails. There was much controversy about the hosting and sponsorship of the World Masters Championships in Keswick in 2005 as well as detailed debates as how best to prepare England international teams for 'foreign' competitions which may be solely 'up' rather than both 'up and down'.[8]

This chapter studies fell running as one way of both understanding and celebrating 'northern' regional identities and local heroes. Sport can be important to how people see themselves and others. People who run up and down northern fells are usually born and bred in the North, work in the North, and they and their families belong in and to northern landscapes. Many great fell runners (for example Ernest Dazell, Joss Naylor, Bill Teasdale, Tommy Sedgewick and more recently Simon Bailey) are often Dales or Lakeland farmers; others work outdoors in landscape gardening, construction, conservation or engineering professions.[9] They belong to, and know their way around, the great outdoors. Stated simply, they are the 'insiders', they are at home in local fell running clubs, they live and train on the fells, they organise their own races and choose favourite events, challenges or sports that are faithfully supported year after year.[10] But like many minority sports, fell running has been largely ignored by policy makers, mainstream athletics and also by national mass media. This is usually not something to worry about unless external funding is necessary to secure championships or to kick-start developments and new initiatives. However, fell runners prefer not to be dependent on external funding.

However, contrary to popular belief, fell running is not a homogeneous northern block. Each region has generated its own classic fell races and fell champions – in Yorkshire there are Burnsall, Buckden, Ilkley Moor and the Three Peaks, in Lancashire various races occur around Pendle Hill, Chew Valley and the Forest of Bowland, in the Lake District, Grasmere Guides, Borrowdale, Wasdale, Kentmere and so on. Many have provided detailed histories of fell running traditions and champions in the Lake District,[11] Peak District,[12] Lancashire,[13] Yorkshire and the North East.[14] These races become the backbone of the English and British championships which are fiercely contested annually by each age group. Wales, Scotland and Ireland have their own national traditions, in part consolidated by recent policy changes in UK Athletics. Each generation has produced its own champions and interestingly there are family dynasties such as the Blands, the Walkers and the Jebbs whose elder members still race, organise and officiate, with Joss Naylor standing out as one famous fell runner celebrated in both local and national media.

On the making of heroes and heroines

Stephen Wagg's chapter in this book[15] helpfully mentions four major periods of British heroes in sport: first, in the eighteenth century, early champions under aristocratic patronage; second, the public school amateurs of the imperial age; third, the rise of the modest, often professional 'ordinary man' in the twentieth century; finally, the sport hero as celebrity, star of global media and authoritative endorser of own brand products. But while such periodisation may make sense of mainstream sports such as football, cricket and rugby it sits uncomfortably with marginalised minority sports which would include fell running. Neither nineteenth-century public school game-playing ideals, nor professional sporting teams and tactics, nor global media stars have had any part to play in fell running. Naturally there are heroes and heroines in fell running, but not as we know them.

There are many key concepts from sports sociology which may help make sense of people's participation in sporting forms and the recent emergence of sporting icons and iconoclasts. But such theories seem less applicable in trying to explain fell running and local heroes and heroines. For example, American sociologists such as Peter Donnelly have championed ideas of sporting subcultures to capture the distinctive world of playing sport as neophytes are introduced by players, coaches and teachers into playing the game 'properly' by deploying subcultural norms and rules of behaviour. Recent theoretical work stresses men in sport – the masculine world of sports teams – of 'locker room' culture where boys are turned into hard men, who are expected to 'put their bodies on the line' for the team, to make sure that they 'get their retaliation in first', to denigrate women and to ridicule any telltale signs of femininity and quintessentially to disappear into post-match drinking games and competition. Indeed, women were excluded from fell running early on, as elsewhere in sport, but by the 1980s[16] they had begun to make a substantial impact on the culture of fell running clubs, on their ideals of 'hardness' and heroism, and on fell records. Hegemonic masculinity is alive and well in running clubs but has been tempered by what could be described as the feminist presence of women fell runners. Their supportive networks encourage women to participate and perform and these friendships occur both within and between fell clubs. Blatant male chauvinism is hard to sustain when women outrun men in races, although some male runners are particularly peeved to be passed by a woman runner. But actions often speak louder than words. Wendy Dodds, profiled as an elite endurance runner later on, had the courage to march into the single (de facto the men-only) shower block available after one filthy Wadsworth Trog, much to the consternation of the men. She had not only run faster than the men showering but mentioned in a loud voice to those women in the ladies changing room, 'that there was nothing worth seeing anyway'. To give another simple example, Angela Mudge is commonly regarded as the best fell runner and there is no mention of gender in that judgement.

In Canada, Robert Stebbins[17] has made his academic career out of working on the idea of 'serious leisure'. He draws a distinction between amateurs, hobbyists and volunteers and casual mass consumption – the popular culture of film, TV, games consoles and radio. His research focused initially on barber shop singers but has expanded to included musicians, sport players, dancers and so on – so that it now covers practically any activity which can offer the individual a 'career'. Such leisure pursuits provide opportunities for skill development, achievement, qualifications, perseverance and status, but most importantly the individual sees him- or herself essentially as a brass band player, bridge player, ballroom dancer and so on.

In the UK substantial interest has developed recently about the idea of extreme sports, particularly surfing. Belinda Wheaton prefers the term 'lifestyle sports' in order to stress that surfers celebrate a distinctive attitude to work, leisure and sport.[18] She hypothesises from her own participation in surfing and her analysis of surfer magazines that participants adopt alternative lifestyles and have the potential to offer a less macho, less competitive sporting culture. There has been growing popularity in adventure challenges – competitions that demand skill in outdoor pursuits such as kayaking, orienteering, mountain biking and climbing. It is slowly dawning on some life-long gym members, writing as journalists,[19] that running and cycling are more fun outdoors than on treadmills or exercise bikes.

But traditional ways of analysing sport and the celebration of sporting heroes just will not work for fell running because at the very core of fell running is a strong sense of inclusion; an egalitarianism; the common bond of being tested by terrain, weather and navigation challenges, by merciless ascents and frankly terrifying descents and by simply racing and finishing. There is inevitably fierce competition amongst elite men and amongst elite women in contesting the national FRA championships, amongst the different age categories of 'vets' and 'super vets', not least within and between fell clubs in relay races and the like, but in general fell runners simply reject elitism. As Allan Greenwood of Calder Valley recounts[20] on his club's origins 'It would be a low-key social running club, dedicated solely to off-road and mountain running' and so to celebrate their 21st birthday in 2008 there was a steady social group run designed to include the whole club. He himself epitomises unsung northern fell running heroes – he loves fell running, has never 'won' any race, has tackled (eventually successfully) the Bob Graham Round, has run the Calder Valley Relay course (50 miles) solo one Saturday, has been married to the legendary fell runner Carole Haigh, and has inaugurated and continues to promote a series of popular races around Ogden Water (near Halifax).

This rejection of exclusivity and elitism is most strongly articulated and practised by the heroes and heroines, both on and off the fell. As we shall see, despite all their heroic performances, records and extraordinary standards set over the years and fells they are modest, self deprecating and 'just ordinary'. Most importantly they are not only 'prepared to' but enjoy mixing both competitively and socially with low-level 'rubbish' performers and they are usually determined to put 'something back into fell running' through marshalling, organising races, acting as 'celebrity' starters and presenting prizes in the pubs afterwards. If Lewis Hamilton is seen as the perfect role model for Formula One motor racing, the people mentioned in this chapter are similarly blessed to inspire by example. But Lewis Hamilton lives in Switzerland for tax reasons, has a pop-star girlfriend and makes millions of pounds/euros/dollars in image rights and product endorsements, whereas fell runners live locally, often have partners who themselves are successful fell runners and work full-time for a living: for example Bingley 3 Peaks winners Ian Holmes works for a company fitting bathrooms, Andy Peace is a postman and Rob Jebb, a BT engineer. They are accessible and make themselves accessible in ways that superstars in other more commercialised sports would not dream of.

Symbolic communities

If sport sociologists have struggled to make sense of the marginal world of fell running, the idea of symbolic boundaries offers a useful prism through which to examine northern fell running clearly. The terms of symbolic boundaries and symbolic community come from the work of Anthony Cohen who in the 1990s developed or 'modernised' social anthropology.[21] Rather than studying the exotic, let us say kinship and witchcraft relationships amongst non-literate island tribes, Cohen's research at the University of Manchester and Edinburgh University[22] approaches ordinary everyday life in modern settings. As an anthropologist, his theoretical starting point is to define people as cultural beings who construct meanings. The task facing social scientists is one of understanding rules and regulations, signs and complex processes of signification that guide people's own everyday lives and shape their dealings with other people. Erving Goffman[23] has framed one key question that underpins all social life, 'What is going on here?' What precisely do these words and actions mean? How can we make sense of what people are doing or saying? For example, writing one's signature could be in the context of signing up for the French Foreign Legion, witnessing a marriage certificate, writing a cheque, signing an affidavit or entering a fell race entry form and thereby affirming that one is running at one's own risk and, in case of accident, one will not sue the race organisers for lack of 'duty of care'.

For Anthony Cohen one answer is that people inhabit and construct symbolic universes – shared worlds of meaning in which 'insiders' understand signifiers such as language, gestures, looks, clothes as well as master statuses of class, gender and race. Skin colour, ethnicity and religion provide important boundaries of cultural significance that one may or may not easily transgress. These constitute symbolic boundaries within which insiders know precisely what, as well as who, you are and what you mean. People disappear, or more accurately, find themselves inside a free-time activity from which they gain tremendous pleasure. For fell runners much of this pleasure relates to traversing the fells, contouring around lakes and tarns, climbing and descending mountains, but equal pleasure is to be gained from running companions, fellow competitors and telling and sharing tales before and after races.

But both local communities and communities of interest are often constructed out of what Raymond Williams[24] termed 'the mutuality of the oppressed' – close-knit networks of neighbours, trade unionists and the like who organise collectively to fight inequalities caused by material poverty or oppression by political and cultural discrimination. In a limited sense, fell runners thrive on the hardship of fell running which gives them a sense of belonging and shared identity before, during and after runs and races.

'Outsiders' or strangers fail to read the signs and just do not know the significance of what is happening or what is really said in conversations. It is not so much that people within these symbolic universes speak in codes that outsiders fail to interpret but rather that conversations usually carry deeper meanings that only insiders fully comprehend. The dynamics of managing 'insider'/'outsider' relations become crucial and, in postmodern times, with heightened difference and diversity, one must be careful not to take people at face value. 'Political correctness' warns individuals that 'traditional' language carrying stigma, prejudices and discrimination along lines of class, gender and race will no longer pass within the public sphere. Of course, in the private sphere, things can be, and are, different.

Fell running clubs

The straightforward answer to the question, 'where do heroes and heroines of this social world come from?' is, simply and unsurprisingly, northern fell running clubs. The myriad of clubs are local; they shape identities and both winning styles and losing styles. So fell running heroes and heroines usually grow up within local clubs with their distinctive races, histories and traditions. It is worth mentioning that the 2008 committee members of the FRA, printed in the annual calendar all carry their club identity after their names.[25] Much is made in the few biographies on fell runners of joining and belonging to a particular club. Unlike in commercial sports, there are few expensive controversial transfers in athlete careers and because of the Amateur Athletics Association's national regulations athletes have to wait six months before they can act as a counter or representative for their new clubs.

This is the intimate world of Bishop and Hoggett's research into voluntary-sector leisure organisations.[26] Clubs provide mutual aid in sport and leisure – they generate a sense of belonging, a personal identity of mutual solidarity, shared enthusiasms and long-lasting and often life-long friendships. These bonds are nurtured over the years by training nights in the week, fell races at weekends and mid-week in the summer months, running as pairs in competitions and competing as club members in regional and national events. Club members have camper vans which provide a haven of comfort and sociability for all on rain and drink-sodden evenings at distant races or during weekend events, such as the Wharfedale TTT, Midsummer Madness Three Day Event and Brecon Fans Three Day Event.

There are also club presentation nights for distinctive prizes, some inclusive such as a prize for 'the most improved runner'. All clubs organise a variety of 'dos' and 'socials'. In a literal sense clubs 'own' athletes and they are expected to turn out and perform for the club whenever deemed necessary. All this occurs within a competitive frame but the glue that binds is a resilient pattern of club sociability from shared lifts, travelling in team minibuses, joint 'recces' of legs of relay courses, teasing and banter that blossoms on Saturday runs, in the pub afterwards, fuelled by legendary running weekends away.

Sociological ideas about sporting subcultures or anthropological accounts of symbolic communities cover the same ground, capturing the nature of social relationships and extended cultural networks. Although made up often of fiercely independent and self-reliant individuals, clubs are essentially democratic, egalitarian and inclusive. Heroes and heroines win in their own right but they also are representatives of their clubs. Each running club develops its own distinctive culture with its own heroes and heroines, both past and present.

But each fell running club remains unique because of its members. For example, Pudsey and Bramley has nurtured a wealth of fell running heroes and heroines over the years – English and British Fell Champions and multiple classic fell race winners which include the likes of Jack Maitland, Sarah Rowell, Anne Buckley, Gary Devine and Rob Hope. But they all belong to a club that traditionally has emphasised the social rather than the serious competitive side of fell running. Most fell clubs describe themselves as drinking clubs with a running problem.[27] Sarah Rowell's important book on fell running, informed by her sports science background and by twenty years of success in off-road running, emphasises the importance of fun.[28] One recent article published by Graham Breeze[29] in *The Fellrunner* is aptly entitled 'Laugh and be Happy – A Profile of Sarah Rowell'. Boff Whalley's profile of Rob Hope (2007 British Fell Champion) stresses his failure to take training seriously in an article aptly titled, 'Run, Drink, Fall Over'. As Hope himself points out he only runs at most one hour a day, leaving him '23 hours to play with'.[30]

Fell running clubs generate manifest and latent cultural boundaries which include 'insiders', such as club members, and exclude 'outsiders'. Very few fell runners remain in the 'unattached' category. One need only read down the results list of any fell race (assiduously compiled for *The Fellrunner* magazine by Dave Weatherhead and Barbara Carney over the years) to notice that 'unattached' runners are few and far between, whichever decile of results or competitors is analysed. Races are categorised by the FRA by distance (i.e. long [12 miles or over], medium [6<12 miles] and short [1<6miles]) as well as height gained ('A', 'B' and 'C');[31] neophyte club members get to know which races traditionally matter in the fell-runners' calendar. Clubs often focus on particular favourite and challenging races, as well as using national and regional races to count towards internal club championships. Club members are naturally expected to run in club vests at races and groups of club members are photographed before important races such as the Three Peaks, Ben Nevis, Borrowdale and so forth. Indeed, adverse comment is made if any club member runs in an ordinary T shirt, but some may justify this absence of team clothing, claiming they are treating the race as 'just a training run' so donning a Helly-Hansen top legitimates a (possibly) lack-lustre performance. Naturally, club members share the experience of simply 'being there' at races, especially when weather conditions go wrong. For example, all runners have witnessed fell races that have been too hot or freezing cold, too misty, too much snow and ice, howling winds and torrential rain, the ground too hard or too soft. These extraordinary races and conditions become deeply embedded in collective memory and obviously there are very different types of races and particular stories 'grow with the telling' and are recounted time and again wherever and whenever relevant. Indeed, new club members are introduced to fell-running culture by these stories; previously faceless members of the club, with their peculiar nicknames, start to make sense once one understands how and where particular individuals have achieved their legendary status and reputations. For example, in my club one 65-year-old carries the nickname 'Tonk' which solely derives from a spelling error (of Tony) on a race results sheet many years ago and it has stuck ever since.

Apart from participation in racing, there are many ties that bind runners together such as shared running regimes, dietary preferences and importantly a (more or less) sympathetic audience to bear witness to lengthy diatribes about running injuries, in addition to any fool's guide to local sports physiotherapists, doctors, osteopaths, chiropractors and 'quacks'. Most individuals seek a variety of scientific and magical cures for chronic injuries to feet, tendons, calves, hamstrings and that 'jewel in the crown' of all ailments – the bad back. As most sports physios, in both NHS and private practice, can testify, the major problem with fell runners is that they cannot wait to resume running, even and often immediately straight after serious injury. It is always 'too much , too early and too often' as rehabilitating athletes drive themselves too hard on the fells just to check out that they are nearly fully fit and ready for racing, thereby exacerbating the initial injury and probably generating new ones. But this does not happen just once to fell runners, it is not one important lesson quickly learned early in their athletic careers – it survives as a recurring and central feature. Although capable of offering good training advice to others, experienced fell runners can rarely apply it to themselves. So it is not uncommon for runners to ignore completely all professional and expensive advice they have paid for. When told to rest or cut down on running, sensible advice is universally ignored. It should be no surprise then that Richard Askwith's award winning book *Feet in the Clouds*, carries the subtitle, 'A Tale of Fell-Running and Obsession'.

After most races, runners discuss race routes – both mistakes and short cuts, particularly trying or pleasurable points in the race and so forth, as well as 'kit', particularly the merits and shortfalls in new fell shoes. In West Yorkshire during the winter months of 2008, a small group independently organised a series of small-scale night races up key local hills such as Pendle and Ingleborough; naturally, there was much discussion about appropriate brands of head torches and night lights to deal with racing in the dark.

Conversations can take place when recovering behind the finishing line, washing down in rivers or in the zinc bath on the village green, as in the Bolton by Bowland race, or most usually in the local pub afterwards. Indeed, the vast majority of fell races are organised from pubs and here is where most runners linger to witness the prize-giving (assuming one is not out there still trying to finish a long-distance race) and one can talk to all participants. Club members, and invariably female partners, also attend races to spectate and to support by looking after gear and dogs, shouting encouragement, providing drinks and food en route and usually taking responsibility for driving to and from venues as competitors can become 'tired and emotional' after the post-race drinks. It is hard to underestimate the amount of support and time offered to young athletes by family, friends and club coaches. One heroic couple in youth fell running is Eileen and Dave Woodhead. Both previously were accomplished fell runners but now concentrate on developing young fell runners by organising attractive inclusive 'fun' fell-running events such as the Bunny Runs at Stanbury, photographing races as well as helping with coaching, organising Halloween 'dos' and weekends. But many clubs have their own youth programme and enthusiastic coaching staff, usually parents of junior athletes, who are prepared to put in hours and hours of 'volunteering', to collect club subs, to take training nights, to enter local and regional competitions and to report results to local running club websites.

One central argument of this chapter is that it becomes a somewhat invidious and in part self-defeating task to name heroes and heroines, not only because of the nature of fell running but also because of the self-effacing character of dominant male and female fell runners. One straightforward resolution to this problem is to call on distinguished writers in fell running matters to provide their own short list. Fortunately, both Graham Breeze (Skyrac), himself something of a Leeds celebrity and key FRA committee member, and Bill Smith, author of the definitive history on amateur fell running, *Stud Marks on the Summits*,[32] have taken on this task for *The Fellrunner Magazine*[33] over the years.

The following table lists their choices with dates of publication.

Table 1 Fell Runners: Heroes and Heroines

Author 'Article Title' Athlete Profiled	Date of publication	Key Achievements at date of publication
Bill Smith 'Wonderwoman of the mountains. A profile of Wendy Dodds' **Wendy Dodds (Clayton-le-Moors Harriers)**	*The Fellrunner Magazine,* February 2002, pp. 9–11	Competed over past 25 years in Lake District Mountain Trial, Karrimor Elite, Saunders Lakeland MM, Lowe Alpine MM, Three Peaks, etc., completed Tranters Round (1978), Bob Graham Round (1979, Munroes, etc.
Bill Smith 'Allan Greenwood – A South Pennine Sportsman' **Allan Greenwood (Bingley Harriers and Calder Valley)**	*The Fellrunner Magazine,* February 2003, pp. 14–16	Race competitor, cyclo-cross competitor, Fell Race Organiser
Graham Breeze 'Scoffer –a Profile' **Andy Schofield (Borrowdale)**	*The Fellrunner Magazine,* February, 2006, pp. 15–17	Member of FRA Champions Committee. Wins include Wasdale, Ennerdale, Duddon Valley, Wadsworth Trog, Old County Tops, Manx MM, Grisedale, Hevellyn, etc.
Graham Breeze 'Sally Newman: Frustrated Pole Dancer? A Profile' **Sally Newman (Glossopdale and Calder Valley)**	*The Fellrunner* Spring, 2006, pp. 10–11	Ladies English Open Champion (2000, 2005) Ladies English Vet 40 champion (2005) Ladies V40 Gold Medal at World Masters(2005) World Masters(2005) Wins at Wasdale, Duddon Valley, Edale Skyline, etc.

Author 'Article Title' Athlete Profiled	Date of publication	Key Achievements at date of publication
Graham Breeze 'Colossus – A Profile of Ian Holmes' **Ian Holmes** **(Bingley Harriers)**	*The Fellrunner,* Spring, 2007, pp. 26–30	5 Open English Championships (1996–2003), 4 British Championships (between 1996 and 2000), British and English Vet champion in his first year as a Vet in 2006; multiple winner on Ben Nevis (5), Jura (4), Borrowdale (2), Langdale (2) and Yorkshire Champion (6)
Bill Smith 'Roger Ingham MBE. A Great Yorkshire Sportsman' **Roger Ingham** **(Parachute Regiment** **Territorial Army** **Volunteer Reserves)**	*The Fellrunner,* Summer, 2007, pp. 26–30	Open (Professional) Fell races – wins at Black Lane Ends, Cowling Gala, One Mile and Two Mile races at Grasmere Sports, and Highland Games – Braemar Athol and Breadalbane. Advocate for the abolition of professional/amateur divide in athletics 1992; youth coach for Skipton AC, fell race organiser and celebrity commentator.
Graham Breeze 'Gary Devine – A tremendous natural talent' **Gary Devine** **(Pudsey and Bramley)**	*The Fellrunner,* Autumn/Winter, 2007, pp. 14–17	English Championship 1989, 1990, British Championship 1990 Yorkshire Championship, Ben, 3 Peaks, Rydal Round. P and B team member winning British Championships (4), British Championship and Calderdale Relay (8), Pennine Way Relay record

41

Table 1 Fell Runners: Heroes and Heroines cont.

Author 'Article Title' Athlete Profiled	Date of publication	Key Achievements at date of publication
Graham Breeze 'Just get on with it: a profile of Angela Mudge' **Angela Mudge Ochil Running Club**	*The Fellrunner*, Spring 2008, pp. 14–17	4 British Championships (1997–2000), 3 Scottish Hill Running Championships, Women's World Mountain Running Trophy 2000, 3 WMRA Grand Prix, World Masters Running Championship (2005), as well as wins at Ben Nevis, 3 Peaks, Pendle, Tour of Pendle, Buttermere Sailbeck and holds a plethora of Scottish fell race records
Graham Breeze 'Hope Springs Eternal A profile of Rob Hope' **Rob Hope (Pudsey and Bramley)**	*The Fellrunner*, Summer 2008, pp. 16-20	British Championships (2007), (2005), as well as wins at Langdale, Burnsall Classic, Kilnsey Sports, Grasmere Sports, Mourne Mountains, Winter Hill Race
Graham Breeze 'Laugh and be happy. A profile of Sarah Rowell' **Sarah Rowell (Pudsey and Bramley)**	*The Fellrunner*, Autumn 2008, pp. 14–19	Silver Medallist World Mountain Running Trophy (1992), 2nd in 1985 London Marathon in British record time, 4 Three Peaks wins, Record holder at Hutton Roof Crags (1994), Skiddaw (1989), Dalehead (1995), Harriers v. Cyclists (1999), Kinder Downfall (1995) England Team Selector

Source: Taken from Breeze and Smith, *The Fellrunner Magazine* (2002–2008)

Conclusion: recognising 'outsiders'

Many fell running clubs have been formed in the last thirty years by enthusiasts to pursue their own distinctive interest.[34] Many fell runners have felt neglected or ill at ease in mainstream athletic clubs with their traditional amateur emphasis on track and field disciplines. Relations between the organising bodies of athletics, the newly formed UK Athletics, and the FRA have become increasingly strained over a variety of issues. This has led to much soul searching amongst the FRA over rules, regulations and qualifications for coaching, procedures for organising races and most recently about litigation and insurance.[35] The precise details and tortuous discussions and positions need not detain us here as they have proved to be both divisive and complicated. But it is fair to say that the FRA fear bureaucratisation and what is viewed as 'interference' in fell running by outsiders, such as UK Athletics. The concern with minimising 'risk' and with codifying qualifications and coach training is generally anathema to fell running clubs and some fail to see any benefit in remaining affiliated to the parent body. However, for fell race organisations there is the growing fear of litigation, inadequate insurance and families or friends embarking on legal proceedings. Even relations between the FRA and UK Athletics' specialist PSG (Policy and Support Group) for Fell and Hill Running, renamed as the Competition Management Group are frosty. This has resulted in much turmoil in the FRA which surveyed members about retaining affiliation and the affirmative result has led to one resignation amongst long-serving FRA officers.

Dave Jones (Pennine) resigned both from the FRA Committee after 19 years service and also as editor of *The Fellrunner* (when he was involved in the production of fifteen Calendars and eighteen issues of the magazine), and he lamented in his final editorial:

> Selwyn Wright once memorably said that the rules of fell-running ought to be written on the back of a postage stamp … Fell-running is a gloriously simple, slightly anarchic activity with a committee composed of active (to a greater or lesser extent depending on the state of their knees, ankles etc!!) participants and has always placed great emphasis on individuality, common sense and a fairly short and straightforward set of rules.[36]

However, back in the 1980s, the 'outsiders' were 'professional' guides and runners. Richard Askwith's book provides an accessible account of the history of tensions reflecting the professional/amateur divide.[37] A more forensic sociological account of this division and its cultural relevance is provided by Frank Kew.[38] This separation was finally abolished in 1992 and was deemed hypocritical as amateurs made more in 'expenses' than professionals could garner from winnings over a year. But the divides ran deep between the Northern Sports Promoters Association (NSPA) and its successor British Open Fell Runners Association (BOFRA) and the AAAs. BOFRA races were the centrepiece of many Dales galas held at Hellifield, Cowling, Hebden and Kilnsey and organisers had no wish to break with local customs and practice. With hindsight, it is easy to minimise or overlook these traditional divisions. At that time they were rigidly adhered to by officials and deeply felt by race organisers. Athletic careers of national performers such as Mick Hawkins and Kenny Stuart were put on hold because they had developed through the junior ranks of BOFRA races and were branded as 'professionals' and banned from amateur competition. Although long forgotten some clubs, such as Wharfedale led by Kevin Rogan and David Hird, retain a strong commitment to organising BOFRA races, offering junior races, developing youth talent and providing BOFRA champions.

It may come as some surprise that for fell runners the clearest boundary sealing and securing their identity is not drawn against inactive 'couch potatoes' but rather against fellow runners. 'Joggers' and 'road runners' are felt to be a different breed. They are 'outsiders' who are 'softies' and fear getting dirty or are dismissed as sad because of their obsession with pounding the urban streets, collecting race T shirts and their constant fretting over mile times, splits and the rest.[39] So completing 5ks, 10ks, 10 miles, Half and Full marathons are really a distraction from the real thing. Fell runners do occasionally compete in road races and cross country competitions but usually as a means to sharpen up for fell races.

As the chapter has suggested, fell running can be a central building block in the construction of a hard northern identity. Dr. Martyn's Problem Page was a long-running spoof column in *The Fellrunner* and he is often called on to administer advice about dealing with women, gays and southerners.[40] People who are from the Midlands and South (or worse still London) are stigmatised and labelled 'softies'. Such 'Southerners', are always apologetic interlopers, who discover fell racing, usually when on holiday. This covers even most accomplished authorities, including even the celebrated Richard Askwith. His book in part maps out the author's several attempts at the Bob Graham Round; for example, trying to memorise the route whilst brushing his teeth in his London flat, as well as his bracing experiences of joining and training with the Keswick club. But he openly acknowledges, as do other contributors to *The Fellrunner Magazine*, that he and they are not from the North. Thereby southerners are denied adequate hills or mountains to train on but also forfeit any claim to be saying anything worthwhile in their articles and letters to the editor and the journal as a whole.

Perhaps the final word should go to Richard Askwith himself.

And more to the point I am supposed to be a fell-runner. That means that I am a member of the same breed as Joss Naylor and Billy Bland and Kenny Stuart and Bill Teasdale; the same as Ian Holmes and Helen Diamantes. I'm finding it tough, am I? Well it's supposed to be tough. If I can't handle it, I should bugger off back to London where I came from.[41]

[1] This article has benefited greatly from help from Graham Breeze, John Capenerhurst, Frank Kew, John Spink and Brett Weedon. Needless to say, all errors and confusions are attributable solely to the author.

[2] R. Askwith, *Feet in the Clouds. A Tale of Fell-Running and Obsession* (London, 2004), pp.1, 6.

[3] Tarquin Cooper, 'Fell-running: run that past me once more', *Daily Telegraph*, 19 July 2008.

[4] Helen Carter and Matthew Connolly, 'Organisers criticised as atrocious weather brings chaotic end to marathon fell race', *Guardian*, Monday 27 October 2008.

[5] Tarquin Cooper, Fell-running: run that past me once more. http://www.Telegraph.co.uk July 19 2008 (accessed 30 October 2008).

[6] For example Wainwright's two-week walk was completed in 39 hours and 36 minutes by Mike Hartley, knocking 7 hours 13 minutes off Mike Cudahy's 1986 time. *Up and Down* No.7 Sept/Oct 1991, p. 5.

[7] See Robin Bergstrand, 'Robin's Rant – where does "Mountain Running" fit in?', *The Fell Runner Magazine*, October 2004, p. 83 when he pointed out that 'mountain running', as practiced internationally, did not exist in the UK. He suggested that UK athletics and the FRA should consider long-term support for such elite athletes. Simon Blease's reply in *The Fell Runner Magazine*, February 2005, p. 88 argued that International Uphill Running is not what ordinary fell running is about. (During the years 2001–2006, the FRA publication carried the full title *The Fellrunner Magazine*, prior to those years and ever since its title was simply *The Fellrunner*).

[8] The alternative fell running magazine (published only in 12 editions by Dave Woodhead during 1991) was entitled *Up and Down*.

[9] Kenny Stuart worked as gardener for Keswick Council; Simon Booth worked for the Environment Agency and now is a Minerals and Waste Planner for Lancashire County Council.

[10] See, for example, 'Champions' Choice', *The Fellrunner Magazine*, February 2004, pp.54-6, when elite athletes Rob Jebb, Ian Holmes etc. choose their favourite races and events.

[11] See, for example, The Lake District Mountain Trial Association, *Fifty Years Running. A History of the Mountain Trial* (The Lake District Trial Association, August 2002).

[12] See, for example, M. Keys, 'The Rossendale Fell Race 1981', at http://www.rossendaleharriers.co.uk/fell%20running.htm (accessed 13.02.2008).

[13] See for example B. Smith, 'From Gradely Hills to Furness Fells', *The Fellrunner*, Autumn, 2008, pp. 30–33.

[14] W. Horsley, 'Kielder Fell Race. A brief history', *The Fellrunner*, Spring, 2008, p. 40.

[15] See 'Fanfare for the Common Woman'.

[16] In 1977 Jean Dawes was the first woman to complete the Bob Graham Round, followed by Anne-Marie Grindley (1978), Ros Coats and Wendy Dodds (1979); at this time 3 Peaks winners included Jean Lockhead, Sue Parkin, Jane Robson, Bridget Hogge and Vanessa Brindle.

17 R.A. Stebbins, 'Serious leisure', in E.L. Jackson and T.L. Burton (eds), *Leisure Studies. Prospects for the Twenty-first Century* (Pennsylvania, 1999).

18 Belinda Wheaton, *Understanding Lifestyle Sports: Consumption, Identity and Difference* (London and New York, 2004).

19 See Peta Bee, 'How I broke out of the gym', http://www.guardian.co.uk, 20.05.2008 (accessed 11 November 2008).

20 A. Greenwood, '21 Calder Valley fell runners get the key to the door', *The Fellrunner*, Spring 2008, p. 64.

21 A. Cohen, *The Symbolic Construction of Community* (London and New York, 1985).

22 See for example, three of Cohen's works, 'A sense of time, a sense of place: the meaning of close social association in Whalsay, Shetland' in his *Belonging: Identity and Social Organisation in British Rural Cultures* (Manchester, 1982), pp. 21–49; 'Of symbols and boundaries, or does Ertie's greatcoat hold the key?' in his *Symbolising Boundaries: Identity and Diversity in British Cultures* (Manchester, 1986), pp. 1–19; *Self Consciousness. An Alternative Anthropology of Identity* (London and New York, 1994).

23 E. Goffman, *Frame Analysis: An Essay on the organisation of Experience* (London, 1974).

24 Raymond Williams, *The country and the city* (London, 1973).

25 See FRA Fixtures Calendar and Handbook 2008, pp. 3–4.

26 J. Bishop and P. Hoggett, *Organizing Around Enthusiasms: Mutual Aid in Leisure* (London, 1986).

27 See, for example, 'Pubs and fell running', *The Fellrunner Magazine*, June 2003, pp. 53–6.

28 See the last part of the introduction to her accessible book *Off-Road Running*. 'That's it. Enjoy, I hope the book helps you get as much fun, enjoyment and satisfaction from running off-road as I do.' S. Rowell, *Off-Road Running* (Marlborough, 2002), p. 8.

29 See G. Breeze, 'Laugh and be happy. A profile of Sarah Rowell', *The Fellrunner*, Autumn 2008, pp. 14–19.

30 B. Whalley, 'Run, drink and fall over', *The Fellrunner*, Spring 2008, pp. 72–3. See G. Breeze, 'Hope springs eternal. A profile of Rob Hope', *The Fellrunner*, Summer 2008, pp. 16–20.

31 'A' should average 250ft climb/mile with <20% on road; 'B' should average 150ft climb/mile with <30% on road; 'C' should average 100ft climb/mile with <40% on road and should contain some genuine fell terrain.

32 Bill Smith, *Stud Marks on the Summits, A History of Amateur Fell Racing: 1861–1983* (Preston, 1985).

33 There is a short profile of Simon Bailey written by Neil Goldsmith in *The Fell Runner Magazine*, June 2005, p.18. See B. Smith, 'From Airedale to Kentdale. A profile of Rob Jebb and Sharon Taylor' in *The Fellrunner Magazine*, June 2004, pp. 50–2; G. Breeze, 'Lloyd and Jackie: a Profile', *The Fellrunner Magazine*, October 2006, pp. 9–11; B. Smith, 'Peak Partners. Profiles of Ali Welch and Aly Raw', *The Fellrunner*, Spring 2008, pp. 18–21.

34 See for example Calder Valley, Black Combe, Keighley and Craven, Dark Peak.

35 See Kevin Shevels, 'Litigation – the death of fell running?', *The Fellrunner Magazine*, February 2005, pp. 65–6 and Alistair McDonald, 'Fell running and litigation', *The Fellrunner Magazine*, June 2005, pp. 62–3.

36 *The Fellrunner Magazine*, October 2006, p. 1.

37 See Chapter 9 'What Price Tradition?' in Askwith, *Feet in the Clouds*, pp. 65–83.

38 F. Kew, 'Professional fell-running in northern Britain: negotiations with the dominant sport culture', in O. Weiss, *Sport in Space and Time* (Vienna, 1991).

39 Many fell runners purposely run without a watch in training and fell races. However, the introduction of GPS measurement has resulted in many fell runners investing in Garmins to measure distance, climb and time during runs. Naturally, there is fierce discussion and a check at the end of runs between athletes whose instrumentation measures the run differently.

40 See, for example, Dr Martyn's Problem Page in *The Fellrunner Magazine*, February 2005, p. 89. Since Britta Sendlhoffer became editor of *The Fellrunner* this intentionally politically incorrect column is no longer running.

41 Askwith, *Feet in the Clouds*, p. 3.

CHAPTER 3

An Extraordinary Joe: the Working-class Climber as Hero

Carol Osborne

Many tales are told of climbers bold
Who perished in the snow
But this is the rhyme of the rise to fame
Of a working lad named Joe.
He came from good old Manchester
That quaint, old-fashioned town
And his name became a legend –
The legend of Joe Brown.[1]

T. Patey, *One Man's Mountains*[2]

This, the first of twelve verses in Tom Patey's *The Joe Brown Song*, unequivocally asserts the Mancunian climber as legendary. Whilst essentially charting over twenty years of Brown's most renowned climbing achievements, in the final verses Patey satirises his friend and climbing companion as 'an also ran'; one who had to make way for the inevitable new generation of climbers; those like Peter Crew who aspired 'to burn Brown off' by repeating established climbs of the highest standards and by audaciously putting up new routes of even greater difficulty.[3] Unfortunately, Patey was killed in a climbing accident in 1970 so did not live to fully witness what he anticipated for Joe in the final verses of his song: namely, that 'The Grand Old Man of the Rock and Ice' would maintain his contribution to climbing, both as practitioner and inspirational figure. This chapter seeks to assess those contributions in the period predominantly before the penning of Patey's song. In doing so, it identifies the complex dynamics that underpin understandings of Brown as a worthy and enduring northern sporting hero.

48

Given the very nature of the pursuit, a climber might seem an obvious choice to posit as a sporting hero. The ascent of vertical, high rocky places is perceived by non-climbers as brave, especially in the context of high peak mountaineering, an aspect in which, in addition to domestic rock climbing, Joe Brown excelled, as will later be shown. Yet, for climbers themselves, over time the perception has been mediated by more finely defined understandings of difficulty or, to be more precise, the ability to challenge established climbing standards as framed by grading systems of the day. When Joe Brown became aware of the issue, the adjectival grading system comprised Easy, Moderate, Difficult, Very Difficult, Severe and Very Severe.[4] It is Joe's early and continued consistency in climbing within and beyond the higher bands of difficulty – thereby consolidating an 'extreme' standard of climbing – coupled with the sheer number of new routes he pioneered, that assured him a high profile in the climbing world at the time of his most prolific activity and ever since.[5]

Yet, in spite of the risk associated with even the most challenging climbs, climbers are generally reticent about being designated heroic. Writing about the psychology of advanced rock climbing, Brown's peer Dennis Gray observed that 'aggressive and competitive factors are most associated with activities requiring boldness and courage. Although I would like to substitute the word "courage" by something like "challenge" I hate to see the word "courage" used for activities like climbing, this word is used too freely and should be only reserved for exceptional situations in which human beings find themselves and usually not by their own free will.'[6] This does, then, allow for heroics to be equated with climbing, due to the unanticipated incidents that are bound to occur in a sport acknowledged to be risky and where participants often find themselves compromised by unforeseen 'conditions', including the misfortunes of fellow climbers.[7] Nevertheless, it is an observation with which the 'hero' under consideration here would almost certainly agree and, as will be shown, it was precisely the exertion of free will that first took the boy Joe Brown out of an increasingly degenerating Manchester millscape in the early 1940s.

In the context of the north of England, beyond the heavily industrialised cities and towns, the mountain landscape broadly identified with the Peak District (impinging upon the counties of Derbyshire, Lancashire and Yorkshire), and the Lake District have provided a natural playground for inhabitants rich and poor, young and old, willing to take up the recreational opportunities on offer. Over time, the North has produced a number of dedicated rambling, caving and climbing clubs, as well as several notable climbing practitioners who have cut their teeth on local crags and climbing outcrops.[8] Yet because of its marginal status within what is typically understood as 'sport', as well as the tendency to equate sporting achievement and interests in the North with football, rugby league and cricket, even the greatest practitioners of climbing have received little mainstream acclaim for their contributions to the sporting life of the region.[9] This in spite of the fact that climbing has not only constituted a part of the patchwork of 'outdoor' activities documented as playing a significant role in the North's recreational and sporting life, but also that of the nation.[10]

Like others before him, Joe Brown was inspired by the sporting challenge the ascent of local crags presented and the search for adventure therein that this implies. When he began to cut a profile for himself in the late 1940s, the type of climber better known to the general public had found mention in a spectacle-hungry press, usually by climbing in the Himalayas where the ascent of Everest had been a focus since the 1920s. Drawing down on a climbing tradition inaugurated in 1857 via the foundation of the socially exclusive Alpine Club, high peak climbing was essentially a rich man's game. Similarly, in spite of the expansion of recreational climbing in the post-war years, the character of the domestic climbing scene was framed by those upper middle-class climbers affiliated to the clubs, such as the Scottish Mountaineering Club (1889), the Climbers' Club (1898) and the Fell and Rock Climbing Club (1906) which were instrumental in cultivating the sport in Britain during the late Victorian and Edwardian periods in Britain.[11]

Born in 1930 and initially raised in 'a very small terrace house in the middle of a large slum area' in the Manchester suburb of Ardwick, Joe Brown therefore emerged from an entirely different social milieu to the one identified with this climbing establishment.[12] His widowed mother moved her family of seven children to the more socially mixed but still mill-defined city district of Chorlton on Medlock, only to be bombed out in the Manchester blitz. Settling in Longsight after this displacement, the profound affinity Joe developed with the countryside was born of 'a desire to explore the outside world'.[13] This seems to have set him apart from the majority of his immediate community, for, in spite of the interwar fashion for walking, they had not the information, wherewithal or disposable income for this exploration:

> The narrowness of interests in and experience of the world beyond our neighbourhood was widespread and unshakeable. … To many people the moorland heights often framed at the end of the dreary streets were merely a boundary marking the limits of a place on earth.[14]

Reminiscing some forty years later in a television documentary, *An Extraordinary Joe*, a glimpse of his boyhood distaste for the mundane which surely underpinned this desire for exploration is revealed: having exhausted the possibilities for mischief and adventure on his doorstep, and buoyed up by his friend Ronnie Dutton, Joe embarked upon a series of excursions and makeshift camping trips to the landscape beyond. The pair focused principally upon 'messing about' down caves, then progressing to climbing at Alderley Edge.[15] By incrementally exploring the local Peak District landscape, Joe and a growing circle of like-minded youths capitalised upon the circumstance of living in relatively close proximity to the fells and crags, just as others of like disposition had done a generation before them.[16] In this period of early exploration, schoolboy poverty and ignorance dictated a rough and ready approach to their activities, his first climbing 'rope' being 'a sash cord … discarded as a washing line by my mother, who considered that it had outworn its usefulness'. In being 'strong enough to give the second man a tug, it seemed quite adequate to use at the time.'[17]

In common with other aspiring climbers of like background, then, for Brown there was neither early introduction to any established climbing network nor instruction in climbing techniques which such connection implies. Instead he enjoyed a self-initiated entry into an activity which in the early years of his participation represented less of a sport and more of a natural thing for an energetic lad to do. By the time Joe was apprenticed to a local builder at fourteen, his regular weekend visits to the crags testify to what would hold as the overarching rationale for his avid participation: pure fun.

That climbing became an integral part of his life from an early age perhaps explains what evolved as a pronounced tendency to understatement; generally in relation to the physical and mental challenges of climbing itself and, more specifically, in relation to his own achievements within the sport. In relation to the latter, Joe put up hundreds of new routes on domestic rock and achieved significant British climbing 'firsts' in the Alps and the greater mountain ranges of the world.[18] However, the active recording of this output was destined to have less to do with Joe himself and more to do with a sporting subculture which, like others, depends upon the documentation of its highest achievements to foster further advances. In the case of Joe, this dynamic suggests that the characteristics of modesty and competitiveness are not mutually exclusive. Indeed, it would be naïve to claim that competitiveness is not a necessary condition of such output, but these achievements can be fundamentally assessed as a by-product of Joe's passion for his sport, rather than born of any original intention to attain recognition as 'the best'. As he put it at the height of his climbing powers and prominence: 'The Beatles didn't set out to dominate the pop world. They made a sound that everyone liked. If the reception had been otherwise the sound would have been just the same. That was how it was with me.'[19]

For those unacquainted with climbing, Joe's statement provides a useful analogy for the purpose of interpretation. The Beatles' sound depended upon the combined talents of the group, even though the defining figures were John Lennon and Paul McCartney. Thus, a critical factor in the formative period of Joe's climbing career during the late 1940s and early 1950s, as well as beyond, must be acknowledged as the company he kept; company that shared a similar process of self initiation into the sport, common social background and an irreverent attitude to life well expressed through the priority given to climbing and easy acceptance of the frugal outdoor lifestyle necessary to facilitate it.

The informality of the friendships cultivated at the local outcrops also ensured that

Joe remained relatively unhindered by preconceived ideas about the difficulties of existing or untried routes. Active route finding was the essence of adventure, at a time when information came by way of privately circulated club journals and when the production of guidebooks specifically for the Peak District was in its infancy. In spite of increasingly moving in circles that contributed to the latter, finding and doing remained the hallmark of Joe's approach, not dedicated documentation of his explorations.[20] This places him within a pre-existing tradition of working-class climbing which reproduced itself via deeds and networks at the crag.

Without access to what in any case was relatively scant information on existing routes, climbing was therefore done in the spirit of identifying a route that might 'go' and getting on with it – regardless of predetermined understandings of difficulty. Thus, at Laddow, early in his career, when other climbers warned Joe about the rock being 'hard' or 'very severe', he claims to have been uncertain about what these terms meant; that existing routes did not leave him compromised led Joe to conclude with hindsight that 'People had a mental blockage about "hard" climbs.'[21] This 'can do' attitude is further exemplified when in Spring 1947 Joe and Slim Sorrell took a break from work and ventured to Snowdonia, North Wales. After 'polishing off' all the routes on Holly Tree Wall and Gribin Facet, attention shifted to the allegedly most difficult route in the district: Lot's Groove. Advice from two of the best climbers in the country, John Disley and John Lawton, to 'top rope' the Groove did nothing to deter them from climbing it 'on sight'.[22] Joe could not understand what the fuss was about, but acknowledged that such achievements were underpinned by his apprenticeship, served grappling with the stiff gritstone problems in the Peak District near to his Manchester home.

The identification of gritstone as a learning and testing ground is important. In the 1995 obituary of Nat Allen, one of Joe's early climbing mentors, Jim Perrin asserts: 'This is the core religion of the British sport, the purest and – the uninitiated would argue – the most difficult of venues and styles.'[23] The positive friction afforded by grit is offset by its smoothness and, therefore, deficiency of positive holds. The fierce cracks, rounded bulges and its relative steepness, make for routes of sustained difficulty, albeit on crags of invariably low height. In the late twentieth century, contributors to the now cult film *Hard Grit* (1998) were unequivocal in their assessment of what the medium represents. Hard grit is 'about belief – belief in yourself. Belief in what the rock can give you. Believing that you're not in a dangerous position when sure as hell you are.' It is about 'climbing at the limits of your capabilities and doing it with strength of mind.' And it is 'about routes that other people can't do'.[24] From this perspective, to climb to the highest standards of the day on grit and, better still, exceed them indicates possession of superior psychological and physical capacities for those practitioners who can master it. In Brown the medium found a perfect combination of attributes: strength of arm coupled with suitable technique (notably expert use of handjams, renowned for taking the skin off the backs of less skilled practitioner's hands, on cracks), suppleness, agility and confidence to master the challenge in front of him. This provides some clue as to the respect he commands within climbing circles past and present.

A full fifty years earlier Joe's own comprehension of 'the difficulty and quality of the routes we [he and others] had been doing with established standards'[25] came into sharper focus through his membership of the Derby-based Valkyrie Club. This association brought him into more frequent contact with other climbers who provided a rudimentary education about climbing, shared their knowledge of trends within the sport and extended his horizons to the loftier crags of the Lake District. There, Joe repeated the climbs of Lakeland's comparable rising star, Arthur Dolphin, the hero of the Yorkshire based Bradford Lads, another largely working-class contingent of enthusiastic climbers.[26] With the fragmentation of the Valkyrie in 1951, those climbers living in Manchester gradually regrouped to form the Rock and Ice – the club Joe felt had 'shaped' his career in the 1950s. The calibre of the Manchester group, fourteen in total, is indicated by Joe's observation that they were all capable of leading Very Severe climbs.[27] The inclusion of 17-year-old Salford-born Don Whillans in the fold, undoubtedly contributed to the group's reputation for bold climbing, something illustrated by an entrée that indicated an ability to climb on equal terms with Joe. Out at the Staffordshire Roaches in April 1951, Whillans opportunely put himself forward not only to follow, but to lead Brown on the second more difficult pitch of a route called Matinee – a climb which had defeated other potential takers that day.[28] This performance in front of a large group of onlookers marked the beginning of a working relationship destined to take on a life of its own, albeit originated and subsequently nurtured in the context of Rock and Ice activities, as member Dennis Gray's observation testifies: 'Whillans and Brown may have been the arrow's tip, but the weight behind the head was often the work of other members.'[29]

Without taking anything away from Don and Joe, what Gray identifies here is the unremittingly collective dedication that went into producing new routes, weekend in and weekend out. Discovering a route did not automatically lead to the immediate climbing of it; several attempts by different climbers, especially one as replete with talent as the Rock and Ice was, followed. Similarly, whilst Brown or Whillans might respectively be responsible for identifying and leading a raft of ultra-challenging new climbs not just with each other, but with different partners, the quality of the partnership was contributory, if not integral, to their achievements. Indeed throughout his climbing career Joe aligned with a number who could hold their own and from whom he benefited, for example, in terms of mentoring and friendship (Nat Allen, Slim Sorrell); shared outlook (Ian McNaught-Davis, Tom Patey, Mo Anthoine); and further innovation which had taken his own achievements as the reference point (Peter Crew). Nevertheless, in much the same way as Lennon and McCartney are accepted as the definitive partnership that underpinned the Beatles' super stardom, the names of Joe Brown and Don Whillans are equated with the phenomenal advance within 'British' climbing from the early 1950s.

The notion that they were advancing within British, as opposed to specifically northern, climbing is accounted for by the pair's less than parochial attitude to their sport. Whilst their expertise and technique were predominantly honed on northern gritstone, as evidenced by an impressive first ascent list that both matched and exceeded the highest standards of the day,[30] they ensured their credibility as all round rock climbers by extending their reach to locations where other top flight climbers plied their trade. For example, on the Eastern Crags of the Lake District, Castle Rock and Raven Crag, they intermittently asserted their authority by tackling and repeating hard climbs on what A.H. Griffin assessed in 1959 as 'fearsome' territory. They are noted too for putting up Dovedale Groove on Dove Crag which had stood 'in inviolate splendour' for almost a decade – this 1953 route itself defied repeat into the 1960s.[31] In Scotland, itself home to a notorious working-class climbing club the Creagh Dhu, they put up the aptly named Sassenach on the 800ft buttress Carn Dearg, under the watchful eyes of Scottish climbers.[32]

However, beyond the gritstone playgrounds their exploits in the Lakes and Scotland can arguably be understood as gestures of their authority when compared with their concerted efforts together, with others and sometimes unseconded, on the Llanberis cliffs in North Wales. For the uninitiated, route nomenclature perhaps best conjures an image of the magnitude (Cenotaph Corner), seriousness (Cemetery Gates), commitment (The Mostest), ingenuity (Cromlech Girdle) and technique (The Black Cleft), their completion required. For climbers, the description of the length and calibre of the routes extends well beyond the limitations that space imposes here and is expressed by the commentators, historians and guidebook writers who, if not climbers of note themselves, are on sufficiently intimate terms with the sport to act as credible arbiters of what counts as groundbreaking, classic and, therefore, essential climbing.[33]

A point upon which several, including Brown, are agreed, is that the 500ft Clogwyn d'ur Arddu, described by his pioneering forerunner Colin Kirkus as 'quite the most magnificent precipice in England and Wales' became synonymous with the Rock and Ice.[34] Yet, more than any other, Joe was integral to that exploration and is generally acknowledged as such. For in offering an inordinate amount of opportunities on a mostly vertical face, 'Cloggy' appealed to his sense of adventure. Thus, he worked until the rock could offer no more by way of surprises and therefore, climbing challenge.[35] Joe's personal sense of 'complete' knowledge quickly translated into discrete recognition of the work he did there, the position summed up by Chris Bonington, an up-and-coming climber during the 1950s: 'In 1955 the routes put up by Joe Brown inspired a superstitious respect; only a handful of climbers were venturing on to even the easiest ones.'[36] When Joe's routes finally succumbed to newcomers at the end of 1950s and into the 1960s, they attained the status of test pieces or classic climbs. Thereafter turning his attention to the southern crags of Snowdonia and notably increasing his standard at Tremadog, he ultimately became *the* name associated with the opening up of Welsh climbing in the post-war period.[37]

Pioneering and repeating climbs that contributed to the consolidation of an extreme standard on cliffs like those found in the Lake District, Scotland and North Wales required Joe to draw down upon accrued experience, sound judgement and a preparedness to extend understandings of sufficient means to climb. He was adept at incorporating innovatory techniques to make a route 'go', ranging from the 'placing' of stones in cracks through which to thread slings, to the limited use of pegs or pitons to protect a serious climb – meaning one where a fall could prove fatal. The use of 'ironmongery' particularly raised the ire of the sport's purists, in fact the majority, who opposed climbing with all but the minimum of aid, meaning rope and, in the post-war years, the gym shoes or vibrams which superseded nailed boots.

Joe himself observed that 'contrary to the impression of cheating, artificial climbing involved complex and precise techniques' and, perhaps more important to a climber like him searching primarily for adventure this rendered the climbing 'very sensational but usually quite safe because the climber was attached to the rock every few feet by the rope running through snap-links on pegs'.[38] As the many descriptions of his climbs in his autobiography *The Hard Years* show, in reality Joe was not unnecessarily liberal with such aid. More critically, coupled with his remarkable movement intelligence, its use proved to be instrumental in raising existing climbing standards beyond expectation, as well as tempering the higher risk of climbing on less viable rock. This rendered Joe a 'safe' climber who openly kept his risky sporting passion in perspective. In doing so he opened the way for others to follow, either in the same style or by incrementally climbing his routes with less aid, something which in Jim Perrin's view, marks him out as 'the great liberating chapter in climbing's history'.[39]

At the time and ever since, insiders have therefore been unequivocal in their assessment of what Joe Brown individually and together with Don Whillans represented in terms of progressing the sport, evidenced by the production of a quantity and quality of routes which others either could not match, or had great difficulty in repeating. But the reputations they achieved, notably as 'hard' climbers, also turned (and turns) upon the lengths to which they were prepared to go to climb: consistently saving every spare penny from manual workers' wages to facilitate an untypical sporting pleasure and, once the hard earned trip was won, climbing with a determination akin to an attitude of 'come hell or high water'. These circumstances are no better expressed than through their oft cited 48-hour 'epic' on the West Face of the Dru during the Alpine season of 1953/54. This saw them achieve an ascent through rain and storm, sleep deprivation, recovery from 'losing' the route, and a descent without food in a frozen state due to bivouacking in sodden clothing. Little wonder that Joe likened the experience to 'a nightmare world', whilst others considered this third ascent a stunning performance given that the first had taken seven days and the second three and a half days.[40] After a serious lull in activity, it was not then members of the Alpine Club who put British Alpinism back on a respectable footing, but two Manchester men from its working-class counterpart, the Rock and Ice.

Had Brown and Whillans done little else beyond the relatively short-lived duration of their partnership, then their place would still be guaranteed in climbing history. However, as already indicated, both maintained a prominent position within the sport via the development of other partnerships. Thus, the profound impression their activities during the first half of the 1950s left upon it does not entirely account for the high status they respectively went on to achieve, but certainly did much to determine perceptions of two distinctive personalities – perceptions which not only framed their future directions within the sport, but had implications for understandings of their heroic appeal.

For Joe, in searching for interpretive leverage, it is important not to conflate the notion of 'hard' climbing with a harshness of character, something which could in turn be explained by the conditions of life implied by his northern working-class background. The opposite can be observed as true for Don Whillans, for whom the limitations of an albeit comparable experience manifested *off* the rock in an observable 'chip on his shoulder' and a demeanour so direct it bordered on the abrasive.[41] Indeed, Whillans has been explicitly written of in the press as the stereotypical working-class northern male. For example, marking his fiftieth birthday in a news report for *The Times*, Ronald Faux observed: 'He has an accent as flat as the cap he often climbs in and his girth is set on a short, immensely strong frame.[42] When Don died just two years later Faux elaborated further: 'In some respects he was an anti-hero, not at all the athletic paragon the public imagine mountaineers to be. He was stout, short and "liked a pint".[43] However, whilst Joe outlived his climbing partner, he can no more be observed as 'the athletic paragon' than Don; he too being short in stature and similarly endowed with workmanlike strength and stamina. Both men rose to the top of their game as *natural* climbers.

Yet, beneath their similar physiological and technical abilities, their 'eye' for routes can be seen as expressive of their essential characters and, therefore, embodied approach to climbing: Don went for more obvious direct lines, Joe for more subtle ones. Drawing a boxing analogy, Jim Perrin likens Joe to a Muhammad Ali or Sugar Ray Leonard, whilst Don is a Mike Tyson, 'clinically efficient, fast and aggressive, reducing the rock's resistance by sheer force of onslaught ...'[44] Off the rock aspects of Joe's subtlety as a climber, expressed by what Ken Wilson observes as 'a rare combination of attributes' translated into his being easier company and more accommodating of others: his keenness, patience, strength and intelligence all adding up to a 'mysterious charisma'.[45] These differences between the two can therefore be understood as the mediating factor in their early relationships with the climbing establishment. For, having both risen rapidly to the summit of their sport, it was Joe who found himself marked for recruitment by the climbing establishment.

In *The Hard Years* Joe says remarkably little about the level or quality of contact he had in his early career with establishment climbers, meaning those who held memberships with the premier climbing clubs. Exposure did, however, undoubtedly occur, as brief comments made about the 'Oxford types' he encountered in North Wales reveal.[46] Brown had met members of the successful 1953 Everest expedition before the acclaimed Alpine trip of 1954. Whilst he assumed that selections for the next large-scale outing to the Himalayas were already decided, the events of that trip may have played no small part in the decision to offer him a place on the 1955 Kanchengjunga reconnaissance expedition.

Arguably, the offer to join this expedition said as much about the attitude of Charles Evans the surgeon who made it as it did about Joe Brown the general builder who accepted it: that the historically persistent curtailment of opportunities to climb at elite level based upon understandings of social class should not be an overarching consideration when weighed against talent and potential to fit in. Certainly, once the expedition was underway, Evans made a point of highlighting how Joe's 'unpretentious ways hide the fact that in recent years he has set a new standard in British climbing …'[47] Thus, firstly, Joe offered up an opportunity for the climbing establishment to break with the precedent of choosing the well-heeled and well-connected for official expeditions and, secondly, he offered up a challenge to it. Not so much by forcing acceptance of an abrasive kind of 'hard' working-class masculinity of the type Don Whillans was perceived to express, but by demonstrating without contrivance that someone from this social background could rise above the perceptions that prevailing understandings of class position implied. Joe's essentially disinterested attitude to the issue of class cannot be observed as having been unduly challenged by this or subsequent sustained exposure to the professional middle classes typically associated with high peak climbing. The acid test for Joe was not so much the social status of an individual as defined by a good education, occupation or title, but simply whether those so privileged were 'a bore, or interesting people'.[48]

Joe's rite of passage into the ranks of the climbing elite and, therefore, potentially wider heroic appeal, thus came with his selection to the 1955 Kanchenjunga expedition. The decision turned out to be well judged, when on the final push for the summit after five hours of upward trudging and scrambling the expedition's acknowledged 'chief expert on rock' came into his own on a challenging rock pitch by picking out the likeliest crack to attain summit success.[49]

In achieving the first ascent of the third highest peak in the world, one identified as posing a greater climbing challenge than Mount Everest, it would be fair to assume that Joe and his climbing partner George Band had secured a place in public, if not sporting, memory.[50] Indeed, Dennis Gray's overtly class-conscious observation that prior to Kanchenjunga the press had been looking 'for heroes from the changing social patterns of Britain in order to interest the public at large in new activities and to capture the attention of a massive new sector with great spending power',[51] would seem to add weight to this assumption. It would, however, be wrong. Commenting on the climbing fraternity's 50th Anniversary celebration of the event in 2005, Ed Douglas came closer to the mark in dubbing this first ascent 'A quiet triumph' – something the unpretentious Joe Brown likely welcomed.[52]

Since this had been an *unanticipated* first ascent on a lesser peak, the usual publicity machine which had become a standard feature of the eight British Mount Everest expeditions since the 1920s had not been set in train. Even the predominantly northern complexion of the expeditionary personnel could not convince the *Manchester Guardian* that there was much value in buying the exclusive rights to the Kanchenjunga story. Ultimately, *The Times* took the rights, but the negotiated terms of copy were scant, thereby suggesting that with the fall of Everest the ability of climbing to capture the public's imagination was considered to have had its day.[53]

Thus an ascent that lent itself to acclaim because it was the highest ever attained by two Britons generated relatively little remark in the national press.[54] Brown and Band did not therefore emerge as well celebrated, let alone heroic figures as a result of their achievement. As Whannel has noted in the context of contemporary sport, narrative is important in the construction of celebrity; it is the story woven around sporting events and the 'sports star' participant that provides the opportunity for audience interaction.[55] In the case of Kanchenjunga the story was missing as the mediating factor in facilitating the recognition of Brown and Band as worthy sporting heroes.

The *Manchester Evening News* was, however, more proactive in taking up the issue of the achievement. Casting Joe as 'a Little Man with Big Ideas', the opportunity to comment upon his 'five feet four' stature matched against 28,000ft of snow and ice was irresistible copy, as was identification of his 'Lancashire grit' in tackling "The Killer" mountain.[56] In this report no concession was made to George Band, Joe's Cambridge-educated partner in the ascent – it was 'Joe Brown the Plumber' who had 'humbled' the overwhelming competition. Although the details of Joe's critical contribution to achieving the first ascent were missing, the message conveyed to the readership was as one that equated his success with northern working-class determination.[57] Explicit identification of heroism in this newspaper was not, however, reserved for those locals searching for challenge of their own free will as Joe had done, but rather for those who responded to unforeseen difficulties, such as the local Scout master who had rescued one of his stranded charges from a 300ft rock face, or the 14-

year-old boy who had rescued two girls from drowning in the Bridgewater Canal.[58]

It is perhaps unsurprising then that Joe's participation in the successful expedition to the spectacular 23, 800ft Mustagh Tower in 1956 only found belated mention in a paper focused upon human interest stories, specifically within announcement of his forthcoming marriage to Burnley schoolteacher Valerie Gray.[59] Whilst Mustagh was appreciated by the climbing community as another significant 'first' within the high peak arena, the wedding was considered to be more newsworthy, related as it was to the local population's more immediate realm of experience – a point subsequently confirmed by Joe's observation that there were probably more journalists at his wedding reception than guests.[60] An excellent climber he may have been, but that did not exempt him either from the practicalities of working life or from the financial considerations an impending marriage implied. Yet, for those who cared to look, Joe Brown simultaneously represented a point of local identification *and* the suggestion of a world beyond Manchester, one that offered extraordinary opportunities to any willing to grasp them.

Certainly for those within his more immediate sporting circle, the Kanchenjunga ascent was pertinent for what it conveyed about the opportunities apparently open to the ordinary working man, coming as it did so close on the heels of the 1953 Everest success. The latter, Dennis Gray observed, 'meant as little to us personally as reading Annapurna had to me and for the same reason: no working class climber had taken part and for most of us even the Alps were beyond our means.'[lxi] Aside from the ascent itself, the significance of Joe's achievement for the climbing community can therefore be observed as the breaking of the class barrier in what to date had been a virtually impenetrable arena to those without the social connections implied by membership or association with the Alpine Club.[62] Through talent and sheer dedication to his sport, Joe Brown had demonstrated that individuals like him could excel in a post-war society that, in theory at least, aspired to promote merit above privilege. However, in the mid-1950s it would perhaps be more accurate to say that Brown's selection *pre-empted* changes afoot in economic and social conditions more generally, rather than being representative of them. From this perspective he might more reasonably be identified as a prototype working-class hero on account of the entrenched attitudes to social class that continued to characterise officially sponsored high peak expeditions.[63]

The point is well illustrated by another of Tom Patey's satirical verses, *Red Pique* (*The Alpine Club Song*). Framed around the event of the 1962 Anglo–Scottish Pamirs expedition, it not only highlighted the particular inclusion of Joe on the successful ascent of Mount Communism, but the class dynamics still at work with regard to selection of appropriate personnel, thus:

Customs change and so alas
We now include the working class
So we invited Good Old Joe
To Come along and join the show
He played his part, he fitted in
He justified our faith in him
We want the climbing world to know –
That the chaps all got on well with Joe.

In the eighth verse, 'Credo', Patey did not spare the Alpine Club mentality from exposure: Our climbing leaders are no fools / They went to the very best Public Schools / You'll never go wrong with Everest Men / So we select them again and again / Again and again and again and again.[64]

It is, then, somewhat surprising that Chris Bonington, noted elsewhere in this song as excluded from the Pamirs expedition, has identified Brown as having 'always been happy to sit back and let opportunity arrive,' as opposed to identifying his action and attitude as integral to the creation of that opportunity.[65] For there can be little doubt that in spite of the resilience of an 'Old School Tie' mentality amongst those who held sway over selections to high peak expeditions, there were those who recognised a fitting combination of calibre and character within Joe that his peers simply did not possess. Moreover, as previously indicated, he showed himself to be proactive in his search for adventure; from a localised contact base along with others of like enthusiasm, he went further afield and at significant moments stretched himself financially to facilitate development of his climbing: in the Alps, on the Kanchenjunga expedition (for which he had to auction his climbing gear to raise the suggested £20 pocket money) and, in 1956, to join the Mustagh Tower expedition. So whilst it was argued at the outset of this chapter that the condition of free choice detracts from the notion of the climber as heroic however risky the climbing encounter, Joe's ordinariness set against the extraordinariness of his activities at the historical juncture of the mid-1950s surely locates him within Campbell's view of a hero as one who 'ventures forth from the world of common day into a region of supernatural wonder [where] fabulous forces are there encountered and a decisive victory won: the hero comes back from his mysterious adventure with the power to bestow boons on his fellow man.'[66]

On the one hand, it is perhaps fanciful to assert that the mountain environment as a region of 'supernatural wonder' could hold much currency for a public drawn by the material temptations of the increasingly vibrant consumer culture of the 1950s. On the other hand, for the overwhelming majority with no direct experience of climbing, the spectacle of high mountains as a 'fabulous force' to be humanly reckoned with and so representative of a 'mysterious adventure' can more readily be asserted as integral to the dynamic which progressed the spectacle of climbing beyond the tired newspaper coverage to the nation's television screens.

The highpoint of this progress came in July 1967 with 'Six Men, One Mountain', the live transmission of an ascent of the Old Man of Hoy, a 450ft sea stack in the Orkneys. This was not the first time that the viewing public had been given the opportunity to watch climbers in action and, in addition to press coverage, since Kanchenjunga Joe had developed a media presence via appearances on radio and television talks and climbs.[67] It was, however, undoubtedly the hitherto most successful televised climb on account of the magnitude of the exercise, its dramatic effect and, in spite of the huge organisational and technical efforts entailed, efficiency of execution.[68]

In pinpointing the location, Tom Patey had astutely predicted that the success of the programme would lie in the motivations of a vicarious audience, compelled by the prospect that those participating could literally come unstuck during transmissions. Whilst the audience was to be disappointed on the latter count, the experience of watching six climbers completing an ascent by three different routes, over a series of six instalments, during one weekend contributed to the suspense of witnessing what Chris Bonington identified as 'a very dangerous bit of work'.[69] The public response was overwhelmingly positive. The press variously declared the programme 'memorable', 'marvellous' and 'spectacular' and the BBC's Audience Research Report summed up the overall public verdict as 'very thrilling viewing indeed'.[70] That audience viewing figures ran into millions was perhaps underpinned by producer and commentator Christopher Brasher's insistence that Hoy should not merely be a Saturday afternoon sideshow scheduled to 'fit in' with *Grandstand*'s mainstream sports, but a high profile exhibition of Britain's best climbers at work, televised in July to avoid the June-time staples of Wimbledon, Ascot and Henley.[71]

All of these conditions give some credibility to Gilchrist's observation that the climbers attained a semblance of celebrity status as a result of this well timed and extensive television exposure.[72] However, then as now, the notion of celebrity neither sits comfortably with climbers who move in an essentially participant-based sporting realm, nor does it necessarily underwrite heroic status – although the spectacle did apparently invoke a sense of the heroic in the eyes of viewers, expressed by one left gasping at this exhibition of courage and skill'.[73]

Particularly in the context of deliberately generated dramatic effects, Joe Brown's performance can be observed as contributing to the sense of amazement viewers registered. This was not on account of behaviour complicit with the drama, but rather, due to the workmanlike ease with which he executed the climb and the lack of concession he made to providing commentary. The latter was left to those more adept at the art conversation on camera – his jocular partner on the climb, Ian MacNaught-Davis and the consummate professional in the team, Chris Bonington, who along with Tom Patey was repeating his first ascent of the Old Man.[74] Due to his distaste for 'rehearsed' television climbs, Joe predominantly led a new route up the South Face of the Old Man, thereby injecting a degree of genuine suspense for the audience and providing an authentic view of a pioneering climber at work. Despite the precariousness of the venture, confirmed during transmission by the crumbling rock either in the climber's hands or giving way 'like [piles of] dinner plates' under their feet, in a suitably matter of fact fashion Joe assessed the ascent as otherwise 'not technically difficult'.[75] But then why would a climber of his calibre identified to the audience as 'the greatest rock climber in the world. … the Master at work' be gripped by such a climb?[76] Chris Brasher, who made that comment, was certainly of the opinion that Joe's contribution was so far above that of the other climbers that he advised Joe that he would request an enhanced fee for him from Artist Bookings.[77]

Joe's subsequent excursions into television and film would keep him intermittently in the public eye, but for someone who otherwise showed little inclination towards cultivating a high public profile it is difficult to assess the acceptance of such work as anything but financially expedient. A return visit to Hoy at the age of 54 for a televised climb with his daughter left him looking no more strained than during his first encounter in his thirties – not surprising for one who was still climbing well up to the extreme standard.[78] It was not an ascent that can be assessed as even remotely replicating the impact of the 1967 broadcast. Chris Bonington identifies the latter as a project never to be repeated, in that it came together at the right time, in the right place with the right people. Hamish MacInness, climber and contracted BBC cameraman, was thereafter challenged by the search for equally spectacular locations and was hindered by the technical insights the making of Hoy had exposed.[79] The BBC's Outside Broadcast Unit had therefore spectacularly over reached itself by producing what Executive Producer Alan Chivers assessed as 'the most outlandish outside broadcast sport ever imagined'.[80] Arguably, as a consequence, climbing could not be envisaged as a regular fixture in the nation's televised sporting schedules. Thus the pursuit neither enjoyed the increasingly consistent exposure of mainstream sports nor the identification of its most gifted practitioners as sporting heroes – although it is unlikely that they would have wished it. In contrast to professional climber Chris Bonington, for whom cultivating a public profile was important, others revealed that accepting the Hoy contract turned less upon making a name for oneself, but more upon the camaraderie of undertaking it, the sociability of a 'piss up' and a 'sumptuous meal' after the event; the gear that came free after the climb and, of course, the payment for providing a rare public display of breathtaking physical prowess on the rock.[81]

Nevertheless, 1967 can be understood as representing a high point in Joe's public visibility. In addition to Hoy came the publication of his ghost written autobiography and a BBC documentary, simply entitled *Joe*. The latter juxtaposed the thoughts and images of Joe Brown the family man with those of Joe Brown the climber, supported and, as one not generally given over to self-promotion, no doubt reassured in the venture by interviewer and friend Ian McNaught-Davis and active climbing partner, Peter Crew.[82] For a climber of Joe Brown's acumen who throughout the years had always needed to earn a living to support both his passion for climbing and a family, engagement with the public face of his sport and, therefore, his own remarkable achievements can be understood as ultimately pragmatic. Both the documentary and book coincided with a relocation to Llanberis in North Wales and the opening of a climbing shop, simply trading under – and on – his name: 'Joe Brown'. Aside from the money, he considered the book to be 'good publicity' and, if his climbing activities had not already implied it, on camera Joe confirmed that 'Manchester doesn't have anything to offer'.[83] Whilst it is unlikely that his affection for gritstone climbing was diminished, at the age of 37 Joe had managed to establish considerably more than a business in the location which had underpinned his early climbing aspirations and high reputation as a rock climber: he was deep in the throes of an equally exceptional second coming, one left relatively (and perhaps shrewdly) unelaborated in his book, as follows:

> After 1960 I made new climbs with upwards of thirty people. Most of them I would consider equal to myself, and several of them – on the grounds of age alone – more advanced in outright daring. One advantage I held was my experience of this class of climbing. ... Only Whillans and a handful of others could match it. The change of attitude towards the companions was so decisive that I grew to regard the new people as equally reliable and well-adjusted to the rigours of mountaineering as my stable and staunchest companions in the old Rock and Ice.[84]

These 'new climbs' were undertaken on the uncharted territory of the Anglesey sea cliffs of Gogarth in the company of Peter Crew and the leading lights of the Alpha Club. The explorations were shrouded in a secrecy which undoubtedly appealed to Joe's passion for thorough exploration.[85] If age had rendered 'the old man' (as Crew called him) a little more circumspect in his approach, it had not clouded his eye for picking off routes or blunted his skill in the execution of them. According to Jones and Milburn, by the end of the 1960s Joe had put up forty-eight first ascents on Gogarth and so was still climbing at the top of his game.[86] He would therefore again find mention alongside others deemed to have produced routes of superior quality in *Extreme Rock*, the companion volume to *Hard Rock* which had earlier announced his contribution to the quality and standard of British rock-climbing as 'outstanding'.[87]

Ironically, in spite of being dubbed 'the new Joe Brown' by the climbing press in the 1960s, of the two it was Barnsley-boy Crew who could not sustain the longevity of the original Master whom he unreservedly identified on film as not only his hero, but 'a demigod almost'.[88] Whilst Joe was undoubtedly the author of his climbing achievements across three decades, such a pronouncement makes it clear that over time the production and reproduction of these, firstly, as extraordinary and, secondly as explicitly heroic, resides respectively within the media world, but more critically within the climbing community itself. Over time the latter has been complicit in the process of constructing Joe Brown a climbing hero – regardless of his own expressed reservation about being designated as such.[89] He did not deliberately set out to impress and, as his own observations about the post 1960 period indicate above, he was willing to embrace the talent of others in light of honest assessment of his own abilities, whilst not placing these or himself above them.

Although Joe's press image has been relatively transient and his televisual presence intermittent, both have tended to posit him as extraordinary on account of his sporting ability, but also ordinary on account of his status as a working man. Whilst high achievements have literally underpinned the construction of a public profile for Joe, so too has a curiosity about the personality behind them. Namely, as one who conceived of his high status in climbing as an inescapable by-product of a recreational passion for it, not an aspiration. In the climbing world, this is well understood, but in spite of it – or perhaps precisely because of it – Joe Brown is variously identified as a 'legend' and a 'hero'.[90] Over time the reproduction of him as such has turned upon several mutually reinforcing elements which together are integral to sustaining the vibrancy of the sport and its culture.

Firstly, the wide-ranging literary output spawned by climbing, from Tom Patey's song that designates Brown 'a legend', through to the encyclopaedias, claimed to be the definitive word on the who, what, whys and wherefores of the sport. In this genre even the household name of Chris Bonington, knighted for his services to mountaineering in 1996, is subordinated as 'one of the best known British climbers of the present era', to the identification of Joe Brown (MBE) as 'One of the greatest mountaineers Britain has ever produced' with 'his influence on rock climbing in particular, [has been] profound.'[91] More recently in the *Who's Who of British Climbing* (2008) Colin Wells has observed that 'Brown is arguably *the* British climber of the 20th century; his skill and vision opening the doors to the modern concept of the sport of rock climbing, while his mountaineering achievements were world class.'[92] Even Jim Perrin, the doyen of the climbing literati who contests the equation of climbing in itself with heroic endeavour concedes that if anyone were to attain that status in his mind he 'might grudgingly have to admit that this little silver-haired grin of a wrestler on his two bandy legs is as close as you could get'.[93]

Secondly, word of mouth, which in the early years of Brown's activity was integral to the emergent working-class climbing culture, secured a reputation that went before him – one he encountered when meeting climbers who had no idea who he was, but would begin talking about Joe Brown …to Joe Brown.[94] The importance of this eputation can also be seen in the formative experiences of climbers, as the parent of 9-year-old girl just beginning in the sport conveys: 'I have told her about Joe and his bility to just walk up rock … I will never forget him at Stanage Edge when I was much younger demonstrating his famous hand jam …'[95]

Thirdly, for those who have not witnessed the climber in action, there are the uidebooks used at the crag week in and week out wherein Brown is named as a ioneer, both in the preliminary historical sections and in the lengthy lists of first scents. Fourthly, and related to this, reproduction resides in the climbs upon which he next generation are obliged to cut their teeth, thereby affirming their rite of passage nto the climbing subculture. For the rising talent, not to mention those already ompetent and with a wish list of routes 'to do', the quality of such climbs resides in heir designation as 'classic' or 'trad'. Hence, of the Right Unconquerable at Stanage, Niall Grimes observes that this 'is probably the most significant route in the country .. First climbed by Joe Brown … by miles the best climber the country has ever seen .. Joe is still the all time, flawless hero of British climbing.'[96] Taking this aptly named oute as a symbolic marker, his rise to heroic status *began* in 1947, but what turned ut to be more critical to Joe Brown's standing was firstly, the way in which he ioneered new routes at standards hardly imaginable and, secondly, how he sustained is credibility by continuing to climb hard alongside the generation that came through n the 1960s. Moreover, whilst North Wales became the main focus of his activity, a ursory look at his list of first ascents and activity in the greater mountain ranges of he world thereafter testifies to a versatility and spirit of adventure that would have seen im rise to the top of the game on any medium.[97]

Further to the routes, a mark of Joe Brown's innovatory quality was that he did ot adhere to established ways of doing, but across the stages of his development as a limber through rock, Alpine and high peak activities he challenged the terms of ngagement: mentally (through refusal of difficulty), physically (through an innovative nd disciplined use of aid) and socially (through movement into climbing stablishment circles). Finally, an attitude born of a genuine conviction that what natters most in climbing is not so much the kudos of high achievement, but the leasure and friendships to be derived from it has perhaps been the defining quality vhich has rendered Joe Brown particularly to those 'in the know' not only a northern porting hero, but an 'absolute hero'.[98]

1   In this collection of dedicated verses Brown joins the esteemed company of Bill Murray, Christian Bonington and John Harlin.

2   T. Patey, *One Man's Mountains* (Edinburgh, 1971, 2005 ed.), pp. 270-273, Part IV Verse

3   *Joe* (BBC 1967), British Film Institute (BFI) / Tape PN NMR5112R. Author's transcript.

4   See Joe Brown, *The Hard Years* (London, 1967), p. 43. Due to the subjective nature of difficulty, the grading system has passed through a fairly complex and contested evolution.

5   B. Birkett, *Lakeland's Greatest Pioneers: A Hundred Years of Rock Climbing* (London, 1983), p. 179.

6   D. Gray, 'Some psychological aspects of advanced rock climbing', *Alpine Journal*, 28, 326 (1977), p. 90.

7   Best known in recent times is Joe Simpson's ordeal on the West Face of Siula Grande. See Joe Simpson, *Touching The Void* (London, 1988). The notion of climbers being designated heroic after extricating themselves from uncompromising situations of epic proportions has, however, been contested. The invariably unsung heroes are those who facilitate evacuation from the mountain at risk to themselves, as opposed to those who survive against the odds. See J. Perrin, 'Man Escapes from Jaws of Death after Conquering Killer Peak – Exclusive', *Yes, To Dance: Essays from Outside the Stockade* (Somerset: Oxford Illustrated Press, 1990), pp. 173–4.

8   E. Byne and G. Sutton, *High Peak: The Story of Walking and Climbing in the Peak District* (London, 1966) details the prime movers and club developments from c.1880 to the 'Years of Fruition' (pp.172–95) in which the nature and 'phenomenal' rise in post-war standards are made plain. For the Lake District see Birkett, *Lakeland's Greatest Pioneers*; T. Jones and G. Milburn, *Cumbrian Rock: 100 Years of Climbing in the Lake District* (Glossop, 1988).

9   Illustrative of this dynamic are R. Holt 'Heroes of the north: sport and the shaping of regional identity' in J. Hill and J. Williams (eds.), *Sport and Identity in the North of England* (Keele, 1996), pp. 137–64; D. Russell, *Looking North: Northern England and the National Imagination* (Manchester, 2004), pp. 236–66.

10 See H. Taylor, *A Claim on the Countryside: A History of the British Outdoor Movement* (Edinburgh, 1997). There is not, however, any dedicated chapter to climbers as an interest group in this account as there is for walkers, natural historians and cyclists.

11 See S. Venables, *Everest: The Summit of Achievement* (London, 2003); W. Unsworth, *Hold the Heights: The Foundations of Mountaineering* (London, 1993); G.B. Bryant, 'The Formation of the Climbers' Club', *Climbers Club Journal*, 1, 1 (August 1898), pp. 1–9; 'The Origins And Aims Of Our Club', *The Journal of the Fell and Rock Climbing Club of the English Lake District*, 1, 1 (1907), pp. 10–14.

12 Brown, *The Hard Years*, p. 23.

13 Ibid., p. 26.

14 Ibid., p. 25.

15 *An Extraordinary Joe* (BBC 1984), British Film Institute (BFI) Tape PN LONU352A. Author's transcript.

16 Bynne and Sutton, *High Peak*, pp. 111–32.

17 Brown, *The Hard Years*, p. 33. Use of makeshift ropes was not untypical during interwar and post-war periods. A. Harry Griffin, *The Coniston Tigers: Seventy Years of Mountain Adventure* (London, 1999), pp. 29–41.

18 It is impossible to place a definitive figure upon this; estimates range from 600 (1984) to currently over 1000. *An Extraordinary Joe*; Joe Brown Shop, First Ascents List, available at http://www.joe-brown.com/first-ascents/index.php (accessed 25 May 2009).

19 Brown, *The Hard Years*, p. 15.

20 The British Mountaineering Council (BMC) is credited with creating stability in relation to comprehensive documentation of gritstone climbing from 1948 onwards. For an overview of the evolution of Peak District guidebooks, process, individuals and northern climbing clubs involved, see N. Allen, 'Peak District Guidebooks', *The First Fifty Years of the British Mountaineering Council* (Manchester, 1997), pp. 115–21.

21 Brown, *The Hard Years*, p. 43. Brown goes on to give several more examples where he and his climbing partners confounded the assessment of others through their exceptional performance on what was considered at the time to be technically difficult rock climbs. See Brown, *The Hard Years*, p.42.

22 Ibid., p. 38. 'Top roping' refers to undertaking protected, prior inspection of a route before it is climbed by dropping an anchored rope from above; whereas to climb a route 'on sight' is literally to do just that: bottom to top assessing the moves required as progress is made. The latter is thus considered a more challenging proposition by climbers, especially when putting up new routes.

23 J. Perrin, 'Nat Allen' (Obituary), *Guardian*, 4 July 1995, p. 16.

24 R. Heap and M. Turnball, *Hard Grit* (Slackjaw Films Ltd., DVD, 2005). Author's transcript.

25 Brown, *The Hard Years*, p. 43.

26 Brown, *The Hard Years*, pp.58–9; Birkett, *Lakeland's Greatest Pioneers*, 'Arthur Rhodes Dolphin', pp. 138–53.

27 Brown, *The Hard Years*, p. 63.

28 J. Perrin, *The Villain: The Life of Don Whillans* (London, 2005, orig. 2004), pp. 64–6.

29 D. Gray, *Rope Boy* (London, 1970), p. 55. For an overview of other key figures post-1945 and associated with the Rock Ice active in Llanberis in the early 1950s, see W. Noyce (ed.), *Snowdon Biography* (London, 1957), pp. 59–112.

30 Definitive guidebooks for Peak District climbing run into several series, see Allen, in *The First Fifty Years of the British Mountaineering Council*, pp.120–21.

31 D.W. Armstrong (ed.), *Buttermere & Eastern Crags* (Fell & Rock Climbing Club of the English Lake District, 1992), pp. 20–25, 336–7.

32 In terms of social background, raw attitude and talent the Creagh Dhu possessed a membership that could withstand direct comparison with the Rock and Ice. See J. Connor, *Creagh Dhu Climber: The Life & Times of John Cunningham* (Glasgow, 1999), a biography about Brown's Scottish equivalent grounded in a history of the club.

33 For an exemplary commentary, history and guide featuring a number of Brown and Whillans classic routes K. Wilson, *Hard Rock: Great British Rock Climbs* (London, 1975).

34 C. Kirkus, 'Potato Medallist' in J. Perrin (ed), *Mirrors in the Cliffs: One hundred mountaineering articles* (London, 1983), p. 197. On Kirkus S. Dean, *Hands of a Climber: A Life of Colin Kirkus* (Glasgow, 1993).

35 Brown, *The Hard Years*, pp. 197–203.

36 C. Bonington, *I Chose To Climb* (London, 1966), p. 102. Bonington notes that there were 11 major routes on Cloggy before 1951. In the period 1951–59, Brown, Whillans and Ron Mosely put up 25 'considerably harder' routes.

37 T. Jones and G. Milburn, *Welsh Rock: 100 Years of Climbing in North Wales* (Glossop, 1986), pp. 149–153.

38 Brown, *The Hard Years*, p. 80.

39 J. Perrin, 'On the Rock with Joe Brown', *Yes, To Dance: Essays from Outside the Stockade* (Sparkford, 1990), p. 19.

40 R. Moseley, 'The Petit Dru by the West Face', *Alpine Journal*, 60, 290 and 291 (1955), pp. 25–30, 28. Account written after 'many conversations' with Joe.

41 C. Bonington, *I Chose to Climb*, p. 148. Bonington was an early and consistent climbing partner on domestic rock and in the Alps. The esteem in which he held Don is reflected in invitations to join his high peak expeditions. See also Perrin, *The Villain*.

42 '50th birthday on K2', *The Times*, 4 May 1983.

43 R. Faux, 'Don Whillans' (Obituary) *The Times*, 7 August 1985, p. 12.

44 C. Bonington, *The Climbers: A History of Mountaineering* (London, 1992), p.160–1; Perrin, *The Villain*, p. 71.

45 Wilson, *Hard Rock*, p. xv.

46 Brown, *The Hard Years*, pp.37–8; p. 70.

47 C. Evans, 'Exploring an Approach', *The Times*, 4 March 1955, p. 9.

48 *Joe* (BBC 1967), British Film Institute (BFI) Tape PN NMR5112R. Author's transcript.

49 C. Evans, *Kanchenjunga The Untrodden Peak* (London, 1956), pp. 11, 120–9.

50 Sir John Hunt, leader of the 1953 Everest expedition, commenting in *The Times*, 29 May 1955.

51 Gray, *Rope Boy*, p. 68. Brown was one of three who became publicly known as 'the Climbing Plumbers', the others were Don Whillans and Nat Allen. In fact, only Allen was a plumber by trade.

52 E. Douglas, 'A quiet triumph', *Summit*, 38, Summer (2005), pp. 36–8. Available at http://thebmc.co.uk/Feature (accessed 23 August 2007).

53 Letter from Assistant Editor (Patrick Monkhouse) *Manchester Guardian* to Sir Edwin Herbert, Royal Geographical Society (RGS), 28 November 1954; Draft Agreement with *The Times*, Kanchenjunga Reconnaissance Expedition, Director's Correspondence, 1954–55, Box 7, RGS Archives, London.

54 The benchmark being reportage in *The Times*, comprising brief report about the summit success of 25 May 1955 on 2 June 1955, p. 6; and subsequently 'Five feet from the summit: how Kanchenjunga was climbed', 9 July 1955, p. 12.

55 G. Whannel, *Media Sport Stars: Masculinities and Moralities* (London, 2002), p. 54.

56 *Manchester Evening News*, 2 June 1955, p.4. Kanchenjunga's reputation as such turned upon an expedition of 1905 when four climbers lost their lives in an avalanche.

57 Douglas, *Summit*, 38. Band explicitly identified Joe as the decisive force in making the summit bid.

58 *Manchester Evening News*, 1 August 1962, p. 5; 2 August 1962, p. 7.

59 Mr Manchester's Diary, *Manchester Evening News*, 29 January 1957, p. 4. *The Times* spared a little over a column inch to the achievement: 'British Baltoro Expedition/ 23,800ft, Karakoram peak sumitted 06 July/ steepest in region last 2000ft. almost vertical', 24 July 1956, p. 8.

60 *Manchester Evening News*, 18 February 1957; *The Hard Years*, p.150–1.

61 Gray, *Rope Boy*, p. 49. With direct reference to Maurice Herzog's *Annapurna* Gray states 'it seemed too far from our mountain reality in 1952 when working class boys didn't go to the Himalaya', p. 40.

62 See S. Venables, *Everest: The Summit of Achievement* (London, 2003), Appendix: 'Mount Everest Expedition Members 1921–1953', for full list of those selected and their credentials.

63 The sponsoring body being the Mount Everest Foundation in the form of a committee comprised of Alpine Club and Royal Geographical Society members.

64 Patey, *One Man's Mountain*, Part IV Verse, pp. 262–4; *The Times*, 'Soviet peak climb by Britons', 17 August 1962, p. 8. Joe and Ian MacNaught-Davis, accompanied by four Soviet climbers, were the first foreigners to make the ascent of the 24,590ft peak.

65 Bonington, *The Climbers*, p. 167.

66 J. Campbell cited in L.R. Vande Berg, 'The sports hero meets mediated celebrityhood', in M. Wenner (ed.), *MediaSport* (London, 1998) p. 135.

67 Artist File: Brown, Joe (Climber), N18/2, 084/1, BBC Written Archives, Caversham.

68 H. MacInnes, *Look Behind the Ranges: A Mountaineers Selection of Adventures and Expeditions* (London, 1979), pp. 137–49.

69 'THE BBC'S REAL-LIFE CLIFFHANGER', *Daily Sketch*, 10 July 1967. The schedule was unprecedented with coverage running between Friday 7 July and Sunday 9 July 1967. The climbers were Chris Bonington, Joe Brown, Peter Crew, Dougal Haston, Ian McNaught-Davis and Tom Patey.

70 *Guardian*; *Daily Mirror*; *Daily Telegraph*, 10 July 1967; BBC Audience Research Dept., An Audience Research Report: Climbers on The Old Man of Hoy, 08 August 1967. File 3, T14/2, 701/3, BBC WAC.

71 Letter from Chris Brasher to Tom Patey, 17 March 1967, Old Man of Hoy File 2, T14/2, 701/2, BBC WAC.

72 P. Gilchrist, 'Reality TV on the Rock Face – Climbing the Old Man of Hoy', *Sport in History*, 27, 1 (2007), pp. 44–63.

73 An Audience Research Report: Climbers on The Old Man of Hoy, 8 August 1967.

74 See C. Bonington, 'The Old Man of Hoy' in Wilson, *Hard Rock*, pp.40–3. The third climber of the Original Route on the first ascent in 1966 was Rustie Baillie.

75 Old Man of Hoy (BBC, 1967) BFI/Tape VB35496/tx. 09/07/67 No.2. Author's transcript. The climb is graded HVS but due to exposed location, stature and medium is intimidating.

76 Old Man of Hoy, BFI/Tape VB35496/TX 09/07/67 No.2.

77 Letter from Chris Brasher to Joe Brown, 1 August 1967. File 2, T14/2, 701/2, BBC WAC. From £25 to £50 although in Artist Fees documentation the total identified is £150, not including subsistence and travel.

78 Old Man of Hoy (BBC, 1984) BFI/Tape UB 80228/Highlights; Jones and Milburn, *Welsh Rock*, p. 168.

79 MacInnes, *Look Behind the Ranges*, pp. 172–5.

80 Old Man of Hoy: 25th Anniversary, BBC2 tx. 07 July 1992. Author's transcript.

81 Points of view raised in discussion during Old Man of Hoy: 25th Anniversary; C. Bonington, *The Next Horizon* (London, 1986) p. 233; MacInnes, *Look Behind the Ranges*, pp. 143–6; T. Patey, 'The Professionals', *One Man's Mountains*, p. 217 'the rewards – although hardly spiritual, mystical, aesthetic or even ethical – are quite substantial'.

82 Peter Crew and Robin Collomb are clearly identified as motivating forces in production of the autobiography. See Brown, *The Hard Years*, pp. 12–17.

83 Brown, *The Hard Years*, p. 13; *Joe* (BBC 1967), British Film Institute (BFI)/Tape PN NMR5112R. Author's transcript.

84 Brown, *The Hard Years*, p. 182.

85 I. MacNaught-Davis, 'Craig Gogarth' in K. Wilson and B. Newman, *Extreme Rock* (London, 1987), pp. 97–99.

86 T. Jones and G. Milburn, *Welsh Rock*, pp. 163–98, exposes the intensity of activity and places Joe's significant contribution into context.

87 Wilson and Newman, *Extreme Rock*; Wilson, *Hard Rock*, p. xiv.

88 C. Wells, *Who's Who In British Climbing* (Buxton, 2008), pp. 115–16; *Joe* (BBC 1967), British Film Institute (BFI)/Tape PN NMR5112R. Author's transcript.

89 Most recently to George Smith: *An interview with Joe Brown* (Al Hughes TV, DVD 2008).

90 *An Extraordinary Joe* (BBC, 1984) BFI, Tape PN LONU352A, pursued a similar strategy in presenting Joe as simultaneously ordinary, but remarkable due to his ongoing taste for adventure and took a particular interest in his motivations and other interests beyond climbing.

91 W. Unsworth, *Encyclopaedia of Mountaineering* (Sevenoaks, 1992), pp. 61, 68.

92 'Climber Joe's royal ascent', *Manchester Evening News*, 14 June 1975, p. 5; C. Wells, *Who's Who in British Climbing* (Buxton, 2008), p. 67.

93 Perrin, *Yes, To Dance*, p. 15.

94 *An interview with Joe Brown* (2008). A predicament identified as 'doubly embarrassing': someone 'talking about me to me' and the question of 'how do you get out of it?'

95 http://www.8000Met.com (accessed July 2007).

96 N. Grimes, *Summit*, 26, Summer (2002), pp. 26–8. Available at http://thebmc.co.uk/Feature (accessed 23 August 2007).

97 First Ascents List, available at http://www.joe-brown.com/first-ascents/index.php (accessed 25 May 2009), provides a selective list for rock, beginning with The Right Unconquerable to Sidewinder (Dinas Mot, 1983).

98 E. Douglas, 'Tough at The Top: The vertical beatnik', *Observer Sport Magazine*, 6 March 2005, p. 46.

CHAPTER 4

Alf Tupper: Real Worlds and Imagined Heroes[1]

Jeffrey Hill

In talking of heroes, there is a certain blurring of boundaries. The real and the imagined rarely seem to be separable. Early in 2007, for example, the *Guardian* newspaper printed an obituary of Fred Norris, who had died at the age of 80.[2] In the 1950s Norris had been an outstanding British long-distance runner whose times took him close to those of the Olympic champion Emil Zatopek, the greatest runner of the era. For most of his active athletics life Norris worked as an electrician at a Lancashire coalmine, but in 1960 he emigrated with his wife and son to the USA. Soon after arriving he ran the Boston marathon. His race was crucially interrupted at a promising stage when a rival in the leading group was attacked by a stray dog. Norris stopped to help, lost time, and finished third. Some would have read this obituary (like all others, a short story of a life) and thought that in it there was a case of life imitating art. The principal themes – worker-athlete, humble northern background, exceptional ability, but prone to unlucky accidents – would undoubtedly have brought to mind another runner of this same period: Alf Tupper, the 'Tough of the Track'. Unlike Norris, Tupper never existed in real life. He had first appeared as a fictional hero in 1949 in the *Rover*, a comic for young males produced by the Scottish publishing firm of D.C. Thomson.[3] After some dozen years as a regular feature in the solidly textual *Rover* the stories were transformed into comic-strip format in its successor paper, the *Victor*, where they ran with gradually diminishing frequency until the early 1990s.

I

Somehow, Tupper has taken on an extra-textual persona; he lives in many people's memory as if a real person. In part this stems from the clever associating of actual events and people in the realist fiction of the Tupper stories. It has been suggested, for example, that the author based his character on a real runner – possibly the Edwardian

71

athlete Alf Shrubb, or more likely the 1920 Olympic champion Albert Hill.[4] The Tupper character has been further fleshed out in the memories of two very successful international athletes of the later-twentieth century, Brendon Foster and Ron Hill. These two runners, both from the north of England, have acknowledged Alf Tupper as the source of their inspiration in athletics. From an early age Hill identified with Tupper because the character had humble northern origins and worked on the railways, as did Hill's own father; but he also admired the character because, as Hill put it, Tupper was always 'up against it', succeeding in adversity through sheer determination[5] It is tribute to the way Tupper was presented to his readers – mainly working-class secondary schoolboys and male adolescents in the early stages of waged labour – as a character in recognisably 'true' social situations, in which he confronted and attempted to solve everyday problems. He was a poor young man, aged about 20, who was also an outstanding 'natural' athlete. His successes on the track owed nothing to family background, scientific coaching or education. He loved to run, and his training methods were completely uncomplicated: regular long runs before and after work. Asked once about his 'secret', Alf replied: 'I ain't got one – I just run as fast as my legs will carry me.'[6] 'The way to keep fit for running,' he claimed, 'is to run.[7] But he was not just a runner, he *raced*; he relished the competition of the track, and his habitual challenge to competitors was a defiant 'I'll run him.' Questioned about the deep resilience he displayed in his races, Alf replied: 'I just don't like being beat [sic]!'[8] Tupper's preference was for the mile (or 1500 metres), but for the opportunity to compete he would take part in almost any running race: cross-country, the six miles, and occasionally even sprints. The stories came onto the market at the same time as some of Britain's greatest achievements in middle-distance running, and Tupper was the fictional equal of champions such as Roger Bannister, Chris Chataway, Chris Brasher, Gordon Pirie and Derek Ibbotson, each of whom achieved honour by setting world records or winning international medals. None, though, was quite so successful as Alf himself, who won the gold medal in the 1500 metres final at the 1952 Helsinki Olympic Games.[9] The combining of a simple will to win in the context of real international athletics success gave the stories immense reader appeal.

Tupper's demeanour on and off the track was truculent, individualist and sometimes aggressive. He was not a conventional schoolboy hero. He matches, in this respect, another real-life runner of the 1950s whose career covered almost the same period as the *Rover* series of Tupper stories: Gordon Pirie. The title of Pirie's autobiography – *Running Wild* – perfectly captured the rebellious nature of his personality and philosophy. He was often at odds with the athletics regime of the day, courting disfavour for his condemnation of, among other things, the prevailing amateur ethos. He followed an unorthodox and demanding training regime, much more scientific than Tupper's simple approach to running, but at the same time he shared with him a belief that athletics was ultimately something to be enjoyed. To achieve a high level of performance, said Pirie, athletes must be prepared to train hard; but they must also develop the 'sheer enjoyment of rhythm, speed, excitement and achievement'.[10] Tupper's credo was similar. 'Running's fun' Alf tells his team mates after beating a group of over-trained East Europeans who 'made athletics a grim, scientific business'.[11] He is, we are told in an early story, 'crazy about running.'[12] Tupper received no payment for his athletics and could only afford to indulge his passion for running by working in regular, paid employment. At a time when the idea of the amateur was being questioned[13] Tupper remained firmly committed to the principle of performing for the joy to be had from sport, rather than for any financial gain. He rejected offers to become a professional, and always saw sport as secondary to his work. In fact, the stories are as much about work and its routines as about athletic competition; readers are told that Alf 'worked for his living, and lived for his running.[14] When, in one story, his employers hesitatingly ask Alf to set aside an evening's training in order to complete a 'rush job', he assures them that 'Running's my sport, mister, but welding is my work, and work comes first.'[15]

By the time Alf disappeared from the world of comics the stories had been consumed by some four reader generations.[16] Tupper brought a real world into the text unlike, for example, the Harry Potter novels of the early-twenty first century, which take the text out of reality. There is no recourse in Tupper to magical explanations and interventions. Like Harry Potter, the exploits of another D.C. Thompson athletic creation – Tupper's comic-book contemporary Wilson, whose feats were extraordinary and demanded a willing suspension of disbelief – provide another sharp contrast. Alf's triumphs seemed achievable, at least for one endowed with outstanding athletic abilities.[17] Whereas Wilson lived in a cave and subsisted on a diet of berries Tupper's settings were mundane: shabby clothes, cheap lodgings and wage labour. Alf Tupper was a working man who shared an ordinary social world with his readers, and the clearest symbol of his ordinariness was seen in his food: Tupper existed almost exclusively on fish and chips.[18]

II

It is, perhaps, from this simple culinary signifier that some of the 'northern' qualities that have been attributed to Alf derive. Signifiers, however, are problematical; the associations they invite are not without ambiguity. To be sure, fish and chip shops were a commonplace in the landscape of the north of England. In the industrial districts, especially those of the Lancashire textile towns with their high levels of employment for married women, fish and chips fulfilled an important need in the work and domestic routine.[19] Here, the fish and chip shops would open at teatime[20] for the queues of customers coming out of the mills wanting a ready-made family meal. Chip-shop technology – the fish-frying ranges in particular – reminded those customers of their regional identity: Stott of Oldham and Ford of Halifax were the principal names emblazoned on them. It was a long and firmly-held belief in such areas that the *best* fish and chips were only to be found there, implying that the art of cooking them had not been fully cultivated elsewhere. But fish and chips, in spite of these strong associations, were not of course an exclusively northern food. In London and the major industrial towns they were also a crucial item in the working-class diet.[21] Tupper's addiction to them, which extended to a virtual elimination of any other food and a constant quest for the 'perfect' plate of fish and chips, does not therefore automatically register him as 'northern'. Nor do other aspects of the stories. His speech, for example, was plain, rough and certainly demotic. It was 'working class', but never given as a northern accent. 'Bloomin' Ada', not 'By Gum', was one of his favourite expressions. His sport, track athletics, was one of growing national prominence in the 1950s and throughout the later-twentieth century it produced a clutch of northern heroes, Hill and Foster among them. It was probably not, however, the sport most readily identified in the public mind with the North. A number of successful football clubs and county championship cricket teams, or the regionally-specific rugby league, would have been far more likely to fulfil the idea of 'northern' sport.[22] Moreover, in the important sense of regional attachment – geography – the Tupper stories were set in the 'midland' engineering towns of Brassingford and Greystone. In their pre-comic strip phase the stories contained much semi-technical detail of workshop practice, labour routines and machinery – all of which, we might suppose, would strike a chord in the minds of readers anticipating an engineering apprenticeship on leaving school, and perhaps among those already serving their time. Industry was a dominant theme, and it was Tupper's economic and social setting rather than its geographical location that was the hallmark of the stories. They composed a picture of British life that was emphatically urban, industrial and class-based, and by so doing rejected those images of 'deep' (and Tory) England that had been assiduously deployed in many forms of popular literature, and most recently in much wartime poster art.[23] In the last analysis, of course, the Tupper stories were commercial products. They provided a template for real situations that would appeal to the massed urban readerships of post-Second World War Britain, and thus avoided restricting that appeal by making the template too regionally-confined. An understated 'midlands' location suited the commercial imperative very well.

If, then, explicit notions of region are largely absent from the text, what is present in abundance is something that contains a latent connection with a sense of region, the provinces and anti-metropolitan feeling: a persistent theme of social tension. The stories are constructed around conflicts which, though portrayed as clashes between individuals, nonetheless seem to have endemic social causes. The stories affirm and reinforce in the reader a vision of a society marked by sharp divisions between those who possess wealth and privilege (and who therefore exercise power) and those who do not. Tupper is without question a spokesman for the 'have-nots', and he has a sporting setting that assists the development of this tension. The Tupper character originated in the mind of the D.C. Thomson writer Gilbert Dalton in the aftermath of the 1948 Olympic Games in London. Tupper was most probably designed in the writer's mind as a sporting icon rather than a social symbol.[24] Dalton was dismayed at the poor performances of British athletes in the 1948 Games, and offered Tupper as a character to arouse in younger readers an interest in athletics. But the sport itself was important: in Britain, in the late 1940s and 1950s, athletics was inscribed with a particular image. Ross McKibbin has included it as one of the 'sectarian' British sports, along with golf, tennis, hunting and rowing; that is to say, a sport with both geographical and social limitations.[25] There were many athletic clubs with a relatively humble location and membership,[26] but the strong links that existed between the governing body – the Amateur Athletics Association (AAA) – and the elite universities of Oxford and Cambridge gave athletics an overall appearance of social exclusiveness. This was reinforced by the sport's amateur ethos, its longstanding hostility to professional running (originally 'pedestrianism'[27]), and its markedly Home Counties leanings. The notion of 'the amateur' had always been a nebulous one,[28] but the idea persisted in athletics as in some other sports (rugby to a great extent, cricket scarcely less so) that to be an amateur was to be upper class, or as Alf Tupper would have it, a 'toff'.[29] To be a 'toff' meant to be characterised by certain types of behaviour, wealth, education and speech that demarcated a superior status and the social exclusiveness that accompanied it. It was this privileged upper-class presence in athletics that Alf Tupper resented and fought hard against. In his running there was always, alongside the athletic challenge, a streak of class conflict: 'I like to have a go at the swanks', he says.[30] Many of his opponents, though excellent athletes, are 'toffee-nosed types' as Alf describes them. The very names connote wealth and privilege: the Hon. Piers Mornington, for example, a Cambridge sprinter known as 'the light blue streak'; Jerrard Tarne, a quarter-mile hurdler whose training is done in the United States; Rakes-Taylor, the supercilious star of the Granton Hall club, who deliberately trips Alf in a race; the haughty Lew Murdoch, who travels from meeting to meeting in a customised motor caravan provided by his rich father and driven by Lew's own personal masseur; and Alf's longstanding rival from overseas Skimba Ru, the son of a Zulu chief. In each of these characters the single-minded pursuit of expected success has leeched from them a sense of common decency. They are contemptuous of those, like Alf, who are outside their social framework, and it is this sense of social superiority that positions the reader against such characters. They are 'snobs'. There is not a single instance in the entire Tupper series of stories where Alf is able to form a friendship with a 'toff'. The social boundary is rigid.

III

This densely-described milieu of status distinctions, giving the text a strong *contextual* reference point, is crucial to the ideological power of the Tupper stories. In this respect they occupy a singular place compared to many other fictions for young readers. In his major study of juvenile sport fiction in America Michael Oriard, drawing on the work of Joseph Campbell and Otto Rank, has argued that the characterisation of the athlete hero derives from heroes of myth.[31] A central feature of the narrative is a *journey* leading through *adversity* to *achievement*, though it is Oriard's contention that in fictions to do with sport this process is an immature one. Achievement is confined to sport, and to the adulation that sporting prowess brings. It stops short of the maturation of human and familial relationships – an 'expansion of consciousness'[32] – to be found in truly mythic stories, and from which they gain their narrative power. Tupper is not set apart from this formula, and there are many ways in which the stories conform to Oriard's typology of athlete-heroes: the 'prowess' hero 'industrious, persistent, honest, brave, steady, generous, self-sacrificing'; the plot movement (involving leaving a small environment and entering a bigger, more challenging one, in which a psychological separation from parents takes place); the presence of various forms of personal and situational adversity; the final triumph and the resulting 'boons' (of a financial or social nature) – each has its place, to a greater or lesser extent, in the Tupper stories[33] Moreover, as Oriard acknowledges, the sport fiction can exercise a powerful social influence: '[P]erhaps most significant, the athlete-hero is the dominant image in the mind of every father who encourages his son to play baseball or football.'[34]

What Oriard's analysis exposes is a conservative textual form in which social context is left hazy. Readers are invited to make tenuous links with historical realities that come in the form of the home, the self-made man, the American Dream, and a vague notion of corporate power. In essence these fictions are, as Oriard notes, purveyors of a 'middle-class morality'.[35] In contrast to the Tupper stories they appear as what might be termed 'de-historicised' texts. The difference for the reader is between, on the one hand, remaining largely 'within the text' and, on the other, bringing a real world into the text.

There is a great deal of real world brought into the Tupper stories. Much of it deals with mentalities that bear comparison with Richard Hoggart's celebrated northern working-class world of 'them' and 'us'. In this dour and somewhat cynical social environment heroism is a hard-won status, founded upon qualities that, whilst beyond the ordinary, are at the same time rooted in a down-to-earth neighbourliness. It is exemplified in Hoggart's memory of the Hunslet rugby league team returning with the cup from Wembley, 'coming down from the City station into the heart of the district on top of a charabanc. They went from pub to pub in all the neighbourhood's main streets, with free drinks at every point ...'[36] This characterisation of northern community and heroism, drawn from personal memory, has been enlarged upon historically by Richard Holt to connect with a range of northern sporting heroes.[37] Though the sporting prowess of the hero changed over time as the nature of sport itself changed, Holt notes that heroes remained invariably male, mostly human, frequently professional and often drawn from the ranks of the labouring class. They were not always born in the North (indeed several were imported from the other side of the world[38]) but critical to their heroism was a perceived relationship of 'the North' with its other, 'the South'.[39] The heroes of the North, Holt maintains, were different from those of the South, because they were defined carefully *against* them. Thus, while northern heroes might originate from overseas, they must (until very recent times) never come from the South.[40] Except as an opponent the South had no place in northern sport. In the northern working-class vision 'North' and 'South' were mapped onto 'Us' and 'Them'.

Cast within this world of blunt oppositions, northern heroes embodied virtues held dear to the localised communities of the region. These are the quintessential qualities that define the region, which the sporting hero simultaneously reflects and proclaims. Holt quotes Jim Kilburn, newspaperman and writer on Yorkshire cricket, as offering a fairly typical interpretation of these heroic qualities: 'cricketers are products of their environment,' said Kilburn, 'and grow as they do grow because of the impulse of their setting ... to contemplate Arthur Mitchell in the acquisition of an unsmiling, purposeful century is to appreciate the hard, unyielding Yorkshire hills.'[41] Such biological-environmental determinism conceals, of course, the part played by writers like Kilburn himself in ascribing a northern image; the picture of Arthur Mitchell's patient century remind us that this 'real' hero figure contains at least some of the same invention that went into the imagined character of Tupper. The rich inventory of 'northern-ness' audited by Dave Russell is not so much an *expression* of an essential northern identity as the cultural determinant of a sense of North.[42] It is, in effect, a language from which an identity is articulated.

There is nonetheless an evident convergence between Holt's composite picture of the real-life northern heroic man and the fictional Tupper.[43]

Northern Hero	Tupper
Tough competitor: 'grit and competitiveness'	Uncomplicated: 'I ain't got a secret I just run as fast as my legs will carry me[44] 'I'll run him'
Strong work ethic	'He worked for his living, and lived for his running'[45]
Effective rather than stylist	'He always looked as if he were fighting his way along'[46]
Blunt sense of humour	Speaks his mind
Respectability and family	Working-class occupation; no family ties
Team sport	Individual competitor
'Open-hearted ... ordinary'	Hatred of 'toffee-nosed blighters'

There are differences, but both profiles might be collapsed into an ideology of 'northernism' informed by conceptions of class, work, respectability and dour common sense. If there is one thread that binds all this together it is perhaps to be found in a particular form of masculinity. In the workplace, where Tupper spends so much of his time, it is expressed in the skilled worker's pride in his work and his status as a craftsman, as well as in the control that this accords to him over his own work. Tupper displays this in a complete lack of deference towards those who imagine themselves above him. Men of whatever position are addressed by the egalitarian term 'mister', and are to be judged by their competence, not by their background or social position. Alf carries this mentality with him into athletics; it is what constitutes his 'toughness'. He is a 'tough' of the track in the mental discipline, physical stamina and sheer ruthlessness he brings to his running. This is what it means to be a *man*. Like Oriard's American sport heroes, Alf is 'in all ways manly'.[47]

As a model of masculinity in the 1950s, however, the Tupper character presents young readers with certain contradictions. To be sure, many young males were still being inducted at this time into a tough hierarchical world of labour, but for those at grammar school a future in the professions beckoned and it is doubtful if Alf provided much of a model for that world. Moreover, for a comic book hero in the age of affluence Alf subverts much of contemporary 'common sense' about growing. The stories, therefore, in spite of their heavy realism, demand a degree of reading against the social grain. This is especially apparent in Tupper's material circumstances. He has few possessions, and what he does own has usually been purchased second hand. He has no home; often he lives where he works, sleeping on the floor and washing at the works tap. In a series of 1952, when Alf is working on the railways in a locomotive depot, he inhabits a disused platelayers' hut at the side of the track. In none of the stories does Alf have a car, nor even aspire to owning one. *Appearance* is not important to him. His hair is a mess, his 'best' clothes are an old sports jacket and flannels, and his usual attire is a pair of overalls. It is frequently remarked in the early stories that he does not wear socks, because they 'make his feet sweat'.[48] His running kit is moth-eaten, picked up at a jumble sale for half a crown (12.5 p). At the start of a crucial mile race the narrator of the story wryly observes: 'All stripped off tracksuits except Alf, who didn't have one.'[49] In the age of the teenage consumer, when youth (and especially male youth) was creating for itself a sub-cultural space defined through style, Alf Tupper bucked the trend; he was completely resistant to fashion, fancy food, music, cars, sex and all the other commodities that Mark Abrams observed as being the badge of the teenage consumer.[50] In an age when such behaviour lent credence to notions of 'embourgeoisement' and the decline of social class, the Tupper character is drawn as an unregenerate representative of an older, male, working-class lifestyle. Thus, while readers of juvenile fiction invariably make a willing suspension of disbelief in order to accommodate their heroes, in Tupper's case the suspension could demand a particularly strong willingness.[51]

One feature in particular underlines Alf's form of masculinity. It relates to Oriard's idea of the 'immature' sport hero, who 'remains a child',[52] and it is a characteristic of mid-twentieth century British juvenile fiction. If, as Hoggart has claimed, sex and sport were the two major topics of interest in the male workplace of this period,[53] the Tupper stories had ample of the latter but of the former there was no sign. In his work on comic-book heroes Brendan Gallagher has observed that 'sex and emotional turmoil were not to be acknowledged or spoken about', an attitude he attributes to the times, when young men had come through the war and were expected to be stoical and not tangle with 'feelings'.[54] There is a suggestion in this that masculinity – and especially perhaps working-class masculinity – involved an unknowingness about intimate emotional relationships, a theme taken up and explored with great sensitivity in David Storey's fine novel of northern working-class gender relations, *This Sporting Life*.[55] Women scarcely featured in Alf's life.[56] His mother had died when he was young, and thereafter the opposite sex was represented either by vile harridans like the alcoholic and devious Aunt Meg, or grumpy landladies.[57] When we consider that readers of the stories would themselves have been experimenting in one form or another with sex – 'exploring their sexuality' to use a contemporary phrase – the omissions seem surprising. But they were not confined to Tupper. In all the D.C. Thomson comics the emphasis was on male society and camaraderie: war and sport provided the dominant subjects of the story lines, and although school stories were rare the comics carried residual traces of an earlier fictionalised school culture. While

Tupper was in almost all respects far removed as a character from the public-school figures in the *Gem* and the *Magnet*, especially the formidable Billy Bunter, there is a similar monosexual – should we say even *misogynist*? – emphasis in both sets of stories. In this they contrasted with fiction aimed at teenage girls, where the idea of the 'feminine career' towards marriage was introduced at an early stage.[58]

Male camaraderie and the absence of women should not, however, be taken to imply a homoerotic element in the stories. Alf is a singular person, sociable in his gruff, laconic way, but he generally does not form friendships that are unconnected to either work or sport. In fact, in the continuing Tupper narrative there are no permanent friendships that fulfil an essential narrative function in the development of character. The runner Flapper Farmer, who appears in stories from the 1950s later repeated in the *Victor*, is a kindred spirit whom Alf befriends for a while; and stories about Alf's army service, and his formation of a running club known as 'Tupper's Trotters'[59] place him in a group situation, usually carrying an informal leadership burden. There is no equivalent, however, of the abiding and spiritual male friendships that have a central place in the two literary works – *Tom Brown's Schooldays* and the Leatherstocking novels of James Fenimore Cooper – that provided the models of male heroism from which Alf Tupper might indirectly have evolved.[60] In the last analysis Alf is a loner. His ruthless dedication to work and sport gives him no leisure time to spend on 'idle pursuits' in which permanent friendships might be developed. His is an ascetic athletic existence.

IV

For all their realism, the Alf Tupper stories remain to the last elusive. They are enigmatic texts capable of yielding a variety of readings. Therein, perhaps, is explained some of their longevity, their ability over many years to reach out to a mass audience with a central character capable of adapting to changing circumstances. The basic theme of Alf's striving for fairness and justice in the workshop and on the running track ties into various historical situations. Alf might be seen as a hero of Mr Attlee's consensual social-democracy, embodying the slogan of 'fair shares for all' that so resonated in the 'People's War' and the 1945 Labour election victory. But equally, through his personal initiative and lack of social ties, and even through his stand against entrenched privilege, he might do service as a Thatcherite hero, reflecting aspects of the radical Right as it unfolded in the 1980s. His truculence is a pre-eminent and, for many readers, an admirable quality. Ultimately, though, this too is problematical; it raises questions about the status quo, but fails to deliver an explicit challenge to it. Alf's obstinacy and determination enable him to withstand the pressures of the rush job and the 'toff'. But neither goes away. In the long history of the stories the same problems recur year after year. Nothing is fundamentally resolved;

life appears to be leading nowhere in particular, except to the next race. His workman's pride ensures that Alf stands up for his rights, but there is little of the class solidarity we might otherwise associate with the skilled worker's mentality, which historically found its expression in independent trades unionism and the labour movement. Alf prefers to follow a lone path, solving problems by individual effort. For the adolescent reader the questions raised by the stories have no clear answer, and any hint of subversion is buried deep within the ambiguities of the text.

Regional identity is one of these ambiguities. It is present to a degree in Tupper, but intertwined with and partially obscured by a number of other themes. The idea of Alf as a 'northern hero' stems as much from what readers bring to the text as from what is inscribed in it. Thus Ron Hill, whose own Accrington childhood seemed to be of a piece with Tupper's background, described Tupper as 'northern'. No doubt he felt that Tupper and his situation reflected something that was essentially of the North, as Hill himself had experienced it. Similarly many other readers have read into Alf's character some of their own experiences. 'I was brought up to admire the independent spirit of the working-class hero,' says a Yorkshire Tupper enthusiast, 'who didn't seek help, certainly not other people's approval, and "got on with it". This is the Geoffrey Boycott mould ... Perhaps it was just a Yorkshire thing ... after all many of us took pride in not having friends ...'.[61] Personal memories and associations of this kind have found a natural outlet in Alf Tupper. He can so readily be made to symbolise the northern side of the boundary in the powerful and lengthy discourse of regional division and identity that developed in Britain during the course of the nineteenth and twentieth centuries. Its industrial pre-eminence and the economic and social problems that accompanied it gave the north of England a position from which its inhabitants came to see themselves as not merely 'northerners' but as representatives of ordinary folk everywhere, a national 'us' standing against a governing-class 'them'.[62] Long before Tupper this articulation of a national popular will had become a feature of popular culture in Britain. In the 1930s it was personified in the stage characters of the entertainers Gracie Fields and George Formby. In the case of Fields, perhaps more so than of Formby, 'our Gracie' was a spiky construction not unlike Tupper in some respects, but the character's ultimate dramatic function was to moderate the tensions implicit in North/South identities. A Lancashire accent and background fashioned a character who spoke for an England seeking social harmony after the General Strike and the travails of the depression.[63] '*Our* Gracie' was a suitably pliable appellation. Tupper inherited many of these characteristics, though he arrived in a period of different consensual politics – Attleeian rather than Baldwinite, with the emphasis on progress instead of 'safety first', and in which a bolder notion of 'the People' prevailed.[64]

As long as the character is remembered and the idea of 'the North' persists, Alf Tupper will continue to be linked to it. For the historian working with literary material and thereby being transported back and forth across the borderland of history and

81

literature, Tupper represents an intriguing case of that process of textual adaptation which takes place when one set of 'meanings' (the author's) is worked over and changed into something different (the reader's and the historian's re-interpretation). The very elusiveness of the Tupper text renders it open to particularly rich appropriations. We should be aware that Tupper was not devised as a fictional symbol simply to express 'northern' virtues, nor to address only readers living in the north of England; and that in its surface narrative the text appears as a plain and rather formulaic moral tale. But from this process of appropriation the text acquires a depth that gives us something far more subtle to engage with. Looking at it from this perspective we might see the story of Alf Tupper as fusing two narratives; one with a powerful national resonance presenting an artful fictionalisation of social conflicts in modern Britain; the other having as one of its principal features the idea of the North, and of what it represents in the larger conflict between privilege and subordination.

1 In preparing this chapter I have benefited from the comments and advice of many people who are 'Tupper fans'. In particular I should like to record my grateful thanks to Alex Jackson and Richard Cox, both of whom spared time to talk to me at length about Alf, and to Peter Lovesey and Ian R. Smith, who not only shared their thoughts but provided me with much valuable primary and secondary material on both the Tupper author, Gilbert Dalton, and the D.C. Thomson organisation.

2 *Guardian*, 17 January 2007.

3 Since the D.C. Thomson archives have not been opened to historians we can only estimate the likely readership of the stories. Kelly Boyd thinks that the comics were read by youths rather than children, and Philip Pullman has noted that these comics were probably bought directly by young readers rather than bought for them by parents. See Kelly Boyd, *Manliness and the Boy's Story Paper in Britain: A Cultural History 1855–1940* (Basingstoke, 2003), p. 20; Philip Pullman, 'Picture stories and graphic novels' in Kimberley Reynolds and Nicholas Tucker (eds), *Children's Book Publishing in Britain Since 1945* (Aldershot,1998), ch. 6.

4 See Brendan Gallagher, *Sporting Supermen: The True Stories of Our Childhood Comic Heroes* (London, 2006), p. 72. Peter Lovesey, author of *The Official Centenary History of the Amateur Athletics Association* (Enfield, 1979), thinks it much more likely that Albert Hill was the model. He cites an entry in Dalton's diary for 4 August 1948 that mentions Hill and 'a notion for an athletics story for next summer.' (Private correspondence, P. Lovesey to J. Hill, 8 April 2008.) I am most grateful to Peter Lovesey for sending me extracts from Gilbert Dalton's diary for the period 1946 to 1949.

5 Ron Hill, *The Long Hard Road: An Autobiography* (Hyde, Cheshire, 1981), part 1, pp. 6–7, 8; also Jon Henderson, 'This Ron will run and run', *Observer Sport*, 21 September 2008, p. 24. Foster claimed that 'Tupper was my hero as a schoolboy'. Quoted in Gallagher, *Sporting Supermen*, p. 72.

6 *Rover*, 8 June 1957, p. 175.

7 *Rover*, 19 January 1957, p.

8 *Victor*, 9 March 1968, p. 22.

9 *Rover*, 9 August 1952, p. 169. Typically, Alf had not been selected as a member of the Great Britain team for these Games, and had made his own way to Finland (a story in itself) to run as an 'independent'.

10 Gordon Pirie, *Running Wild* (London, 1961), p. 24. Pirie, a critic of the amateur ethos prevailing in British athletics in the 1950s, was trained by the German coach Waldemar Gerschler, and followed the punishing routines that had brought success for Zatopek. 'I have often trodden a lone path,' said Pirie, 'and so have been called conceited, awkward, self-opinionated, rebellious – and even a bad sport.' (p. 9.) See also Wray Vamplew, 'Douglas Alastair Gordon Pirie (1931–1991)', *Oxford Dictionary of National Biography* (Oxford, 2004) http://www.oxforddnb.com/view/article49928.

11 *Victor*, 5 January 1980, p. 9.

12 *Rover*, 22 April 1950, p. 67.

13 The Wolfenden Committee on Sport (1957–1960) had commented on the concealed payment of amateur sportsmen, though its members were divided over the values of amateurism and the Committee offered an ambivalent statement on amateurism in its

final report. See Central Council of Physical Recreation, *Sport and the Community* (London, 1960), p. 97. See also Jeffrey Hill, *Sport, Leisure and Culture in Twentieth-Century Britain* (Basingstoke, 2002), pp. 155–7.

14   *Rover*, 24 April 1952, p. 179.

15   *Rover*, 24 April 1954, p. 70.

16   Alex Jackson interestingly noted how he, a *Victor* reader, had been inducted into the Tupper stories by his father, a reader of the earlier *Rover* stories. (Interview, Preston, 13 August 2008.)

17   See Gallagher, *Sporting Supermen*, pp. 16–43.

18   See Jeffrey Hill, "'I'll run him": Alf Tupper, social class, and British amateurism', *Sport in History*, 26, 3 (2006), pp. 502–19.

19   See John K. Walton, 'Fish and chips and the British working class, 1870–1930', *Journal of Social History*, 23, 2 (1989), pp. 243–66, and the subsequent book *Fish and Chips and the British Working Class, 1870–1940* (Leicester, 1992). Also Gerald Priestland, *Frying Tonight: the Saga of Fish and Chips* (London, 1972).

20   That is, between 4.30pm and 6pm – unusual in many other parts of the country.

21   In the Tupper stories, however, it is usually cod or haddock, the northern staple, that forms the centrepiece of Alf's meal; in London the fish content was often rock salmon or skate.

22   These are the two sports given prominence in the chapter on sport in Dave Russell's *Looking North: Northern England and the National Imagination* (Manchester, 2004), chapter 8, where athletics figures scarcely at all.

23   For example, the impressive poster series of Frank Newbould, 'Your Britain – Fight for it Now' (see J. Darracot and B. Loftus, *Second World War Posters* (London, 1972) and the popular inter-war novels of Warwick Deeping, especially *Sorrell and Son* (London, 1925), reprinted fifteen times within two years of its first appearance.

24   Dalton (1903–63), the son of a journalist, was born in Kidderminster. He reported on sport for various national newspapers but after the Second World War seems to have devoted his time in prodigious amounts to writing children's fiction, primarily for the D.C. Thomson organisation. Dalton wrote the Wilson stories (sometimes under the pen name W.S.K. Webb), based on an idea by William Blain, an editor at Thomson's. (Ian R. Smith, 'The truth about W.S.K. Webb', *Track Stats*, 36, 3, 1998, pp. 54–7: copy provided by author.) See also Frank Keating, 'Dalton's millions', *Spectator*, 9 December 2006, p. 87. I am grateful to Peter Lovesey and Ian R. Smith for sharing with me their thoughts and information on Gilbert Dalton and his character Alf Tupper.

25   Ross McKibbin, *Classes and Cultures: England 1918–1951* (Oxford, 1998), pp. 357–8.

26   There is an interesting fictional portrayal of such a club in Jim Peters and Bob Hoare, *Spiked Shoes* (London, 1959). I am very grateful to my colleague Dilwyn Porter for bringing this book to my attention.

27   See Peter Lovesey, *Wobble to Death* (London, 1970) for a fictional account of the sport.

28   On amateurism see: Richard Holt, *Sport and the British* (London, 1989), ch. 2; Lincoln Allison, *Amateurism in Sport* (London, 2001); D.J. Taylor, *On the Corinthian Spirit: the Decline of Amateurism in Sport* (London, 2006); A. Smith and D. Porter (eds), *Amateurs and Professionals in Post-War British Sport* (London, 2000); and the special issue of *Sport*

in History, 'Amateurism in Britain: for the love of the game?', 26, 3 (2006).

29 The strength of the amateur image in athletics is well brought out in the story of Roger
    Bannister and the first sub four-minute mile in 1954, where in spite of Bannister's
    rigorous 'professional' preparations for the race the myth of his being a talented amateur
    persisted. (John Bale, *Roger Bannister and the Four-Minute Mile: Sports Myth and Sports
    History* (London, 2004), especially chapter 1.)

30 *Rover*, 29 April 1950, p. 66.

31 Oriard, *Dreaming of Heroes: American Sports Fiction, 1868–1980* (Chicago, 1982), pp.
    36–8. See also Christopher Brooker, *The Seven Basic Plots: Why We Tell Stories* (London,
    2004), p. 4 (emphasises the 'test' of the hero, driving the story and providing a moral
    focus for the central character).

32 Oriard, *Dreaming*, p. 39.

33 Oriard, *Dreaming*, p. 30.

34 Oriard, *Dreaming*, p. 36.

35 Oriard, *Dreaming*, p. 47.

36 Richard Hoggart, *The Uses of Literacy: Aspects of Working-Class Life, with special reference
    to publications and entertainments* (London, 1957), p. 92. The local nature of this
    heroism is well illustrated in Lindsay Anderson's film of David Storey's novel *This
    Sporting Life*. Anderson has a scene in which Machin the rugby player performs a 'turn'
    in a working-men's club, singing 'Here in My Heart' to the delight of his local audience.
    (Lindsay Anderson, dir., *This Sporting Life*, Independent Artists, UK, 1963.)

37 Richard Holt, 'Heroes of the north: sport and the shaping of regional identity', in J. Hill
    and J. Williams (eds), *Sport and Identity in the North of England* (Keele, 1996), ch. 7.

38 Ted McDonald, the great Australian cricketer who played for Lancashire in the 1920s,
    was from Tasmania, which accounted for a certain 'mystery' he was thought to possess.

39 See also Russell, *Looking North*, pp. 36–7. The 'North/South' relationship is also
    discussed in Russell's 'Sport and identity: the case of Yorkshire County Cricket Club,
    1890–1939', *20th Century British History*, 7, 2 (1996), pp. 206–30.

40 There are odd exceptions in the modern period; in football, for example, David
    Beckham and Paul Ince at Manchester United, Rodney Marsh at Manchester City, and
    (a little earlier) Reg Attwell at Burnley. Earlier in the twentieth century the exceptions
    are harder to identify: Charles Buchan at Sunderland is the main one.

41 Holt, 'Heroes', p. 146.

42 Russell, *Looking North, passim*.

43 Holt, 'Heroes', p. 161.

44 *Rover*, 8 June 1957.

45 *Rover*, 24 April 1953, p. 179.

46 *Rover*, 24 April 1954, p. 54.

47 Oriard, *Dreaming*, p. 30.

48 *Rover*, 14 June 1952, p. 52.

49 *Rover*, 24 April 1954, p. 56.

50 Mark Abrams, *The Teenage Consumer* (London, 1959).

51 This is usually seen in the acceptance the hero's detachment from normal parental

supervision. In most Enid Blyton stories, for example, the child heroes mostly act out their adventures as an autonomous group pitted against villainous adults. Tupper's lone existence, without family or home of any kind, is an extreme form of this convention.

52   Oriard, *Dreaming*, pp. 39–40.

53   Hoggart, *Uses of Literacy*, p. 91.

54   Gallagher, *Sporting Supermen*, p. 50. Ian McEwan explores aspects of this issue in his novel *On Chesil Beach* (London, 2007).

55   David Storey, *This Sporting Life* (London, 1960).

56   See E.S. Turner, *Boys Will Be Boys: the History of Sweeny Todd, Deadwood Dick, Sexton Blake, Billy Bunter, Dick Barton et al.* (London, 1948).

57   Aunt Meg is developed most fully in a Victor series of 1973, when the story of Alf's tragic childhood is told. This is the only time the character is represented at an age other than his usual early manhood, and the stories actually subvert some of the previous narrative themes about Alf's social class. (See *Victor* issues February–May 1973.)

58   The classic examination of this is Angela McRobbie, '*Jackie*: An Ideology of Adolescent Femininity', in B. Waites, T. Bennett and G. Martin (eds), *Popular Culture: Past and Present* (London, 1982), pp. 263–83.

59   See *Victor*, issues of February and March 1963.

60   See, for example, D.H. Lawrence on Fenimore Cooper's stories of Natty Bumppo. D.H. Lawrence, *Studies in Classic American Literature*, ch. 5, in E. Greenspan, L. Vasey and J. Worthen eds, *The Cambridge Edition of the Works of D.H. Lawrence* (Cambridge, 2003).

61   E-mail correspondence with Richard Cox, 15 May 2008.

62   See Rob Shields for the idea of the 'space myth' of the British North, in which the North could be seen as the 'land of the working class'. Rob Shields, *Places on the Margin: Alternative Geographies of Modernity* (London, 1991), ch. 5.

63   See Patrick Joyce, *Visions of the People: Industrial England and the Question of Class 1848–1914* (Cambridge, 1991), pp. 307, 318, 322– 6.

64   See N. Hayes and J. Hill (eds), *Millions Like Us? British Culture in the Second World War* (Liverpool, 1999). It is worth noting that the popularity of both Gracie Fields and George Formby quickly waned after 1945.

CHAPTER 5

'This Incredible Yorkshire Lass.' Beryl Burton and the Importance of being Northern

Dave Russell

In his pioneering article on the history of the northern sporting hero, Richard Holt defended his exclusion of the northern 'heroine' by virtue of the fact that in the North, 'female achievements were ignored. Animals were more readily accepted than women as the objects of sporting admiration ... northern men did not want their women to appropriate the grit, competitiveness and guile that they saw as belonging to themselves and their animals'.[1] It is ultimately impossible to disagree with this as a statement of general principle. Sport has long been a decidedly male republic, a site for the making of certain forms of masculinity that, to varying degrees, demanded the exclusion or minimisation of the female presence; changes have certainly occurred in recent decades, but the broad argument still stands.[2] Nevertheless, as other chapters in this book also testify, there have been notable exceptions to this exclusionary northern world view. Perhaps the most striking example is presented by the Yorkshire cyclist Beryl Burton, who probably enjoyed a higher level of public visibility, for a longer period, than any other northern woman athlete of the twentieth century. Indeed, although clearly not as significant a figure as, for example, Gracie Fields, Thora Hird and Hylda Baker in entertainment, Kathleen Ferrier in music or Bessie Braddock and Barbara Castle in politics, she can be seen as one of the public figures whose life and work has contributed to popular notions of what constitutes a 'northern' woman.

One of the greatest athletes of either gender of all time, Burton was an almost invincible force within British women's cycling from the late 1950s until the early 1980s.[3] As the magazine *Cycling* recorded in 1960, 'so completely is women's racing dominated by this lass from Morley, that only the minor places are usually open to speculation'.[4] However, Burton's sporting career was, especially in its earlier stages, not only remarkable but also potentially transgressive. Although competitive cycling had long acknowledged women's capacity to operate highly effectively in some of its most demanding disciplines and, more generally, there had been some loosening of attitudes to women's role in sporting activity, there were still many barriers as to the level and nature of women's participation in post-1945 Britain. Lingering concerns rooted in Victorian medical theory that saw competitive sport as a threat to women's physical heath and thus their capacity for motherhood, deeply imbedded notions of what constituted 'suitable' female public behaviour and the many economic restraints that structured women's sport, particularly amongst the working class, formed a powerful potential brake on women's sporting practices. Moreover, Burton's adoption of an unusually physically demanding discipline and her ability to match and sometimes outperform elite male cyclists within it made her a highly unorthodox sporting woman.

In fact, Burton was widely seen not as a challenge but as an inspiration; she was, simply, a sporting 'hero', someone of exceptional talent to be admired, not derided. The situation was well captured, albeit at a humorous level, in a cartoon in *Cycling* magazine which shows a vicar telling his wife, 'I christened sixteen babies Beryl today – and five of them were lads'.[5] In an earlier study, I have argued that of the many factors allowing Burton the space and opportunity to challenge the social and cultural norms surrounding women and sport in the late–middle twentieth century, the most significant was her highly public performance of her roles as wife and mother.[6] While there is no attempt to challenge that central point here, this chapter is concerned to give more weight in the argument to the role played by both her self-presentation and her wider representation as a typical 'northern' or 'Yorkshire' lass. While the English North might ultimately be a secondary and subordinate place within the national culture, as Burton was to discover, northern identity was nevertheless a strong and, for many, desirable cultural resource that could be an enabling device of considerable potency. The fact of her being northern gave increased licence to the exercise of her prodigious talent.

Born Beryl Charnock in Leeds in May 1937, Burton, the daughter of a motor mechanic, was raised within the skilled working class.[7] Academically bright, she not only unexpectedly failed her eleven-plus examination but suffered a complete nervous collapse during it, resulting in the onset of chorea (colloquially St Vitus Dance) and rheumatic fever. Partially paralysed for several months, she spent fifteen months in hospital and convalescence. In later life she attributed the intense determination that defined her cycling career to a desire to compensate for her academic 'failure' and subsequent illness. At fifteen she obtained an office job at Montague Burton's tailoring factory in Leeds where she met Charlie Burton (no relation to the company family), an accounts clerk and keen amateur racing cyclist. Settling in Morley, a small industrial town immediately to the south-west of Leeds, they married days short of Beryl's eighteenth birthday in 1955 and Denise, their only child and eventually an outstanding cyclist in her own right, was born the next year.

Although showing some sporting ability, mainly as a swimmer, Beryl had no interest in cycling until Charlie introduced her to it in 1954. Her rise from novice to elite rider was rapid and all the more remarkable because of the success she achieved across an unusually large range of cycling disciplines. Although her extraordinary physical stamina and mental resilience were ultimately best suited to the long-distance time trial – an event in which riders, setting out in staggered starts, attempted either to cycle a set distance in the fastest time or to cover the greatest distance in a set time – she was also highly successful in track and road races over various distances.[8] (She also competed in cyclo-cross, a form of cross-country cycling.) Although only beginning serious competition in 1956, Burton won her first national title, the 25-mile time trial, in June 1958. The following year she won the gold medal in the women's pursuit at the cycling World Championships as well as four national titles and the coveted title of British Best All-rounder (BAR), an award given to the rider recording the fastest average speed across three time trial distances (25, 50 and 100 miles). This was to be the first of twenty-five consecutive BAR titles. Overall, from 1958 until 1986 when, aged 49, she took her last two British titles, she won seven world and ninety-seven national titles to complement her BAR successes, breaking three world records as well as numerous others at national level and at individual courses and events en route. In 1960, fellow rider, Joan Kershaw, contributed an article to Cycling tellingly entitled 'The eternal second' in which she commented on Burton's technique in road races. 'There comes a hill. Beryl attacks and breaks clear. And then every other rider gives up hope…'[9] Although inevitably she did suffer defeats and setbacks, Burton's dominance led to one official suggesting to her in 1961 that she should retire and let others have their chance.[10] Although she began to lower her expectations of success from the late 1980s and despite suffering often poor health, she continued to cycle competitively until her death in May 1996. Indeed, the heart failure that claimed her life, probably the result of damage from her childhood illness, occurred during a training ride near her Harrogate home.

Throughout her career, Burton remained an amateur, helping to both support her cycling and supplement the wider family income through a series of mainly manual jobs, including a long period as a labourer on a rhubarb farm in Morley.[11] The wider significance of these jobs will be considered below. After her successes in the World Championships of 1959 and 1960, some commentators expected and even hoped that she would join the very small band of professional women riders.[12] Leading male professional, Reg Harris, argued, for example, that rather than have a future 'comprising constant repetition of her past achievements' she could be the 'cycling ambassador' who captured 'the imagination of the cycling public but also the world of sport and the millions of television viewers'.[13] Although approached by Raleigh to turn professional in 1961, she declined, partly because she felt the rewards were insufficient to justify the risk, but largely because 'constant repetition of her past achievements' in the amateur world was precisely what attracted her. Fully aware that the regulations then in existence would not allow her to return to amateur racing and, as will be seen later, genuinely committed to the 'social' ethos that accompanied it, she was not prepared to leave this distinctive sporting culture.

She was certainly acutely aware of the economic consequences of her decision. As the co-writer of her autobiography noted, she 'has been known to give a wry smile and comment that if she had been a tennis player or born in France she would have been a millionairess'.[14] Even those riding in international competitions had to pay their own expenses and were given extremely modest living expenses; when arriving for her first World Championships in Belgium in 1959 she could not even afford a track suit.[15] As late as 1975, her material reward for success in the National Championships came in the form of 'a Marks and Spencer's cardigan worth £7 and a £6 track-suit-top' from which the maker's name had to be unstitched to avoid the contravention of advertising regulations. Burton's position was certainly better than most.[16] In 1960, the Cycle Industries Association gave her and Charlie a three-wheeler car to improve their travelling arrangements while other modest perks were often available to her.

Arguably her greatest triumph came in September 1967 when, only days after victory in the World Championship road race, Burton became the first ever woman cyclist (and one of the first woman athletes in any discipline) to beat a national record that was also available to men. Riding in a women's twelve-hour time trial that immediately followed the equivalent men's event, her distance of 277.25 miles carried her 0.73 of a mile further than the day's leading male competitor, Mike McNamara. Moreover, the draw dictating the staggered starts saw her set off as the first woman immediately behind McNamara, the last male rider. She was therefore able not merely to cover more ground but physically to overtake him, thus rendering her victory all the more emphatic. Feeling as she passed that 'some gesture was required on my part' she offered a consoling sweet from her supply of energy food. '"Liquorice allsort, Mac?" I shouted, and held it toward him. He gave a wan smile. "Ta, love", he said, popping the sweet into his mouth. I put my head down and drew away.'[17] While her 'victory' over McNamara in 1967 is remembered because it resulted in a British record, she frequently matched or recorded times better than those of leading male cyclists throughout the 1960s and 1970s.[18] This achievement was acknowledged by her becoming the first ever woman invited to ride in the *Grand Prix de Nations* in 1968, effectively the world time trial championship and open only to elite male professionals.[19]

One of the leitmotifs of Burton's autobiography was her criticism of the media, and the press in particular, for its poor coverage of her career and her sport more generally.[20] Of the reaction to her successes at the 1960 World Championships she noted tartly, 'I was a double world champion in an international sport and it might have been a ladies' darts final down at the local as far as Britain was concerned.'[21] There was undoubtedly much substance in her criticism. Women's sport in general received far less attention than its male equivalent and women's cycling specifically, a sport largely of the lower-middle and working classes, lacked the social cachet that allowed, for example, women's tennis its annual spell in the Wimbledon spotlight. Crucially, it was not an Olympic sport until 1984 and women cyclists were, therefore, denied the opportunity to gain the spotlight that could fall every four years on some of their more fortunate sisters in other sports. Thus her two Yorkshire contemporaries and social peers, Anita Lonsbrough and Dorothy Hyman, gained far more media attention for their respective gold medals in swimming and silver in athletics at the 1960 Rome Olympics than Burton could ever hope to attain for winning her two golds in the cycling World Championships in the same year.[22]

Nevertheless, Burton, at least in regard to her own exposure, arguably protested a little too much. She received an MBE in 1964 and an OBE four years later. That the *Guardian* recognised the latter award by including her photograph alongside boxer Howard Winston, racing driver Graham Hill and Manchester United Football Club's iconic manager, Matt Busby, all similarly honoured for services to sport, gives some indication of her place in the contemporary sporting pantheon.[23] Again, public voting saw her made *Daily Express* 'Sportswoman of the Year' in 1967 (she was also runner-up to Lonsbrough in 1960 and was voted into the top six on ten consecutive occasions between 1959 and 1968) while in the same year, she was voted Sportswriters' 'Sportswoman of the Year' (she had been second here too in 1960) and elected runner-up by viewers to the immensely popular heavyweight boxer Henry Cooper in the BBC's 'Sports Personality of the Year' award. There were also television interviews and occasional appearances in newsreel.[24] On her death, one cycling journalist termed her a 'household name' and this is not an unreasonable epithet, particularly in regard to the 1960s.[25] Burton was, then, the recipient of a not inconsiderable degree of media attention and, from the very outset of her career, it rooted her resolutely within the county of her birth.

As the English county with arguably the strongest resonance and purchase within the national imagination, Yorkshire's sporting representatives were always far more likely than most of their counterparts to be situated spatially by the media, although Londoners, Lancastrians and north-easterners might perhaps have similar claims. For the *Daily Mail* in 1960 she was 'the 23-year-old Yorkshire mother' and 'the wonderful cycling girl from Morley, Yorkshire'. For the *News of the World* in 1967 she was a 'Yorkshire housewife', for a 1968 television documentary 'a 31-year-old Yorkshire lass and world-class athlete' and for the *Daily Express* in 1970 'Yorkshire Beryl'. In 1975, a lengthy feature in the *Sunday Times* magazine chose to report most of her comments in its (generally accurate) version of a Leeds accent. Recalling the joys of first staying in a hotel she recalls, "'E" I thought to meself "I could live like this for the rest of my life". There were 'lectric kettle in room, teabags *and* coffeebags'.[26] *Cycling*, the sport's main journal was similarly anxious to place her. In two months of 1960 alone she appeared as 'this lass from Morley', 'Beryl Burton from Morley in Yorkshire' and the 'curly-haired mother from Yorkshire'.[27] Interestingly, her many obituaries in 1996 showed the same focus on place.[28]

This is not to suggest that Burton's presentation as quintessentially 'Yorkshire' was a media construction. She was clearly happy for her autobiographical ghost to claim at the outset that 'Beryl was and remains an ordinary Yorkshire lass'.[29] She made absolutely no attempt to moderate her accent and lived her whole life in Yorkshire. Although she eventually abandoned the environs of industrial Leeds for the prestigious spa town of Harrogate – Charlie was manager of a cycling warehouse there – she remained a member of Morley Cycling Club for most of her life. Morley in its turn was proud of the athlete who represented it so well. As with Lonsbrough and Hyman she was honoured at a number of civic dinners during the 1950s and 1960s and her death was commemorated by the construction of the town centre Beryl Burton Gardens, which incorporated a 900 square foot mural by a Yorkshire artist of her in cycling action.[30]

Nevertheless, it is undoubtedly the case that coming from the North generally and Yorkshire specifically set Burton's career within a context of widely accepted regional characteristics and attitudes that were always available to colour and shape its meanings.[31] Although it might be argued that regional 'character' has increasingly hardened into cliché and reflex comic response from the later 1960s, at the time when Burton emerged on the sporting scene there were still many who believed firmly in such a phenomenon and interpreted at least some of the contemporary social world through its lens. Some defined traits – a certain egalitarianism or, at least independence of opinion, directness of speech, a pleasure in understatement, respect for modesty and 'ordinariness' and an accompanying dislike of boastfulness and 'fuss' – appear to have been available to, or applicable to, almost any northerner. However there was also space within the national imagination for strong sub-regional and/or county stereotypes within which these perceived characteristics could be either softened or exaggerated. Brusque, blunt, rough-mannered Yorkshire has often been seen as the ultimate site of an extreme intransigent northernness with sport, especially cricket, playing a major role in this discourse.[32]

There has always been a powerful gender dimension within the construction of regional identities, with particular characteristics differentially distributed amongst men and women. Admittedly, this is not a straightforward process. Northern men and women can be imagined in a variety of ways and a survey of the novels, plays, films and other popular cultural forms that have shaped and driven so many ideas of regional identity would illustrate every conceivable version of northern masculinity and femininity that might be required by the exigencies of plot and narrative.

Nevertheless, gender has been a permanent and critical factor. The North has generally been coded as 'masculine', a site of hard work dominated by men, legitimised, from the mid-nineteenth century, by notions of the male breadwinner norm. The South, if not necessarily feminine, has certainly been seen as effete, a softer, less demanding place. Again, most of the North's key cultural archetypes are men: the bluff Yorkshire 'tyke', 'Bob Cranky', the hard-working but harder drinking Newcastle collier and Andy Capp, Reg Smyth's 1957 cartoon creation for the *Daily Mirror*.[33] More specifically, those characteristics relating to physical prowess and to the sporting virtues of 'grit, competitiveness and guile' that Holt has noted, have undoubtedly been associated with the northern male, and especially those of the working class.

A set of clearly agreed female characteristics have, in their turn, often been rooted in a particular element of the domestic or private sphere; 'homeliness' and 'neighbourliness' were certainly commonly claimed. Crucially, however, many such representations have also stressed northern women's power within households. This has arguably been at its most pronounced in the depiction of women in textile Lancashire, where higher than average levels of female employment may objectively have increased their authority. Whatever the cause, what Jeffrey Richards has termed 'the north west as matriarchy' has been a significant feature within representations of Lancashire life. The shrewd and confident 'Lancashire lass' or Lancashire 'mill girl' and her strong, powerful mother were ubiquitous in later nineteenth and twentieth-century popular culture.[34] Their equivalents were not perhaps as common in Yorkshire but they were there, wielding power by tongue as much as anything else. Yorkshire dialect writing and many comic forms that drew from it was richly populated by quick-witted women who could reduce erring males to size with ease: 'tha' wor born lazy, an' aw wonder tha' doesn't engage a chap to draw breath for thi'.[35] Yorkshire women were also attributed with a markedly phlegmatic, unexcitable character. In her posthumous 1936 novel, *South Riding*, Winifred Holtby has one of her characters observe, 'she enjoyed scenes, you know. Not like a Yorkshire woman'.[36] If northern and, in this context, Yorkshire women, were, then, usually denied full association with the sheer physical toughness claimed for their men folk, they were seen as part of an imagined landscape in which a wider tenacity and strength was a key constituent and were thus allowed to be viewed as determined, forceful and resilient in numerous other ways.

Burton's life, sporting career and the manner in which these were represented, resonated powerfully with many of the key elements of accepted northern/Yorkshire character. As will be discussed at a later stage, widespread acknowledgement and even expectation of 'Yorkshire stubbornness and determination' limited any challenge that her physical prowess might have presented. This toleration of an incursion into more 'masculine' terrain was made easier by her consummate performance of a variety of more clearly gendered concerns.[37] Her roles as wife and mother were important here, claiming for her both 'homeliness' – she produced home-made cakes for a *Sunday*

Times interviewer in 1975, albeit with the decidedly northern-inflected disclaimer that she 'wasn't a fancy baker' – and status as a powerful, organising figure within the home.[38] She was intensely proud of her marriage, her daughter and her domestic skills and readily accepted her 'traditional' domestic obligations. Marriage and childbirth would often end or at least curtail women's sporting careers but Burton's early experience of both resulted in her overcoming and adapting to these potential barriers before they had manifested themselves as such. In fact, inverting the assumption that women, once married, would not normally continue as elite athletes, she argued for family obligations, and hers in particular, as a perfect training for sport.

> I certainly think married women might be better suited to longer distances because they are used to keeping up the pressures in their daily domestic life, which consists of one job after another. I find that in the middle of one job I'm already thinking about the next. You develop more of a drive than men, because so much more has to be fitted into the day.[39]

Charlie's relationship with Beryl was utterly central to her success; having introduced his wife to the sport, he was only too willing to nurse her precocious talent. Burton's debt to the man who served as her mechanic, support worker, driver and general factotum, was widely acknowledged within the cycling world and not least by Burton: her autobiography was dedicated 'To Charlie, without whom none of this could be possible' and the book and her other public utterances are full of praise for him.[40] Crucially, however, Charlie was never in any sense Burton's coach. She remained in charge of her own training and racing regime, always the dominant partner in the sporting relationship. Indeed, for all her acceptance of the role of wife and mother, her cycling career in many senses inverted the 'standard' hierarchy within marriage and dictated the terms of the relationship more widely. Only late in her career did she announce with typical forthrightness that 'Charlie's lost interest ... Now he's got fed up, doesn't come out with me as much and I miss a shoulder to lean on. He reads books and goes out walking.[41]

Family life more widely was also based around her needs as a cyclist, with her intense powers of organisation and levels of energy allowing her to maximise every sporting opportunity. Soon after Denise was born, a sidecar was added to Charlie's bike so that Denise could be taken out of the house and training, club activity and competition thus resumed with limited disruption. Charlie's mother was 'very anxious because somebody had said that all the bumping around would affect Denise's spine' but Burton chose to ignore the heavy hint and argued that it was better to have her daughter 'sleeping in the country air than at home. And we were happy as a family involving Denise in our activities'.[42] Training rides took place every evening and most weekends were structured around the need to be ready for competition early or

Sunday mornings with extensive travel a key part of events. The way in which Burton organised her career, with family life and sport collapsed into one, inevitably meant that Charlie and, perhaps even more importantly, Denise, frequently featured in media coverage of Burton's career. In 1967, for example, a *Cycling* race report noted mother brushing her daughter's hair only minutes after winning the women's national 100 mile trial title. Crucial, too, were the family photographs that were so often used to illustrate her success. The weekly newspaper *Cycling* was probably the most common source of such images, but they also found their way into the national press.[43] Two of these are reproduced in her autobiography, including one that, as with the hair-brushing story, shows Burton in motherly mode, giving her daughter a drink at a hot Herne Hill race track. Another, drawn from the *Daily Mirror*, shows the seven-year-old Denise aloft on her parents' shoulders at the medal ceremony in the 1963 World Championships in Liège. Such representations were vital in defining Burton to the world not just as a great athlete, but as a woman at the heart of a family.[44]

Marriage and motherhood also added much to the sense of Burton as 'typical', an exceptional athlete perhaps, but tightly connected to daily realities. A cluster of phrases frequently attested to her 'ordinariness', 'modesty' and loyalty to group norms and expectations in many other senses; her frequent appellation as a 'lass' with all the rootedness in place and social order that the word can carry is significant here. Burton's commitment to amateurism and the highly specific meanings that it held within cycling was critical to her 'democratic' status. She loved the camaraderie that the sport engendered. In part this stemmed from the essentially upper-working and lower middle-class social tone of competitive cycling, which created a degree of cohesion and social comfort. Probably more important, however, was that cyclists felt themselves part of, in Burton's words, a 'kind of freemasonry', united in their specialist skills, knowledge, pleasures and suffering.[45] That the time-trialling community was such a small subset of the wider cycling world added much in this regard. Although cycling as an activity embraced hundreds of thousands of people, with millions more drawn in at certain moments, above all during the *Tour de France*, its competitive dimension comprised a number of small, essentially private worlds; according to one estimate in 1978, perhaps only 4–5,000 men and 350 women regularly took part in trials.[46] These trials, utilising quiet roads early on Sunday mornings, were, moreover, almost secret events with key elements within them known almost only to the competitors. Burton made this point herself when noting that the critical moment in her duel with McNamara in 1967 was a matter of 'just two riders' in a 'country lane' with no cheering crowds, no 'excited television reporters, the occupants of the odd car that passed unaware of the drama'.[47]

Cycling, especially time-trialling has, then, much in common with the northern climbing and fell running worlds discussed in this book by Carol Osborne and Peter Bramham respectively. Although 'stars' has perhaps been more prevalent in cycling than in these sports, they were expected to know their place as exceptionally talented figures within a wider, self-sustaining community that demanded and deserved their full commitment and expected little ostentation.[48] Beryl made a point of dressing well for public events in honour of her sport as much of herself, but managed to maintain the notion that, while enjoying doing so, it was not too significant an act. Talking of her new hairstyle at the 1967 Sportswriters' Association dinner she commented that 'I brayed [rushed] over to Margaret's this morning to get it done.' In her normal fashion habits, however, she was typically austere, buying out of habit, so her daughter claimed, the cheapest clothes available to her.[49] As noted, she retained a deep loyalty to the Morley Club, wearing its colours long after she had left the town and took every opportunity to promote it at all stages of her career; following the presentation of her British title trophies at an Albert Hall concert in 1960, she sold its raffle tickets to the assembled guests.[50] In her autobiography, Burton remembered with obvious pleasure a private party organised by the club after an official Road Time Trial Council celebration of her twenty-fifth B.A.R. in 1984.

> I sat on the floor and munched cake, drank apple juice and realised that this, really, was what it was all about. The fellowship of like-minded folk who, in their various ways, were part of the greatest sport in the world ... To be part of it gives you something nobody else has.[51]

It is not unsurprising that, on her death, *The Times* felt that she had always remained the 'down-to-earth Yorkshire club cyclist she had been since taking up the sport in her teens'. Letters to *Cycling* were replete with similar sentiments. 'You represented' one correspondent claimed, 'the best of "old-fashioned" club folk, riding all types of event ... and mixing with your mates, fellow competitors, without any "side" or bigheadedness.' Another recalled how, having cycled to an event as a spectator, she had then lent a stranger a part from her bike so that he could take part in the competition following damage to his own.[52]

The sense of Burton's normality and understanding of daily life owed much to her decision to continue in paid manual work throughout her career. Interestingly, she saw manual labour as a boon, 'toughening my body and my will, without coaches, facilities or grants'.[53] It was a financial necessity initially but even as Charlie began to move up the occupational scale and the terrace streets of Morley were exchanged first for an estate house in the Leeds suburbs and, later, one in Harrogate, Burton continued in employment. In the 1970s, she worked two hours each morning as cleaner in a local shop and dismissed the idea that this was 'rather undignified work for a holder of the OBE', before once again taking up farm work.[54] While there may well have been fitness benefits as she claimed, this appears to be more a determined effort to be 'useful', to have a function beyond sport. When, in 1963, the BBC invited her to appear in a tableau of British champions as part of the *Sportsnight*'s 'Review of the Year', she demanded and received a £5 payment for 'broken time' alongside her travel and hotel expenses; this essentially ceremonial and decorative function had to be placed within the financial context that governed her 'real' life.[55] There are here great similarities with the fictional career of Alf Tupper, so well explored by Jeff Hill elsewhere in this volume. As Hill notes, when, in one story, Alf's employers hesitatingly ask him if he was willing to set aside an evening's training in order to complete a 'rush job', he assures them that 'Running's my sport, mister, but welding is my work, and work comes first.' Burton's real life career shows how cleverly this fiction sheds light on attitudes within the working- and lower-middle class amateur sporting culture of the post-war period. Burton was almost obsessed with the need to excel in sport while balancing it with other necessary commitments. A highly public argument with her daughter in July 1976, when Denise beat her mother to win the National Road Race Championship and Beryl refused even to shake her hand, had at least some of its roots in her annoyance at Denise's perceived unwillingness to 'do more' domestically.[56] In a later *Guardian* interview with the two women, Beryl recalled her feelings when Denise told her that she could not manage the demands of full-time work, training and domestic obligation. 'Can you imagine what I felt when Denise said she couldn't cope? I've had to cope with training, racing, a full-time job, and cooking, washing and ironing when I get home.'[57]

This intense pleasure in managing, in being reliable and permanently busy was absolutely central to her self-image and one of the key narratives that she chose for her self-presentation. Indeed, one of her claimed motives for writing her autobiography was that she wanted 'people to see what an ordinary person can do if they have determination and drive'.[58] Her decision not to compete following her late selection as a substitute rider for the British team in the inaugural women's *Tour de France* in 1984 is depicted in her autobiography not as pique but as a refusal to let down colleagues at the Harrogate potato farm where she was then working.

> I had told the boss that I had not been picked in the team, and we had re-arranged some work schedules accordingly, so other people were involved in all this, and I was not going to muck them about.[59]

For all the element of artifice here, with Burton obviously anxious to project herself as 'ordinary' and the cycling world equally concerned to paint its hero in the most virtuous shades, maintaining a sense of place within a community of hard-working people genuinely mattered to her.

For Burton, however, 'knowing her place', was not in any sense associated with subservience. Her 'place' was demotic Yorkshire; she fitted and could be fitted well into a county stereotype renowned for a certain egalitarian directness. *Cycling* reported the whole of her acceptance speech at the 1967 Sportswriters' Association dinner and praised her for diving 'straight into her subject with the characteristic bluntness that has become her trademark'.

> Mr Chairman, fellow Yorkshire landowner the Rt Hon. Earl of Harewood – we pronounce that Hairwood in Yorkshire, like the village near Harrogate – members of the Sports Writers' Association, I suppose the rest must be ladies and gentlemen, there are at times when even a woman is lost for words.

Words were clearly the last thing she was lost for as, having had some gentle but healthily democratic fun at the expense of the Queen's first cousin, she cracked jokes and enthusiastically 'talked cycling' for several minutes.[60] Again, while Burton rejected any display of pretension or ostentation, she knew her worth, socially – a quiet steady upwards move along the housing ladder was perfectly acceptable – and, crucially within the sporting arena. Although a television presenter's description of her as a 'modest and charming world champion' has many echoes in other reportage, she was well aware of both her standing and the gap often present between her and her competitors. When a Belgian journalist at the 1967 World Championships asked 'timorously' if the absence of his compatriot Yvonne Reynders had helped Burton secure gold, she replied, 'Frankly it didn't matter … she would have been at the back shattered with the others any way'.[61] By 1981, the *Observer*'s David Hunn could describe her as 'like many champions … confident to the point of arrogance'.[62]

This powerful sense of self and the streak of superiority that accompanied it lead directly into the final and perhaps the most important element within her role as northern hero. Simply, she was an extraordinary competitor, willing to push herself way beyond the physical limits that might have been expected to constrain her. The legendary competitiveness, 'grit' and determination of Yorkshire sporting stars (albeit mainly male ones) was one of the most deeply embedded of all English cultural signifiers. Burton personified these characteristics in a striking and undeniable fashion and was recognised for it. In 1978, for example, she received the C.A. Rhodes Memorial Award, admittedly an award given by a Yorkshire cycling body, in recognition of the 'true Yorkshire grit and courage' shown in fighting back from her serious injury the previous year. Thus constructed, any unseemly competitiveness could be explained and excused. Burton never pedalled 'for foon'.

Burton was undoubtedly blessed with certain physiological advantages, including an exceptionally low pulse rate and 'soft, sinewy muscle … noticeable only at times of supreme effort'.[63] Moreover, her favoured cycling discipline, the longer distance time trial, was one in which women were unusually well-equipped to compete with men. As Kenneth Dyer's pioneering socio-biological study illustrates, gender similarities in terms of energy reserves and leg muscle power, coupled with the 'smaller

Fred Trueman   Raymond Illingworth

Geoffrey Boycott

Brian Statham

Clive Lloyd

Andrew Flintoff

Ellery Hanley

Joe Brown

Alf Tupper

Beryl Burton

Anita Lonsbrough

Dorothy Hyman

Jane Tomlinson

Rebecca Adlington

William Sudell

Jackie Milburn

John Conteh

William Bellhouse AKA 'Cyclone Billy'

Horace 'Skid' Skinner

body frame and rounded contours' that provide women with 'important advantages' in restricting air resistance, give distance cycling generally lower performance differentials than virtually any other sport.[64]

Nevertheless, whatever her 'natural' advantages' – and, of course, the effects of her childhood illness may sometimes have counter-balanced these – her success and the abnormal longevity of her competitive career were ultimately due to Burton's punishing training regimes and iron self-discipline. Much of her training was undertaken on the A64 Leeds–York road at the side of which she could sometimes be found vomiting, having pushed herself too hard.[65] Aside from her pre-cycling illness problems, she also suffered a number of serious injuries from which she set about recovering with intense dedication. The worst stemmed from a training crash in 1977 which left her (aged 40) with a double fracture of the leg and head wounds requiring 56 stitches. She regained fitness so aggressively that her muscles expanded to a size where her skin attached itself to the plaster cast, causing a painful infection. In 1983, she fought through diagnoses of both anaemia and concussion of the spine.[66] Burton was, as she readily acknowledged, an intensely competitive individual by nature. 'Whether I'm sat knitting or up biking, it don't matter ... I've got to come first' she acknowledged in an interview in which she also admitted avoiding some cycling social events because the very discussion of racing made her agitated.[67] This same competitiveness spilled over into her relationship and rivalry with Denise. By the mid-1970s, mother and daughter were serious rivals with the former admitting that in competition against each other, 'there's no friendship, it's daggers drawn'. In 1978 she acknowledged that, while proud of her daughter, 'I can honestly say I don't get all excited if she's done something and I've done it already.'[68]

Clearly, the various characteristics discussed in this essay cannot be claimed as distinctive to the North or to Yorkshire. 'Ordinariness', modesty and a lack of pretension are attributes accorded to many sporting and other heroes from many other places. In England, they are certainly associated with working-class culture generally and perhaps London's East End especially; the death of Bobby Moore in 1993 resulted in much journalism declaring him a 'perfect gentleman', a model representative of the old East end community as it should be remembered. Extreme competitiveness, too, is obviously hardly something that can be ascribed only to the athletes of just one region. Again, the stereotype cannot be lived up to in all aspects. Beryl, the composite Yorkshire woman in so many ways, did, indeed, have a most un-Yorkshire like 'scene' with Denise. Nevertheless, as argued earlier, universal attributes had long been distributed in greater profusion to certain places than others within the national imagination and Burton's career was played out within a clear set of public expectations. In actuality an extraordinarily brave and driven competitor, she became doubly so in the regionalist discourses which embraced and inscribed her.

At the same time as she was being viewed within the framework of a

Yorkshire/northern stereotype, Burton, or, at least, representations of her were also reinforcing that stereotype, both generally and in a specifically gendered form. Her emergence as a sporting figure in the late 1950s and early 1960s was highly important here, for this was in many senses a particularly 'masculine' moment in terms of the cultural representation of a North suddenly made modish by the 'New Wave' and social realism.[69] While there was space for women in this northern 'moment', as *Coronation Street* was to demonstrate, it was largely the male (West Riding) voices of writers such as John Braine, Stan Barstow, David Storey and Keith Waterhouse and their leading characters that dominated the landscape. Burton, in a modest way, kept open a space for women in the real world that fed into positive and enabling regional imagery. Care must obviously be taken not to exaggerate Burton's cultural role; women's cycling was never large enough to carry too heavy a cultural burden. Nevertheless, her career illustrates much about how regional stereotypes operate in both a general and an individual context. Whatever the interpretation placed upon it, it was most certainly one that demands the greatest respect. It is hard to deny that she was objectively 'an incredible Yorkshire lass'.

1   Richard Holt, 'Heroes of the north; sport and the shaping of regional identity', in Jeff Hill and Jack Williams (eds), *Sport and Identity in the North of England* (Keele, 1996), p.139.

2   For women's sport in Britain, and attitudes to it see K.F. Dyer, *Catching up the Men* (St. Lucia, Queensland, 1982); Martin Polley, *Moving the Goalposts. A History of Sport and Society Since 1945* (London, 1998); Jennifer Hargreaves, *Sporting Females. Critical Issues in the History and Sociology of Women's Sport* (London, 1994); Jean Williams, *A Game for Rough Girls: A History of Women's Football in Britain* (London, 2003); K. McCrone, *Sport and the Physical Emancipation of English Women, 1870–1914* (London, 1988); P. Vertinsky, *The Eternally Wounded Woman: Women, Doctors and Exercise* (Manchester, 1990).

3   For an autobiography, Beryl Burton, *Personal Best* (Denby Dale, 1986).

4   *Cycling*, 6 July 1960.

5   Ibid., 14 October 1967.

6   Dave Russell, '"Mum's the word": the cycling career of Beryl Burton, 1956–1986', *Women's History Review*, 17, 5 (2008), pp. 787–806. Some of the material used in the essay in this volume is drawn verbatim from this earlier article and I am grateful to June Purvis, editor of *Women's History Review*, for allowing this.

7   This sketch is largely drawn from *Personal Best*.

8   She regarded her best event as the 100 miles time trial. *Cycling*, 21 March 1970.

9   *Cycling*, 9 November 1960.

10 *Personal Best*, p. 47.

11 On amateurism in this period, Richard Holt and Tony Mason (eds), *Sport in Britain* (Oxford, 2000) and Adrian Smith and Dilwyn Porter (eds), *Amateurs and Professionals in Post-war British Sport* (London, 2000).

12 Their main activity involved timed rides between London to Brighton, Land's End to John 'O'Groats or similar.

13 *Cycling*, 14 September 1960.

14 *Personal Best*, foreword.

15 Ibid., pp. 16, 25. See also pp. 74–5.

16 'The Lady is a champ', *Sunday Times*, magazine, 7 September 1975, pp. 26–30.

17 *Personal Best*, p. 98.

18 See, for example, *Cycling*, 6 May 1967, 12 August 1967, 10 August 1968, 1 November 1969, 11 May 1996, 18 May 1996.

19 *Personal Best*, pp. 109–13.

20 During her career, the latter may have worried her more. See *Cycling*, 21 March 1970. For greater development of this topic, Russell, 'Beryl Burton, 1956–1986', pp. 801–3.

21 *Personal Best*, p. 39. See also pp. 21, 27, 85, 115.

22 Holt and Mason, *Sport*, pp. 46, 60.

23 *Guardian*, 8 June 1968.

24 For example, she appeared on BBC *Sportsnight*'s 'Review of the Year' on a number of occasions. Some newsreel material can be seen in Kate Siney's three-minute documentary, *Beryl the champion of the world* (2006), available on

http://www.channel4.com/culture/microsites/0-9/3MWbicycle/index.html. Accessed 20/1/2009.

25   Dennis Donovan in *Cycling*, 18 May 1996.

26   *Daily Mail*, 6 August, 15 August 1960; *News of the World*, 3 September 1967; the interview – the source, as yet unidentified – is used in Kate Siney's *Beryl the champion of the world; Daily Express*, 6 August 1970; 'Lady is a champ'. See also *Guardian*, 7 June 1978, 2 November 1985.

27   *Cycling*, 6 July, 13 July, 3 August 1960.

28   *Times*, 8 May 1996; *Guardian*, 7 May 1996; *Cycling*, readers' letters, 18 May 1996.

29   *Personal Best*, p. vii.

30   For example, *Morley Observer*, 6 November 1959; *Yorkshire Evening Post*, 28 August, 14 November 1997. Harrogate cared too, with her name given to a cycling path avoiding some of the most dangerous stretches of the A59 Harrogate to Knaresborough Road.

31   See introduction to this volume.

32   Dave Russell, 'Sport and identity; the case of Yorkshire County Cricket Club, 1890–1939', *Twentieth Century British History*, 7, 2 (1996), p. 214 and Steve Wagg's contribution to this volume.

33   For 'softer' versions of masculinity, Dave Russell, *Looking North: Northern England and the National Imagination* (Manchester, 2004), pp. 157–60.

34   Jeffrey Richards, *Stars in their Eyes. Lancashire Stars of Stage, Screen and Radio* (Preston, 1994), p. 12; Russell, Looking North, pp. 161–3.

35   *Halifax Original Illustrated Clock Almanack*, 1885, p. 36.

36   1949 edition (London: Collins), p. 454.

37   'The Texas bicycle chain massacre', *Guardian*, 2 November 1985. The article dealt with Burton's involvement in the Waco 500 mile race. She and another 269 of the 302 starters failed to finish.

38   'Lady is a champ'.

39   *Personal Best*, p. 99.

40   Ibid., p. 166.

41   *Yorkshire Post*, 16 June 1979.

42   *Personal Best*, pp. 13, 15–16.

43   For example, 13 July 1960.

44   *Cycling*, 12 August 1967, 28 October 1967.

45   *Personal Best*, p. 18.

46   Dyer, *Catching up*, p. 187.

47   *Personal Best*, p. 98.

48   This was also true of rugby league stars. Simon Kelner, *To Jerusalem and Back* (London, 1996), pp. 11–13.

49   *Cycling*, 23 December 1967; *Guardian*, 7 June 1978.

50   *Cycling*, 7 December 1960.

51   *Personal Best*, p. 166.

52   *The Times*, obituary, 8 May 1996; *Cycling* 18 May 1996.

53 *Personal Best*, p. 14.
54 *Yorkshire Post*, 16 June 1979.
55 Hand written expenses sheet, BBC Written Archive Centre, Caversham, T14/1799/5.
56 *Personal Best*, p. 142. This incident, returned to below, is discussed in more detail in Russell, '"Mum's the word"', pp. 799–801.
57 *Guardian*, 7 June 1978.
58 Ibid., 2 November 1985.
59 *Personal Best*, p. 168. On the women's event, C.S. Thompson, *The Tour de France* (Berkeley and Los Angeles, 2006), pp. 132–8, 232–3.
60 Cycling, 23 December 1967.
61 Kate Siney, *Beryl the champion*; *Cycling*, 9 September 1967.
62 *Observer*, 21 June 1981.
63 *Personal Best*, p. 173. Her resting pulse rate in 1985, when she was aged 48, was 40. *Guardian*, 2 November 1985.
64 Dyer *Catching up*, pp. 185–91. Dyer is one of the few academic writers to discuss Burton. Skating and long-distance swimming show similar trends. *Catching Up*, pp. 191–8.
65 'The Lady is a champ'.
66 *Personal Best*, pp. 146, 163.
67 'Lady is a champ'.
68 'Lady is a champ'; *Guardian*, 7 June 1978.
69 Stuart Laing, *Representations of Working-Class Life* (London, 1986).

CHAPTER 6

Fanfare for the Common Woman: Sporting Heroines, the North of England and Social Change

Stephen Wagg

This chapter looks at four sporting heroines from the north of England – two from the early 1960s and two from the beginning of the twenty-first century. It examines the ways in which these four young women and their experiences were framed by the local media and by the prevailing culture of the(ir) time and region. In doing so, its principal purpose is to illustrate, not so much the changing nature of female sporting heroism – although it will certainly comment on this – as the changed nature of the social circumstances in which sporting heroism in the north of England has been achieved and rendered.

Community, the civic and the Olympics in Yorkshire, 1960

This first section originated in work I did in 2006 for a collection of essays on sport and the Cold War. Having begun to trawl the British popular press of the 1950s and 1960s for derogatory references to hefty, unfeminine female athletes from behind the Iron Curtain, I found instead a powerful discourse about the Girls Next Door, whether from East or West.[1] Although this did not apply wholly or solely to women (there were, of course, a number of Boys Next Door), women nevertheless emerged as the dominant motif of Olympism and, thus, in some cases, of sport heroism. These young women stepped, temporarily, out of ordinary life; were perhaps successful and, if so, mounted the Olympic rostrum, dipping their heads proudly to receive their medals; they comported themselves with a mixture of joy and embarrassment; they returned to civic receptions and large crowds, composed in significant part of people whom they knew by name; they had had a thrilling time but were 'glad to be home'; they returned to ordinary life – as typists, clerks, teachers, dentists, sisters, girlfriends – and were seen no more. Just to reiterate, the concern here is not with the gendered or domestic nature of the lives of these sportspeople but with their straightforward ordinariness – the simple fact that they lived lives much like millions of others at the time.

Two athletes who approximated to this description were Anita Lonsbrough and Dorothy Hyman, two young Yorkshire women who won medals in the Rome Olympics of 1960. This account of their Olympic experience is culled from the pages of the popular national sports press but, more especially, from the *Yorkshire Post*. It gives, I hope, an insight into the nature of sporting heroines in the North but it doesn't seek to make statements exclusively either about females or about the north of England. Ultimately, for example, receptions styled as 'traditional Yorkshire welcomes' were probably not that different from welcomes accorded in similar circumstances in other parts of the country. Nor do I claim that Yorkshire or the north of England had some kind of monopoly either on community spirit or on civic pride. What does emerge is a strong sense of the way in which Olympic sport, amateur sport generally and the people who practised it were handled in the north of England and, perhaps, more widely in Britain at the time.

Rome, 1960, was, politically and culturally, between two worlds for British athletes and their public. On the one hand, this was the first Olympiad to be seen on any scale by television audiences. Grainy, black and white images of these competitors threatened to turn them into objects of, perhaps brief, fascination – embryo celebrities. On the other hand, most of the people who competed for Britain that year were neither the self-financing genteel amateurs of the inter-war period, nor the sponsored full-time athletes of today. The Byers Report on the financing of British Olympians would not be delivered for another eight years and, meanwhile, athletes would often be sustained, as the stories of Lonsbrough and Hyman show, by their communities, their families, their municipalities and their own dedication. These were the days, and probably the high tide, of the local state and of strong public provision. In this regard, although Lonsbrough and Hyman were self-evidently 'northern lasses', the fact that they were from Yorkshire probably matters less than the fact that they were from *somewhere*. Where, after all, are contemporary British sport heroines such as Paula Radcliffe or Kelly Holmes *from*? Radcliffe and Holmes inhabit a globalised world of athletics practice and body preparation; they're *from* the sum total of international training camps and gymnasia to which their fitness programmes and status as elite athletes have taken them, and, as athletes, regardless of where they were born, they're from, so far as I can judge, nowhere in particular.

What is a local sport heroine?

Let us take sport heroism first. Drawing on the introduction to this book, a good starting point is Richard Holt's and J.A. Mangan's observation that 'heroes epitomise the qualities their society esteems'.[2] They cite Michael Oriard's assertion that, in the

United States, the athlete hero represents the rags-to-riches openness and democratic ideals of that society[3] and Wiley Lee Umphlett as saying that 'spectators, in identifying with their sport heroes, are really spectators of themselves'.[4] Sport heroes are also acknowledged sources of collective identity, status and pride, be it in national, supra-national[5] or, as in this chapter, regional or local contexts. And, as Marshall Fishwick observed, heroes reflect the age: in the eighteenth century they were 'enlightened gentlemen', in the nineteenth century self-made men – 'In our own time we are seeing the common man become heroic.'[6]

We also saw how, in Richard Holt's periodisation of British sport heroism, sport heroes of the pre-imperial and imperial eras gradually gave way to the modest, often professional 'ordinary man' (Jack Hobbs, Stan Matthews) of the twentieth century who came from, and often remained among, 'respectable, kindly, ordinary' folk; and how the latter, in turn, was eclipsed by the sport celebrity, creature of the postmodern sporting landscape inhabited by such as Alan Shearer, 'an icon on Tyneside but not a hero in the old *community* sense [my emphasis]'.[7] Women, understandably, have seldom been a part of this picture, given their historic struggles to be allowed to participate in sport at all.[8] Holt notes some of the pioneers of women's sport and the 'Golden Girls' of 1960s Olympiads – in particular the jumper Mary Rand and the sprinter Ann Packer[9] – but by the time the principal academic writer on women's sport, Jennifer Hargreaves, had produced a book on heroines of sport, in the year 2000,[10] the debate seemed to have moved on. In this book Hargreaves, quite properly, concentrates on female sportspeople in specifically marginalised groups (black South Africans, lesbians, the disabled) and calls, while she is about it, for a return to the '1970s anti-individualistic feminist principle that commodified heroines/stars should be replaced by "real women"'.[11]

All of this commentary helps to contextualise Anita Lonsbrough and Dorothy Hyman. They were Holt's 'respectable, kindly, ordinary' folk; they were Hargreaves' 'real women'; they were the means, adapting Umphlett, by which Yorkshire spectators viewed themselves; above all, they were rooted, as I've said, in their communities and in the civic, in a municipal culture which they took for granted.

Before Rome: when in Yorkshire ...

On Saturday 30 July 1960, scarcely a month before she was due to swim for Britain in the Olympic Games, Anita Lonsbrough won the Yorkshire Amateur Swimming Association's Group Championship 200 yards breast stroke race at the Cambridge Road Baths in Huddersfield, her home town.[12] Although there's no reason to think that this was an untypical preparation for British Olympians of the time, there is nevertheless a sense, in the pages of the *Yorkshire Post*, of some North–South, us-and-them tension in the run-up to Rome. For example, the Barnsley shot putter Arthur

Rowe was reported to be 'in the black books of the Olympic Games team selectors' because he had refused to compete in a meeting at the White City in London, preferring to take part in the National Coal Board sports day at Mansfield. He did so, he said, 'in appreciation of the way the Coal Board has treated me in the past'.[13] '"Play for us or else" seems to be the policy,' grumbled the sports editor of the *Yorkshire Post*. 'The rights and wrongs of that are for the moment no concern of mine; I am concerned that our Olympic Games team should not get off on the wrong foot. It seems to me that Rowe could show his fitness quite as well at Mansfield as at White City. In fact he did so.'[14] There was also some disquiet in Hull where 41-year-old gun maker and marksman Joe Wheater, due to represent Britain in the clay pigeon shooting event, was complaining in mid-August that shooters had been excluded from the opening parade in Rome.[15]

Generally speaking, though, the world that Lonsbrough and Hyman left temporarily behind bathed them in civic pride, while affirming their status as amateurs, fending financially for themselves. Anita was given an official send-off by the Mayor of Huddersfield, Alderman Norman Day, and Mrs Day accompanied, significantly, by Alderman Arthur Gardiner, chairman of the Town Council committee which controls the municipal baths and his wife Councillor Mrs A.L. Gardiner. A similar send-off was accorded to 17-year-old swimmer Jean Oldroyd of Dewsbury[16] and this seemed to make the two young women semi-official emissaries of their local swimming baths. Meanwhile, rather belatedly, a fund had been set up to assist local athletes competing in the Olympics (of the 270 British competitors, eleven were from Yorkshire) and officially opened by the mayor of Wakefield, Ald. Leonard Boston 'himself a keen cyclist and sportsman. But it has got off to a slow start, only £5 having been received so far'. A benefit dance was scheduled for 17 August at the Embassy Ballroom in Wakefield.[17] As regards the *Yorkshire Post* Dorothy Hyman arrived in Rome virtually unnoticed. Wheater and Lonsbrough were identified as the county's best prospects for medals and, as if to confirm the latter's status as the Girl Next Door, the paper informed readers of where her door could actually be found – on St. Peters Street in Huddersfield.[18]

It was the nuns: Lonsbrough in victory

The day after Anita Lonsbrough won the gold medal for the women's 200 metres breast stroke she was predictably feted in the popular national newspapers. In Rome Desmond Hackett of the *Daily Express* interviewed Anita's mother, who responded in 'a frank and warmly friendly Yorkshire fashion'. Her father, a regimental sergeant major in the Coldstream Guards, had stayed behind in Huddersfield because he 'reckoned he was a jinx'. 'Mum,' wrote Hackett, 'wanted Anita to show me the medal, but Anita said: "I left it in the hut. If I started to carry it around they would think I was just a big show-off".'[19] In the *Daily Mail*, Lonsbrough made clear to Harry Carpenter the minimal professional help that has supported her journey toward Rome. The nuns at St Josephs Convent School in Bradford 'made me take up breast stroke swimming. But for them I would never have won a gold medal'. The rest was ascribed to family and locality. Anita's mother told Carpenter: 'My husband and I taught Anita to swim when she was three. She was always mad on games'. 'She has true Yorkshire grit,' adds Carpenter. 'Early in 1959 she underwent a nose blockage caused by a childhood accident. Afterwards she smashed the world record.' Carpenter pressed home Lonsbrough's ordinariness: 'Normally she touches no liquor, never smokes, seldom dates boys; indeed, has no steady interests other than swimming and making out car licences at Huddersfield Town Hall.'[20] In the *Post*, Arthur Sunley, the President of Huddersfield Amateur Swimming Club, told of the club's pride in Anita, pointed out that she had only been swimming competitively for three years and expressed regret that Harry Chambers, chief instructor at Huddersfield Baths and therefore sometime tutor to Anita, had not lived to see her success. Mr J.H. Wilkin, Huddersfield Borough Treasurer, commented, with the slightly municipal stiffness characteristic of the period, that 'All these triumphs have left her completely unspoiled. Her popularity with all the members of my staff clearly testifies to that.'[21] 'She won the race,' wrote British Olympian Chris Brasher elsewhere in the same issue, 'through her calmness and her Yorkshire determination.' Amid all the tabloid hyperbole and the invocation of home, hearth and region, it's perhaps surprising to find from Brasher's article that Lonsbrough actually had a coach – Ray Scholey from Oswaldtwistle in Lancashire.[22] In an editorial the *Post* commented that 'Huddersfield can now take pride in the fact that it has at least two claims to world fame – its choir and Miss Lonsbrough. It would be a fitting gesture if the choir could take part in the welcome home celebrations … .'[23]

Stanley Lonsbrough's gift to his daughter to mark her achievement was to take her to Scarborough to watch some county cricket. There she would also attend the *Black and White Minstrel Show* and be toasted by its cast. She told well-wishers that she wanted to catch up on some sleep but, despite limping with a swollen ankle, that she expected to swim at Bingley the following week.[24] Seven days later she received a civic reception at Huddersfield Town Hall and it was announced that she would be given a testimonial gift at a 'Cavalcade of Sport' at Huddersfield's Theatre Royal in October. Anita Lonsbrough was voted BBC Sports Personality of 1962, was made an MBE in 1963 and now writes on swimming for the *Daily Telegraph*.

Dorothy Hyman: the conviviality of the short distance runner

Dorothy Hyman was beaten into second place by the legendary Wilma Rudolph in the women's 100 metres in Rome. Nineteen and from a mining family she worked as a tracer at the National Coal Board offices in Ardsley in South Yorkshire. When she took her silver medal, the *Post*, as with Lonsbrough, printed her address: Bloemfontein Street, Cudworth, near Barnsley. Her coach, Denis Watts of the Amateur Athletic

Association, had sent her instructions by post and her father Jack, a miner, had seen that they were carried out. Dorothy had done all her training after work, with only one day off a week – 'when she had her hair done'. Jack had promised her a radiogram if she were to win a medal. Councillor Albert Glover, chairman of Cudworth Urban Council called for 'civic recognition' of Hyman's achievement. Later it was announced that she would run a lap of honour at the new track at Thurnscoe belonging to her athletics club Hickleton Main.[25] On her return home the *Yorkshire Post* reported a 'typical Yorkshire welcome' for Dorothy: she was met by her family but mobbed by villagers from Cudworth and Thurnscoe and greeted by station master Mr J.P. Walsh who was wearing a top hat in honour of the occasion. 'Today,' said the *Post*, 'a triumphal procession will carry her back to Cudworth in time for the children leaving school to be able to meet her.'[26] The following day the Doncaster staff of the *Yorkshire Post* reported that Dorothy Hyman's reception in Cudworth (population 8,870) had been tumultuous, 'rivalling the V-Day celebrations'. The reception, featuring the Grimethorpe Colliery Band, had been recorded on colour film at the expense of Cudworth Council. Hyman told the crowd: 'When you have been born in a place and lived there all your life it is completely overwhelming for people who have known you to turn out as Cudworth people have turned out for me today.'[27]

Hyman won a gold medal at the European Championships in Belgrade in 1962 and captained the British women's team at the Olympics in Tokyo two years later. She retired after the games at the age of 23. Her achievements are commemorated in the sports centre in Cudworth that bears her name. She remained in her home community of Barnsley and coached athletics in the Barnsley area until 1989. In 1994 Jon Culley of the *Independent* sought out Dorothy for a 'Where Are They Now?' feature and reported that she had worked for 30 years as a planning assistant with British Coal, taking redundancy in 1990. She had then begun work as at a day care centre for the mentally handicapped.[28] She seems to have continued her support for participation in community sport and recreation: in 2006 she re-emerged briefly to decry the apparent decline of regional athletics, especially among females: she took part in an Educational Action Zone project in Yorkshire schools to raise awareness of sport. 'When I was watching the Yorkshire County Championships last year,' she said, 'I noticed there were only enough competitors for a women's final. In my day there were enough for several heats. That's so sad because it means that there's not much competition. I asked what the winning time was for the women's 100m and it was 12.6 seconds and that's poor. That is why we need to help and encourage children; we need to put the passion back into sport.'[29] In March of 2009 she switched her attention to senior citizens, appearing with the local mayor at Barnsley Metrodome to promote free swimming for the over-60s.[30]

Local heroines and the north of England in the 1960s

Making the necessary allowances for the cloying prose of national sports pages and the starch-and-treacle style of the *Yorkshire Post* around this time, a number of things can be said about Anita Lonsbrough and Dorothy Hyman as local sport heroines. They were among the last female members of Holt's third category – civic heroines who came from, went back to and, especially in Hyman's case, remained among the common people. They were not 'Golden Girls'. Mary Bignal (later Rand), their contemporary, was. The press hung around the glamorous Bignal, who liked, to adopt the 1950s/1960s idiom, to 'date'. They touted stories of engagement and, by implication, sex. She was, however reluctantly, celebrity material. But Lonsbrough and Hyman were embarrassed and impatient with press talk of boys. There was no regular fellow. They were athletes, there solely to compete. They had stepped out of ordinary life, won trophies, returned, been heroines for ten days and then stepped back in to that ordinary life. They were sustained largely by their families, the council, their own dedication and that of their coaches – in Dorothy's case via the Royal Mail. They were pre-celebrity and non-celebrity. Probably without knowing it, they stood for public provision and the idea that sport was part of community life – there for the enhancement of all therein.

These case studies of Anita Lonsbrough and Dorothy Hyman are thrown into sharp relief when compared to two contemporary sport heroines from, approximately, the same region. Direct comparisons, as will be apparent, will not always be possible here, but, in general, these two latter case studies show a greatly altered cultural and political landscape and, most importantly within that, a radically revised sense of the civic.

A sporting life and a death foretold: Jane Tomlinson and the public sphere

Jane Tomlinson was not an Olympic, nor even an elite, athlete. She gained public prominence as a sportswoman only after, and because, she was found to be dying. Her final years were spent raising funds, via sporting feats, for the continued public provision of health care in a northern city and coping reluctantly with the celebrity that that entailed. Her death, in 2007, was in some senses a muted and egalitarian version of the death of Princess Diana 11 years earlier; it called up notions of the heroine and female icon in a north of England now styled by many commentators as 'postmodern'.

Jane Goward was born in Wakefield in 1964, the year of the Tokyo Olympics. She married Mike Tomlinson in the mid-1980s, settled in the small town of Rothwell – just south of Leeds – and had two children. In 1990, still only 26, Jane was told that she had breast cancer and underwent a mastectomy; ten years later she learned from doctors that the disease had returned, was now terminal and she was unlikely to survive longer than six months. Her life, as I noted earlier, thereafter became closely bound up with the worlds of sport and health care provision.

Jane Tomlinson became known for the essentially non-competitive, endurance sports of 'fun run' marathons and long-distance cycling and took up both activities only when told that she had a short time to live. In 2002 she received a special award on the BBC 'Sports Personality of the Year Show' and when she died in September 2007 *The Times* carried an obituary written by Rob Hughes, of the paper's sport staff. This obituary detailed her achievements, in and through these sports:

Aug 2000 scan reveals multiple secondary cancers. She is given six months to live, but decides on the same day she is going to run the London Marathon

May 2001 takes part in her first race, the 5km Race for Life

2002 completes Great North Run in Newcastle in 1hr 51min, four minutes ahead of her husband Mike

Apr 2002 completes London Marathon

May 2002 wins Woman of Achievement Award in Leeds in recognition of her courage in running the London Marathon

Aug 2002 crosses the line in the first half of the field in the London Triathlon

Dec 2002 wins Helen Rollason Award at Sunday Times Sportswomen of the Year awards. Also honoured at BBC Sports Personality of the Year show

Mar 2003 cycles from John o'Groats to Land's End on tandem with her brother Luke Goward

Jun 2003 awarded MBE in Queen's Birthday Honours

Aug 2003 completes the Ironman UK Triathlon, the only person to finish a triathlon while having chemotherapy

Jun 2004 Jane and Luke complete 2,000-mile, five-week tandem bike ride from Rome to Leeds

Jun 2006 cycles 4,200 miles across America

Jan 2007 Jane and Mike launch Run For All, a 10km charity run held in Leeds in June. It will become an annual event

Monday, Sept 3 Jane dies, aged 43, after raising £1.75m for charities, including Macmillan Cancer Relief, SPARKS, Damon Runyon Cancer Research, Yorkshire Cancer Centre and Bluebell Wood Children's Hospice. Within 24 hours of her death, £50,000 more was donated.

A number of things are significant, and important to note, about the later life and death of Jane Tomlinson.

First, she was an authentic sporting heroine. Her heroism expressed itself through sport, while plainly transcending it. It derived from her sporting feats and, more importantly, from the fact that they were accomplished while she waited to die. In her running and cycling, she seemed, in the public perception, to challenge not only the physical terrain and the pain inflicted on her own body, but death itself. She 'defied the experts', wrote the *Yorkshire Evening Post* a few days after her death.[32] 'We thought of Jane as invincible even though her passing was pre-ordained', wrote Rachel Robinson, a fellow cancer-sufferer and one of many people to record their tributes on the *Yorkshire Evening Post* website. 'It's as though we forgot [her illness].'[33]

Second, although Hughes' *Times* obituary refers to her 'Yorkshire grit',[34] the reception accorded to Tomlinson, in her final years and in death, generally speaking was free of regional allusions, stereotypical or otherwise. On the contrary, Jane and her exploits were defined by globalisation and by links between the local and the global that she herself has forged. At her passing, for example, the *Yorkshire Evening Post* immediately identified her as 'an amazing ambassador for Leeds'[35] and an obituary in the *Daily Telegraph* noted that, at the height of her fundraising, she was receiving 2,500 letters a week.[36] A fortnight later Sheena Hastings of the *Yorkshire Evening Post* observed that Tomlinson's bravery had 'made her a household name' and taken her and her reputation beyond these shores – notably, via a 4,000 mile cycle ride across the United States in 2006. An accompanying colour photograph showed her pedalling through the Grand Canyon.[37] Moreover it was noted that: 'Jane's death has made headlines right around the world with newspapers and TV stations in places as far afield as the USA, Australia and the Middle East today carrying stories about her life and achievements. Closer to home, tributes continued to pour in with the Queen herself saying she was "saddened" to hear of Jane's death.'[38] Here Jane Tomlinson is praised, in essence, for becoming widely known – for transcending place, both social (the monarch has been aware of her) and geographical.

Third, Jane's death was notable for the public expression of emotion and regard. The *Yorkshire Evening Post* website was awash with tributes. Gary and Tracey Wigley, for example, wrote: 'I have loads of memories of Jane but most of all I have admiration for her and her family. If the world leaders had a quarter of Jane's determination, dedication and compassion this world would be a much better place to live. This sad day should be remembered by naming it the Jane Tomlinson Day. I would ask the YEP to put this to the people of Yorkshire. Thank you Jane.' A message from 'Barbara and Harry' read: 'Leeds has lost its own people's princess.' 'Dave' wrote: 'God has one fab angel by his side now.' And so on.[39] All this ran counter to some of the historic notions of Yorkshire people, long depicted as unsentimental, grouchy and emotionally closed. Until the 1990s the Yorkshire County Cricket Club, with its regular internal disputes, had typified this view, along with myriad literary and media depictions.[40] And feminist writers, reflecting on the 'Yorkshire Ripper' murders of 1975–81 which had taken place principally in West Yorkshire, had claimed that a broad strain of misogyny ran through the culture of the region.[41] Postmodern culture, however, has a more central place for the emotions so many of the citizens of postmodern Leeds unabashedly communed with the Tomlinson family in their grief.

Fourth, and most important, the phenomenon of Jane Tomlinson had a latent politics which entailed a complex interplay between the public and the private, the civic certainties of the Lonsbrough–Hyman era having long since evaporated.

Most of Tomlinson's adult life was deeply intertwined with the National Health Service. She was first treated for cancer at St James Hospital in Leeds in 1990. She then trained as a radiographer at Leeds General Infirmary. Her brother Luke Goward, who cycled from Rome to Leeds with her in 2004, was a casualty nurse; his wife Karen was also a nurse, at St James'. And Paediatric Services at Leeds Teaching Hospitals NHS Trust was among the many benefactors of her prodigious fundraising. Furthermore, Jane, while seeking publicity – between 2005 and 2007 she and her husband Mike produced three copious, diary-format books of autobiography[42] and her various sporting feats were covered widely by the international media – invariably eschewed celebrity, seeking to place the causes for which she worked at centre stage. According to Hughes, she and her husband always slipped away early from awards dinners, professing themselves to feel 'like gatecrashers' in a roomful of sport stars.[43] 'I am just an ordinary mum and wife. I never did any of this to win a prize' she recalled thinking when she received her BBC award in 2002[44] and, after her death, her husband insisted that a statue of her would be a waste of money.[45]

Here Tomlinson parallels Lonsbrough and Hyman in their reluctance to 'get above themselves' and their determination, despite evident gratitude, that there should be 'no fuss'. But, despite her self-effacement – or, perhaps, because of it – Jane's project carried with it the strong implication that the treatment of illness was now in large part a matter for private initiative – be it through personal forbearance, individual donation to, or acts of, charity or commercial provision. The money raised by the Tomlinsons – estimated to be around £1.75 million in September 2007 – was divided between health charities and a needy public sector: the children's sports charity Sparks, Macmillan Cancer Support, Martin House Children's Hospice in Boston Spa, Leeds, the Paediatric Acute Services at Leeds Teaching Hospitals NHS Trust and the Bluebell Wood Children's Hospice in Doncaster.[46] In this sense, Jane Tomlinson embodied, and called up, community values in the absence or inadequacy of public provision, with increasing amounts of the NHS budget being diverted away from clinical care.[47]

Thus, motivated by the desire not to sit at home and feel sorry for herself, Jane Tomlinson entered an already established nexus of participation sport ('fun runs'), health promotion, private donation and corporate sponsorship. Like Lonsbrough and Hyman, Tomlinson was the modest young woman next door; but, unlike them, her marriage of the ordinary to the extraordinary formed the basis of an ongoing media phenomenon. In this context, she became a private promoter of the public good – giving, and encouraging, voluntary support for a range of medical research and treatment in the voluntary and state sectors. The publicity generated by her cycle rides, marathons and global known-ness became, like all publicity, a currency and a host of bodies and individuals, public and private, were able to deal in this currency. While, for Lonsbrough and Hyman, the mayor and local councillors had been virtually the sole stewards of public acknowledgement, civic dignitaries were simply some among many of the persons wishing to be pictured smiling on the photograph that was Jane Tomlinson's life. Leeds City Council, for example, is just one of ten listed sponsors of the Leeds 10K Race for All, which Jane helped to inaugurate in 2007 and which bears her name; the others include Morrisons, the supermarket chain, Gatorade, the sports drink firm and ASICS the running technology company, along with local media such as the *Yorkshire Post*. The race's website mingles company and council logos with tributes to Tomlinson from sport celebrities (Olympic rowing champion Sir Steven Redgrave, athletes Paula Radcliffe and Kris Akabusi, England rugby coach and ex-captain Martin Johnson), photographs of fun runners and information about cancer charities in a contemporary melange of public–private partnership.[48]

Proud to be from Mansfield: the feting of Beccy Adlington

Some of these same social changes are manifest in the reception accorded to Rebecca Adlington, a swimmer who won two gold medals for Britain at the Beijing Olympics in August 2008 – the first British female to do so since Anita Lonsbrough, 48 years earlier.

Rebecca Adlington was born in 1989, in the North Nottinghamshire town of Mansfield. She is, therefore, identifiably from somewhere, although this may have much to do with the specific facilities for her sport – had she been a specialist in another athletic discipline it might have been necessary for her to move around the world, on athletic scholarships, to different training camps, and so on. Adlington has, at the time of writing, lived all her life with her family in Mansfield. She is therefore, in a literal sense, the Girl Next Door. Indeed like Lonsbrough's and Hyman's before her, Rebecca's local paper, the *Mansfield Chad* (formerly the *Chronicle and Advertiser*), frequently gave the location of that door, on Ryedale Avenue in the town. But in another sense Beccy Adlington could not be construed as a Girl Next Door, stepping briefly out of ordinary life. She was a full-time swimmer with an exacting training regimen, the details of which were soon published by Motley Health, a website advising on fitness:

> **Monday:** From 6am to 8am, swimming about 7,000–8,000 metres per two-hour session in the Olympic pool at Nottingham Uni. After the morning swim, she goes home to have breakfast and rest. She would then go running or circuit

training for an hour at around 3pm, before returning to the pool around 5pm for another two-hour training session, and then another gym session before bed.

Tuesday: Up at 5am for a high intensity session. In the afternoon it is an aerobic session, involving steady swimming for endurance training. These sessions are repeated on Thursday and Friday evening.

Wednesday: Just one 2 hour session in a 50m pool in the afternoon, followed by an hour of weights in the gym, which is next to the pool. Total training session is about 4 hours.

Thursday and Friday: Another 5am start, with both morning and evening sessions in the pool.

'It's all sleeping, training, driving and occasionally finding time to eat. That's what my life is about.' Rebecca Adlington, 2008.

Saturday: 7am start for one session in the pool. She says that 'by the end of the week I've swum 65,000–70,000m. For the rest of the day, I get to indulge my passion for shopping. I am into shoes in a big way. I have dozens of pairs.'

Sunday – Rest Day: Sleep until 10am and then just relax for the day.

The longer you do it, the harder it gets. Every year is harder. To keep improving it has to be like that. I pushed myself harder than ever in my training cycle up to the Olympic Trials. I've been crying in training, I've been in so much pain. Sometimes I finish training so tired I wonder: 'What am I doing this for?' Then you do an amazing swim and you know why." Rebecca Adlington, 2008.[49]

This, of course, did not prevent her being styled as a Girl Next Door in other senses, but, as with Jane Tomlinson, the feting of Beccy Adlington entailed a relationship between the local and the global very different from that visited upon Lonsbrough and Hyman. They had been global for a few days and then vanished back into the local. Beccy, like Jane, had, so to speak, brought the global right here, to our town, and the link between the local (Mansfield) and the global (the Olympics, world fame) would remain for as long as it could be sustained. Similarly, there was a changed role for the civic authority.

Mansfield is around 25 miles south of Sheffield. In matters of local culture and regional identity it seems to be on the border between the North and the Midlands. For most of the last century it was a colliery town – it is identified as such in D.H. Lawrence's *Lady Chatterley's Lover* – but all the local pits had closed by the late 1990s. Nearby Annesley Colliery, where the England fast bowlers Bill Voce and Harold Larwood both worked in the early 1920s, was designated a Conservation Area in 1999. In 2005 the East Midlands Development Agency, based in Nottingham, appointed a new Executive Director of Regeneration. The person in question, Diana Gilhespy, expressed herself 'delighted to be joining the team at *emda* – one of the most successful development agencies in the country. In its relatively short life it has put the East Midlands on the map both nationally and internationally.' Ms Gilhespy, a notice on the *emda* website continued, had 'for the past 8 years [...] worked at Mansfield District Council heading up regeneration and marketing, helping the town to restructure from its coal mining past and high unemployment, to a vibrant town and district with good work opportunities'.[50] This kind of discourse – with its implications of 'raising the profile' of a region, creating good news stories about it and thereby attracting people to it – defines quite aptly the role of councils and regional development and myriad public and/or private bodies in the post-industrial era. Globally visible sport heroes are, of course, a huge boon in the pursuit of these policies – indeed, soon after Jane Tomlinson's death, Yorkshire's regional development agency Yorkshire Forward, as sponsors of the Yorkshire leg of the Tour of Britain cycle race, announced that this leg would be named after her.[51] This provides some context in which to make sense of Adlington's homecoming.

Rebecca Adlington, to be sure, had benefited from local facilities. She had learned to swim at the age of six at the Sherwood Baths in Mansfield Woodhouse[52] but her Olympic preparation was done in Nottingham with the Nova Centurion Swimming Club. This was an elite squad made up of the best swimmers drawn from the county's various clubs and funded by Nottinghamshire County Council. This was fully consonant with contemporary political thinking on the Olympic Games and on sport in general which, while recognising the importance of sport participation, placed a high value on 'performance': the Blair government's *Game Plan* strategy document of 2002 is a good example.[53]

This had two clear implications for the watchers of Beccy's Olympic progress back in Mansfield. One was that her own local council – the Mansfield District Council– was relegated to the role of cheerleader because, since her identification as an elite swimmer, she had been swimming in another council's baths. Beneath its motto 'Creating a District Where People Can Succeed' and a headline which read 'Mansfield Backs Beijing-Bound Heroes' Mansfield DC instituted an on-line blog, hosted by the Chad, 'which will allow local people to post their good luck messages to Rebecca Adlington (swimming, Olympics), Sam Hynd (swimming, Paralympics), Charlotte Henshaw (swimming, Paralympics), Arnie Chan (table tennis, Paralympics) and Chris Martin (discus, Paralympics)'. It was also announced that, as for Lonsbrough and Hyman more than three decades earlier, the Council's Executive Mayor, Tony Egginton, had hosted 'a special send-off event for the athletes'. This time, though, 200 community leaders and representatives from local sports clubs and businesses had been invited along.

Second, as I have argued, Adlington could not be rendered, as Lonsbrough and

Hyman had been, as a Girl Next Door, taking brief time out from an ordinary life. As we have seen, she had no conventional job or workmates; she was a full-time swimmer, spending most of her waking hours in the water. This, though, proved a small obstacle for the ravenous local media of Mansfield who readily surmounted it in two ways. First, Rebecca, if not definable as ordinary in the sphere of production, instead became a Girl Next Door through *consumption*. She was immediately styled as '[i]nspirational Rebecca, who enjoys shopping and watching DVDs in her leisure time'[55] whose self confessed weakness was designer shoes: 'Christian Louboutins', she told the *Chad*, were her favourite.[56] Beyond this Adlington was ordinary simply by being from Mansfield – an ordinary town like thousands of others seeking 'regeneration' and now gifted with a global celebrity who, as *Chad* readers were frequently reminded, resided in their midst, on Ryedale Avenue. Second, whatever ground there might have been for supposing that Rebecca had lived an ordinary life, there would, unlike for Lonsbrough and Hyman, be no foreseeable return to it for Adlington. This became part of the burgeoning media narrative that surrounded her: 'Rebecca Adlington: My life has changed forever' read a headline in the *Chad* in early October.[57]

Following the award of her Olympic medals Rebecca Adlington became an ongoing story for the Mansfield media – a walking news item. On the *Chad* website she was constituted as a subsidiary site category in her own right. Beneath the principal categories of 'Home', 'News', 'Sport', 'Community', 'Your Say', 'Newspaper' and 'Health Info', visitors could select from 'A–Z', 'Contact', 'Order pics', 'Notices', 'Video', 'Book ads', 'Forums', 'Leisure', 'Slideshows', 'Blogs', 'Podcasts', 'Facebook', 'What's On' and, finally, 'Rebecca Adlington'.[58] In mid-October 2008, two months after her successful swims, web visitors clicking on the 'Rebecca Adlington' category could choose from twenty written stories, two videos, a 'Photo Special' and a slide show.[59] Among these stories and representations of Beccy there were accounts of aspects of her success that recalled the 1950s and 1960s: she (along with local Paralympic swimmer Sam Hynd) received the Freedom of Mansfield; she (again with Hynd) was given a civic reception at County Hall in Nottingham; she paid tribute to her family's sacrifices; and there was a further tribute to her coach, Bill Furness.[60] But, equally, some were rooted in the tautology of publicity – simply making public the fact that Adlington was now a public figure: former Olympic athlete and now television personality Roger Black offered great praise to Rebecca and predicted a media-oriented future for her: 'The reality is that every sport needs a superstar and swimming now has one.' Beccy, he remarked, in the familiar lexicon of the publicity business, 'is going to be massive for the next four years'[61]; Mansfield Town Football Club announced that their showers will be named after Rebecca[62]; three weeks later, Yates's a local bar that had changed its name to 'The Adlington Arms' in her honour now announced that it was reverting to its original name, indicating that the value of Adlington publicity, as currency, might carry a time limit: 'It was a temporary thing as a homecoming for Rebecca but there was a bit of a mixed reaction to changing the name,' said the bar's manager Dan England. 'It was meant as a celebration but there was not enough reason to justify keeping it — if there had been a better reaction we might have kept it longer'[63]; another story announced that the swimmer herself would be appearing on television:

> Mansfield's Olympic swim star Rebecca Adlington is under the spotlight when BBC TV's *Inside Out* returns tonight. A new series of *Inside Out* starts on Wednesday September 17th at 7.30pm on BBC1 East Midlands. Since many Mansfield viewers will have aerials pointed at *Look North* and won't see *Inside Out East Midlands* on analague or on channel 101 the East Mid[land]s programme is also available on Sky on channel 980 and on Freesat on channel 952.[64]

These latter stories are, again, predicated on the brief conjoining of the local (Mansfield) and the global (the Olympic Games, an international media event recently concluded in faraway Beijing). For as long as the phenomenon lasts, Adlington, like Tomlinson, is made an ambassador from her place of birth/residence to the world of mass media, publicity, sales and the seeking of profile; while local folk grapple with the notion that someone from their town is going to be 'massive', entrepreneurs queue to pay homage in pursuit of commercial advantage. Rebecca, inevitably, returned the compliment, the now-global paying tribute to the local: 'I'm proud to be from Mansfield' she told a huge crowd on her return to the town.[65] But, meanwhile, her phone had been ringing since she began to promise victory in Beijing. As a national newspaper observed, she

> received phone calls from the producers of the BBC quiz show *A Question of Sport* even before she'd won her first gold. She is almost certain to get kit deals from the likes of Speedo or Adidas and could be endorsed by a bank or pharmaceutical company, for instance, to the tune of £150,000 a year. The new golden girl of British sport still receives an annual £1,000 grant from Mansfield district council for travel and accommodation costs. Over the weekend, she said she 'got the feeling' her Lottery funding would go up from its current level of £12,000, but added: 'I wouldn't accept anything that comes in the way of my swimming.'[66]

A leading publicist affirms Beccy's prospects:

> Mark Borkowski, author of *The Fame Formula*, said: 'She [Adlington] compares well with Olympians like [rowers] Steve Redgrave and Matthew Pinsent, in that swimming is not an exclusively middle class sport. Adlington

has so much genuine heroism about her ... and that ordinariness will serve her well.'[67]

To sum up: heroism has not gone away, nor, drawing on the definitions with which I began this chapter, has it been especially redefined, but, as Holt noted, it now jostles with and, beyond a certain point, cannot be distinguished from, celebrity. Anita Lonsbrough and Dorothy Hyman practised their sport in a society still dominated by the production of goods, in which public provision was taken for granted, wherein there was a strong sense of the civic and sport, for many, was no more than a welcome diversion. For them, as returning medal winners, and for the northern towns which welcomed them home, a town hall reception, a few words of thanks and a modest treat (a radiogram, a trip to see the *Black and White Minstrel Show*) sufficed to mark their achievements; they then went back to ordinary life – family, friends and work. But, for Rebecca Adlington and, in a very real sense, for Jane Tomlinson, being who they were *became* their work. Tomlinson, of course, was privately uncomfortable with her own celebrity, but this was out of self-effacement, rather than political critique. For Adlington, her 'ordinariness' – residing in her origins in an ordinary town, her lack of pretension and her liking, as a consumer, for ordinary things (shoes, DVDs, burger and chips) together became a commodity. Becky Adlington reflected her time. In a world where sport was a media spectacle, she herself became a media spectacle; in a world where sport, like health, sought private financing, she became a commodity – even better, a commodity who loved commodities. Following Umphlett, she was the people who beheld her: millions of young women, steeped in television, could see themselves in her. After all, along with the burger and chips and the shoes, she liked to watch TV, and wanted to be on it. 'I'd absolutely love to do *Strictly Come Dancing*', she said when she came back from Beijing. 'I don't dance at all but I watch it every time it's on. It's just the best programme on television ... Do you think I could get on *Top Gear* as well'. The producer of the popular 'laddish' motoring programme said he would arrange it: 'She's a fantastic British hero ... and we love that on *Top Gear*.'[68]

---

[1]   Stephen Wagg, '"If you want the girl next door ..." Olympic sport and the popular press in early Cold War Britain', in Stephen Wagg and David L. Andrews (eds), *East Plays West: Sport and the Cold War* (London, 2007), pp. 100–22.

[2]   Richard Holt and J.A. Mangan, 'Prologue: heroes of a European past', in Richard Holt, J.A. Mangan and Pierre Lanfranchi (eds), *European Heroes: Myth, Identity, Sport* (London, 1996), p. 2.

[3]   Michael Oriard, *Dreaming of Heroes: American Sports Fiction* 1868–1980 (Chicago, 1982), p. 26, quoted in Holt and Mangan, 'Prologue: heroes of a European past', p. 3.

4   Wiley Lee Umphlett, *The Sporting Myth and the American Experience* (London, 1975), p.170, quoted in Holt and Mangan, 'Prologue: heroes of a European past', p. 2.

5   Ibid., p. 3.

6   Marshall W. Fishwick, *American Heroes: Myth and Reality* (Westport, 1954), p.225, quoted in Holt and Mangan, 'Prologue: heroes of a European past', pp. 4–5.

7   Richard Holt, 'Champions, heroes and celebrities: sporting greatness and the British public', in *The Book of British Sporting Heroes* (London, 1998), pp. 13, 18 and 21.

8   Jennifer Hargreaves, *Sporting Females: Critical Issues in the History and Sociology of Women's Sports* (London, 1994).

9   Holt 'Champions', p. 23.

10 Jennifer Hargreaves, *Heroines of Sport: The Politics of Difference and Identity* (London, 2000).

11 Ibid., p. 5.

12 *Yorkshire Post*, 1 August 1960, p. 8.

13 *Yorkshire Post*, 2 August 1960, p. 8.

14 *Yorkshire Post*, 11 August 1960, p. 10.

15 *Yorkshire Post*, 13 August 1960, p. 7.

16 *Yorkshire Post*, 13 August 1960, p. 7.

17 *Yorkshire Post*, 8 August 1960, p. 5

18 *Yorkshire Post*, 18 August 1960, p. 9.

19 *Daily Express*, 29 August 1960, p. 10.

20 *Daily Mail*, 29 August 1960, p. 9.

21 *Yorkshire Post*, 29 August 1960, p. 1.

22 Chris Brasher, 'Miss Lonsbrough sets an example', *Yorkshire Post*, 29 August 1960, p.8.

23 *Yorkshire Post*, 29 August 1960, p. 6.

24 *Yorkshire Post*, 7 September 1960 p. 7.

25 *Yorkshire Post*, 3 September 1960, p. 1, 6 September 1960, p. 1.

26 *Yorkshire Post*, 13 September 1960, p. 7.

27 *Yorkshire Post*, 14 September 1960, p. 9.

28 Jon Culley 'Where are they now?: Dorothy Hyman', *Independent*, 23 August 1994. www.independent.co.uk/sport/where-are-they-now-dorothy-hyman-1385334.html (accessed 31 May 2009).

29 http://www.britain.tv/articles/publish/olympic¬¬_games_commonwealth_games¬ doroth (accessed 9 October 2006).

30 'Olympic star takes the plunge for free swimming for over 60s', *Sheffield Telegraph*, 16 March 2009. www.sheffieldtelegraph.co.uk/news2/Olympic-star-takes-the-plunge.5071999.jp (accessed 1 June 2009).

31 Rob Hughes 'Iron lady: Jane Tomlinson 1964–2007: the bravest woman I ever met has left us, but the legacy of her amazing heroism remains', 7 September 2007. http://www.timesonline.co.uk/tol/sport/more_sport/article2413914.ece (accessed 7 October 2008).

32   'Jane's Appeal gets £50, 000 boost in just two days'
     http://www.yorkshireeveningpost.co.uk/jane/-Jane39s-Appeal-gets-50000.3178931.jp
     (posted 19 September 2007, accessed 7 October 2008).
33   'Jane Tomlinson: our amazing ambassador',
     http://www.yorkshireeveningpost.co.uk/jane/Jane-Tomlinson-Our-amazing-
     ambassador.3177099.jp Posted 19th September 2007 (accessed 7 October 2008).
34   Rob Hughes 'Iron lady'.
35   'Jane Tomlinson: our amazing ambassador'.
36   http://www.telegraph.co.uk/news/obituaries/1562293/Jane-Tomlinson.html Posted 6th
     September 2007 (accessed 8 October 2008).
37   'A moving end to Jane Tomlinson's incredible journey'.
     http://www.yorkshirepost.co.uk/highlights/A-moving-end-to-Jane.4444607.jp (posted 1
     September 2007, accessed 7 October 2008).
38   'Tomlinson family: pay tribute to Jane through charity donations'.
     http://www.yorkshireeveningpost.co.uk/jane/Tomlinson-family-Pay-tribute-
     to.3173931.jp (posted 5 September 2007, accessed 7 October 2008).
39   'Jane Tomlinson: our amazing ambassador'.
40   See, for example, 'Muck or nettles', my other chapter in this book, originally published
     in *Sport in History*, 23, 2 (2003–4), pp. 68–93.
41   See, for instance, Nicole Ward Jouve, *The Streetcleaner* (London, 1988) and Joan Smith,
     Mysogynies (London, 1989).
42   Jane and Mike Tomlinson, *The Luxury of Time* (London, 2005); *You Can't Take it with
     You* (London, 2006); *How Good is That?* (London, 2008).
43   Hughes 'Iron lady'.
44   *The Luxury of Time*, p. 5
45   Mike Tomlinson: 'We don't need a statue erecting in Jane's memory',
     http://www.yorkshireeveningpost.co.uk/news/Mike-Tomlinson-39We-don39t-
     need.3186062.jp (posted: 8 September 2007, accessed 7 October 2008).
46   'Jane Tomlinson: an inspiration to millions',
     http://www.yorkshireeveningpost.co.uk/jane/Jane-Tomlinson-An-inspiration-
     to.3170551.jp (posted 4 September 2007, accessed 7 October 2008).
47   For the documentation of the privatisation of the National Health Service see Alison M.
     Pollock *et al*, *NHS plc* (London, 2005).
48   http://www.runforall.com/ (accessed 8 October 2008).
49   'Rebecca Adlington – Olympic double gold medal winner – her swimming workout',
     http://www.motleyhealth.com/articles/2008/08/rebecca-adlington-olympic-gold-medal-
     her-swimming-workout.html (posted 17 August 2008, accessed 9 October 2008).
50   Press Release: 'New regeneration director at *emda*',
     http://www.emda.org.uk/news/newsreturn.asp?fileno=2841 (posted 27 July 2005,
     accessed 8 October 2008).
51   'Cycle race honours Jane Tomlinson',
     http://www.yorkshireeveningpost.co.uk/jane/Cycle-race-honours-Jane-
     Tomlinson.3190084.jp (posted 11 September 2007, accessed 10 October 2008).

52 'Meet Rebecca Adlington – Mansfield's Olympic champion', http://www.chad.co.uk/adlington/Meet-Rebecca-Adlington--Mansfield39s.4377563.jp (posted 11 August 2007, accessed 9 October 2008).

53 See www.sportdevelopment.org.uk/gameplan2002.pdf (accessed 10 October 2008).

54 'Mansfield backs Beijing-bound heroes', http://www.mansfield.gov.uk/index.aspx?articleid=2010 (accessed 6 October 2008).

55 'Meet Rebecca Adlington – Mansfield's Olympic champion'.

56 'Olympic champ Becky to walk tall in Mansfield', http://www.chad.co.uk/adlington/Olympic-champ-Becky-to-walk.4410812.jp (posted 20 August 2008, accessed 10 October 2008).

57 http://www.chad.co.uk/adlington/Rebecca-Adlington-39My-life-has.4543280.jp (posted 1 October 2008, accessed 9 October 2008).

58 http://www.chad.co.uk/ (accessed 10 October 2008).

59 http://www.chad.co.uk/sectionhome.aspx?sectionID=13954 (accessed 15 October 2008).

60 http://www.chad.co.uk/adlington/Adlington-and-Hynd-given-Freedom.4493577.jp (posted 15 September 2008, accessed 15 October 2008). http://www.chad.co.uk/adlington/Becky-and-Sam-honoured-at.4551875.jp (posted 2 October 2008, accessed 15 October 2008). http://www.chad.co.uk/adlington/39Sacrifices-have-been-made39.4543410.jp (posted 1 October 2008, accessed 15 October 2008). http://www.chad.co.uk/adlington/39She-would-not-have-done.4543368.jp (posted 1 October 2008, accessed 15 October 2008).

61 http://www.chad.co.uk/adlington/EXCLUSIVE-Olympic-legend39s-tribute-to.4423693.jp (posted 25 August 2008, accessed 15 October 2008).

62 http://www.chad.co.uk/adlington/Football-club-showers-renamed-after.4428297.jp (posted 26 August 2008, accessed 15 October 2008).

63 http://www.chad.co.uk/adlington/Pub-rebranded-in-honour-of.4492777.jp (posted 15 September, accessed 15 October 2008).

64 http://www.chad.co.uk/adlington/Becky-under-Inside-Out-BBC.4485089.jp (posted 11 September 2008, accessed 15 October 2008).

65 http://www.chad.co.uk/adlington/I-am-proud-to-be.4424576.jp (posted 25 August 2008, accessed 15 October 2008).

66 Amol Rajan, 'Ready, steady, go – the race to turn gold into millions', *Independent Beijing Supplement*, 19 August 2008, p. 7.

67 Ibid.

68 Amol Rajan '*Top Gear* will open its doors to Adlington'. http://www.independent.co.uk/sport/olympics/top-gear-will-open-its-doors-to-adlington-906525.html (posted 23 August 2008, accessed 16 October 2008).

CHAPTER 7

Football's First Northern Hero? The Rise and Fall of William Sudell

Neil Carter

'Of course, this'll make him more popular than ever ...
And yet ... What great cause is he identified with?
He's identified with the great cause of cheering us all up'.

Arnold Bennett, The Card[1]

Introduction

The status of sporting hero has usually been conferred on men and women for their exploits on the field of play. In recent years, more attention has been paid to those on the sidelines. In particular, through association with the success of their teams, football managers have increasingly been perceived as heroes. Partly through changes in the football industry, developments in the media and the emergence of a cult of celebrity, they have become emblematic figures for the clubs that they manage. When we think of football managers who have been bestowed this status, names like Clough, Shankly, Busby and, latterly, Ferguson spring to mind.

In the mid-nineteenth century Thomas Carlyle had ascribed the notion of hero to various 'men': Gods, Prophets, Poets, Priests, Writers and Kings.[2] Unsurprisingly, he had not thought of football managers, mainly because they had not been invented when he wrote about heroism, and it is highly unlikely, even if they had, that Carlyle would have thought them worthy of the title. For Carlyle, heroes had to be conspicuous and admired for their achievements, if not their noble qualities. This interpretation could indicate a reflection on wider changes in society since Carlyle's era. Through the growth of popular culture, 'hero-worship' has become more democratic, moving away from elites to those lower down the social ladder. The growth of commercialised sport, and especially association football, in Britain from the late nineteenth century has mirrored these social changes.

One managerial figure who has been rarely acclaimed as a hero is William Sudell. His recent rediscovery notwithstanding, Sudell has been a largely forgotten figure in the history of football, but under his leadership Preston was 'the' club of the 1880s. In 1889, Preston North End, known as the 'Invincibles', won the first ever Football League and FA Cup double and retained the League again the following year.[3] Sudell's achievements with Preston were only part of the modernising role he played in the development of professional football in the 1880s. He was an early football entrepreneur and at the forefront of the game's move to professionalism in 1885.[4] Furthermore, he was a model for future football managers. He thought about tactics and pre-match preparation as well as looking to buy the best players. Sudell also knew the worth of good relations with the press. His fall was spectacular, however. In 1895, he was jailed for three years for embezzlement and lived out the latter part of his life in South Africa.

A northern hero?

To what extent was William Sudell a sporting hero of the North? Which communities did he appeal to and what particular qualities did he possess that gave him a legitimate claim to this title? In terms of northernness, many commentators have noted that identity is generally a nebulous as well as a multi-layered concept. Hill and Williams have suggested that the north of England is as much a state of mind as a place and that:

> Being a Northerner is a creation of the imagination, a product of cultural traditions, assumptions and memories. No doubt this is why notions of the North and of what constitutes Northernness have varied over time and between places.

Moreover, 'One person's awareness of being a Northerner is not necessarily the same as another's and, indeed, the same individual can subscribe to differing forms of Northern identity at different times.'[5]

While Sudell was from the North and Preston was located in the heart of Lancashire, it is perhaps in the category of 'new urban hero', that Sudell can be placed.[6] Sudell's reputation was forged against the background of a nineteenth-century civic culture that was a particular feature of northern towns and cities. His image was a product of the town's social make-up and his own aspirations in addition to his association with the football club. Nevertheless, it can also be argued that, to a lesser extent, the celebrity he achieved in Preston through the exploits of the football club had wider consequences for perceptions of the North and especially football in the North.

The construction of a northern identity

If Sudell was a heroic figure in the rise of Preston North End, how was this image transmitted? What sources can be used to outline this process? Sudell seems to have left no personal papers or records. In addition, there is no trace of any archives of Preston North End FC from this period. Moreover, there are no published or even unpublished autobiographies or biographies of him.[7] As with much of sports history, the image of Sudell has largely been constructed through contemporary local newspapers. From the late nineteenth century, the reporting of sporting events by newspapers had given sport a cultural legitimacy. However, newspapers had their own agendas. They were businesses and due to the need to sell papers some would put a gloss on stories for their particular market. Jeffrey Hill has further cautioned that newspaper reports are as much a form of 'fictive narrative' as they are straight-forward recorders of facts and that history itself 'is concerned with the act of narrating – both the narrating contained in the sources themselves, and the narrative imposed by the historian on them'.[8]

The period from about the 1880s to the 1950s represented the heyday of the provincial press. From the late nineteenth century, their political positions were subsumed in the themes of community, locality and 'our town', which provided the main tropes of local newspaper reportage. The voice assumed by the local press was the voice of 'us', the locality; the local paper spoke, or was felt to speak, for the people of the community it served.[9] Sport came to play an essential part in the make up of the late Victorian provincial newspaper. Publications like the *Athletic News* and the *Bolton Cricket and Football Field* also helped a nascent sporting press form a symbiotic relationship with football. Through reporters like Jimmy Catton and John Bentley, they shaped a distinctly northern footballing sub-culture, which promoted the professional game.[10] As a consequence, the press also played an important role in framing particular myths and legends, and as a consequence, relatively simplistic North–South stereotypes.

What was the role of the press in presenting Sudell as an emblematic figure for Preston North End? During this period, the management of early football clubs was usually reported in terms of its directors. At Preston, however, the press recognised Sudell as the dominant figure. He was the first managerial figure whose relationship with the performance of the team was personalised by the press. After winning the FA Cup in 1889, it was reported that Sudell 'took his great victory and the result of many years of hard work, with as much composure as he accepted the defeat last year'.[11] For the following season the *Athletic News* predicted that 'Mr Sudell will keep the team up to its present high standards'.[12]

The attention in the press through the exploits of the Invincibles turned him into a local celebrity, enhanced his standing in the town and he became the public face of the club. On the day of the 1888 FA Cup final, the *Preston Herald* devoted a whole page to a preview of the game. Sudell received the biggest write up, and while there were sketches of the players, Sudell's was the largest, suggesting his overall importance. He was also given a full column to pontificate on the benefits of professional football.[13] After eventually winning the cup the following year, the team was granted a reception by the Mayor. Sudell was greeted with an ovation and a rendition of 'For he's a jolly good fellow'. The town's MPs later queued up to be photographed with the double winning team. In 1890, Sudell was presented with a memento of this triumph, an event that was presided over by a town Alderman and a number of its councillors.[14]

Sudell, football and civic culture

As suggested in the opening quotation, Arnold Bennett's 'card', Denry Machin, characterised the optimism and civic pride of provincial Victorian and Edwardian England. As Denry showed by associating himself with a successful football team, it could have important effects for those who were trying to climb the town's social ladder. To a certain extent, Sudell's story was not dissimilar to that of 'Denry' – but without the happy ending.[15]

What is known of his early background? Sudell was no working-class hero. He was born in Preston in 1850, the youngest of four children. The Sudell family tree included a seventeenth-century Guild Mayor of the town, although William's father was of more modest means, the manager of a warehouse. Nevertheless, young Billy attended a private school in Cheshire. On his return to Preston, he obtained a position at the cotton mill of John Goodair. He aspired to a middle-class lifestyle and worked his way up the company ranks and eventually became the mill's manager. The owners or family members had traditionally undertaken the management of companies. However, due to the increase in the size of businesses and a growing a division of labour by the late nineteenth century, managerial hierarchies emerged. Sudell later ran the factory himself, earning a salary of £500.[16] This allowed him to move up the property ladder and by 1891; he could afford to have two servants living-in and to keep a private carriage.[17] Sudell was part of a nascent salaried managerial class that reflected the overall growth of the technocratic, professional middle classes. The identity of this group at this time though was generally weak. It sought a broad middle-class identity, rather than one based on their occupation.[18]

Civic culture was deep-rooted within Lancashire but had shifted during the nineteenth century. Initially, across the Victorian urban landscape, there had been a proliferation of societies and institutes that formed the basis for middle-class political, social and cultural networks.[19] These networks formed the agencies behind the construction of civic buildings like town halls, museums, libraries and concert halls as well as civic benevolence and philanthropy through the building of new hospitals and schools.[20] Preston, allegedly the setting for Dickens' *Hard Times*, exhibited the symbols of this civic culture. Like other Victorian cities and towns, a town hall was built in 1867. Moreover, Preston was famed for its Guild that dated from the twelfth century in which public parades took place every twenty years.

Undoubtedly Sudell aspired to be part of Preston's social elite. Before the football club, he had already immersed himself in other areas of Preston's civic life, indicating his desire to climb the social ladder. In 1874, through his boss John Goodair, he joined the local Volunteer Force, which was an important local institution where men of influence met and where the less celebrated might make a mark. The Volunteers were also keen on manly sports, and, as in the army, rank reflected social hierarchy. Sudell joined as an officer, eventually rising to the rank of major. In addition to his connection with the football club, he was vice-President of the town's Bicycle and Swimming clubs as well as a number of football and cricket clubs.[21] Victorian civic culture generally was an overwhelmingly male-dominated environment from which women were largely excluded. Whereas women were mainly involved in voluntary organisations that had a social welfare element, male societies provided opportunities for drinking and merriment.[22]

Sudell also took on the duties of a local guardian in Fylde, administering the poor law in this area. In 1879, it was reported that he had attended 15 of the local board's fortnightly meetings for 1878–79. Two years later, he was nominated for re-election to the Clifton Board of Guardians.[23] Voluntary and charitable activity gave members of the middle classes access to 'one of the most important ladders to social status available in Victorian towns and cities'.[24] However, even these activities were subject to social gradations. Those, like Sudell, in the urban middle ranks involved themselves at less prestigious levels of local government such as health boards and Poor Law administrators.[25]

He was later the vice-Chairman of the Preston Licensed Victuallers' Association. In 1888, the town's MPs, Aldermen and councillors attended its annual dinner. In a speech, Sudell spoke of his pride in his Preston ancestry and promoted the virtues of the town's workers. He claimed that:

> There was not a better class of weavers or spinners to be found anywhere than those in Preston; and so long as they had workpeople second to none in the kingdom he did not see why the town should not prosper.[26]

While Sudell's words can be construed as perhaps being somewhat embellished, they nevertheless do indicate a sense of civic pride. As a further indication of his standing in the local community, in 1888, he was approached by a 'strong and influential deputation of burgesses', that is, some of Preston's great and good, to stand in a forthcoming local election in Park Ward. It was reported in the normally conservative *Preston Guardian* (which paid more attention to political matters rather than local sport) that:

Mr Sudell is exceedingly popular throughout the ward, and already he has received numerous promises of support. He is thoroughly acquainted with business matters, and if elected – which by many is looked upon as a certainty – he will prove a decided acquisition to the Corporation, especially at the present time, when questions of vast importance are under consideration.[27]

Interestingly, Sudell chose to stand as an Independent candidate against two Conservatives, which may have been because he did not want to antagonise Liberals or Tories who supported North End. However, within a couple of days, Sudell mysteriously withdrew his candidature.[28] While Sudell may have thought that he wouldn't get elected, he also perhaps wanted to devote more of his energies to running the football club.[29]

Although he played football and cricket, and also skated, Sudell did not excel on the sporting field. His talents lay in organisation. In 1867, he joined Preston North End cricket club and became its treasurer. He later organised an athletics festivals at Deepdale, Preston North End FC's ground. In 1876, he became President of the cricket club and started running it. That winter a football section was started. Initially it was the rugby code, or a form of the handling game, that was played. Rugby was the town's preferred winter game and Preston Grasshoppers its leading and oldest club, formed in 1869 by the town's premier cricket club Preston CC. By 1881, North End had switched codes. Football, through the Lancashire Cup locally and the FA Cup on a national stage, provided towns with more opportunities than rugby for civic recognition. Combined with the success of the Lancashire clubs in the FA Cup, it provided the springboard from which soccer began to overtake rugby.

Within Victorian civic culture, football played an important role in providing a sense of place and belonging as well as constructing and promoting broader town and city identities. At the same time, prevailing class relations shaped this construction of citizenship. Football, however, generated a sense of urban community through which supporters achieved a 'symbolic citizenship' as well as promoting notions of 'otherness' in relation to those from outside the town or city.[30] Sudell's association with Preston North End can be seen in the context of this burgeoning urban civic culture, and the success of the Lilywhites helped to promote the town of Preston on a national stage. On a more personal level, it raised Sudell's name and status within the town.

The growing interest in football was reflected by an increase in spectators as well as the enclosing of the ground and the building of stands, which improved the amenities and prevented spectators outside getting a free view of the game. Initially, many women went to games, perhaps mainly because it was free. This concession was withdrawn when 2,000 female spectators attended a game at Deepdale on Easter Monday 1885.[31] During the 1880s, attendances were generally erratic and dependent on the quality of the opposition, and a good run in the cup. The formation of the Football League had been a response to these fluctuations and the League had attempted to ensure high quality opponents on a regular basis. In the first five years of the League, it has been estimated that Preston's average attendance figures were between 6280 and 7650. However, there were some big crowds at Deepdale. In November 1884, 12,450 watched Bolton Wanderers and between 14,000 and 15,000 saw Preston play Sunderland in January 1893.[32]

Football clubs, therefore, became important local institutions that were run on a voluntary basis. Even when professionalism was legalised and football clubs converted themselves into companies, they were largely run by local businessmen and other members of the middle classes for little financial reward. For these men it was something new and exciting. It gave a warm feeling inside as well as enhancing their standing within the local community.[33] It is possible that the success of the club affected Sudell's ego. At the 1886, 1887 and 1889 AGMs, for example, he offered to resign on each occasion. At the first AGM, the players also threatened to resign if this happened while at the others his offer brought a chorus of 'no's'. [34]It gave the impression that Sudell believed that the club could not do without him.

What consequences did the growth of football have for northern identity? Rather than any attachment to a shared regional identity, the loyalties of northern supporters have traditionally grown up around individual towns and cities.[35] In the late nineteenth century, 'northern football' only existed in the abstract as it was cross cut by allegiances and loyalties that transcended both regional and county boundaries, and acted as 'the closed world of the vendetta'.[36] Blackburn Rovers supporters, for example, were unlikely to have taken much satisfaction from Preston's triumphs in the 1889 and 1890 seasons, and Preston fans vice versa at the time of Rovers' successes. By contrast, while Lancashire and Yorkshire enjoyed a fierce rivalry in cricket, there was a sense that both counties would prefer for the other to win the county championship rather than either the southern counties of Surrey or Middlesex.[37]

The football rivalry between northern towns can be partly explained by the development of professional football itself. While football as a game was not invented in the North, as a spectator sport, it was. Although organised football had strong roots in South Yorkshire and the Midlands, it was in Lancashire that football first became a proto-business. Importantly, the Lancashire cotton towns of Accrington, Bolton, Blackburn, Burnley, Darwen and Preston were not only forerunners of professionalism but except for Darwen, they were original members of the Football League, and these local derbies built on old local rivalries based on geography and trade. So fierce could the rivalries be that on one occasion, in 1888, Preston North End refused to play Blackburn Rovers in the Lancashire Cup due to the abuse they claimed that their players had received in Blackburn.[38]

Sudell and football management

While civic culture and local rivalries provided the background for Sudell's association with Preston North End, it was the success that the club enjoyed under his management that made his reputation. Sudell was a pioneering figure in the development of football management, and has been described as the game's first professional manager. Although Herbert Chapman has been referred to as the 'grand-daddy' of football managers, Sudell in many ways pre-dated him.

To a certain extent, Sudell's management of the team reflected his background as a member of the emerging technocratic and professional middle classes, and it also contrasted with the gentlemanly amateur values of others in football. Sudell always stressed the benefits of professionalism and was keen to liken football to a science. In 1887, when questioned on professionalism, he stated that:

> I consider football is played more scientifically now than ever it was, and that is solely due to the fact that in a professional team the men are under the control of the management and are constantly playing together. Professionalism must improve football, because men who devote their entire attention to the game are more likely to become good players than the amateur who is worried by business cares. No purely amateur clubs will ever be able to hold their own against a professional team.[39]

However, Sudell was also an early football entrepreneur and, although it is unlikely that he could predict the rapid boom in the game's popularity, he soon became aware of its commercial possibilities. He realised that the better the quality of the 'product' and the spectacle the greater would be the demand. To gain some respectability, and perhaps deflect ideas that he looked to profit from the club, he also described football in terms of rational recreation and its social benefits, at the same time reflecting contemporary eugenic theories.

> Football is not only a cheap amusement for the masses, for those who witness it as well as those who take part in the game but it has higher recommendations to those who do not wish to see the physical qualities of our race gradually decay under the enervating influence of the conditions under which a greater portion of our people live in the large towns and cities.[40]

Sudell's position at Preston was unusual. In the early days of the professional game, teams were picked and recruited by committee rather than by one man but at Preston Sudell *was* the committee. From 1876 to 1893, he was the club chairman and ran it in an increasingly autocratic manner, and from 1889 there were no annual general meetings for four years.[41] He had total control over team affairs at Preston and, in modern parlance, was a 'hands-on' manager. He travelled with the players to games, and was described by one as a father to the team.[42] Other early managerial figures included Aston Villa's George Ramsay and Tom Watson of Sunderland and later Liverpool, although both were given the title of secretary. Unlike Sudell they were both salaried officials employed by the club. Secretaries looked towards their middle-class directors while the day-to-day handling of the working-class players was left to the trainer. Secretaries took their direction from the directors who usually picked the team, although they may have had some input in the selection.

Throughout the history of the game successful football managers have required three basic qualities: judgement of a player, tactical acumen and motivational skills. On the pitch, many Lancashire teams had recruited Scottish players and Preston was no different – although in his recruitment, Sudell may have benefited from that ingredient all successful managers need: luck. From the summer of 1883, Preston's policy of recruiting Scottish players centred on Edinburgh. By contrast, other Lancashire clubs had focused on Glasgow. Sudell had acted on the advice on Tom McNeill, a native of the Scottish capital, who was a foreman in the *Preston Herald's* composing room.[43] The most famous of these Scottish 'professors' was Nick Ross, a full back who later played centre-forward.[44] In addition, John Goodall joined in 1885 and gained a reputation for his 'scientific' play.

It was perhaps in the area of tactics and the style of play that Preston employed that Sudell was able to stamp his own personality on the team. In this era, tactics were usually placed in the hands of the captain. At Preston, however, Sudell made himself responsible for them. In this era, football was characterised by rushes of players up and down the field and heavy shoulder charging. Sudell devised the tactics using a blackboard and sometimes chess pieces set out on a billiard table.[45] Tactical innovations were not new and teams such as the Royal Engineers and Queen's Park had been early pioneers. Unlike most other teams, Preston played with 2 full backs, 3 half backs and 5 forwards. This became known as the attacking centre-half formation and endured until 1925 when the offside law was changed. As a result, and also due to the quality of their players, Preston was noted for a more systematic style of play than other teams. It was said of them that they were not a particularly 'fast lot but their combination and manipulation is beautiful'.[46] They developed a measured short passing game that embodied Sudell's promotion of a more cultured and systematic form of football. In one game against Bolton in 1885, it was reported that North End was 'machine like ... in working the ball along the ground' whereas their opponents did 'their work in rushes'. At the 1889 Cup Final, the forwards of Wolves went in for 'very hard and determined play', Preston, by contrast, 'plodded away with a distinct system'.[47]

Sudell also believed in pre-match preparation. On one occasion, he hired a bus and four horses and drove the team to Blackburn to watch them play against Everton so that the players could spy on both teams. On another, a cobbler accompanied the team, enabling the players to alter their footwear in light of the underfoot conditions.[48] It was said that what made Preston supreme was the 'thoroughness of their training and their complete subordination of self to the interests of the side'.[49] Depicted, perhaps melodramatically, as a martinet by William McGregor, the founder of the Football League, Sudell was nevertheless strict with the players and in particular did not like them to drink.[50] The players recognised his contribution. After winning the FA Cup, the team captain, Fred Dewhurst, had wanted Sudell to accept the cup and give a speech.[51]

The impact of Sudell's management was not lost on other clubs. When Aston Villa's committee was forced to resign in 1893 *en masse* due to complaints of mismanagement, it was argued that the club lacked someone like Major Sudell who could improve its fortunes.[52] At the AGM of Burnley in 1894, there had been criticism of its board by the members. It was reported that, 'The argument was that while Mr Sudell was the manager, the North End were the champions. Therefore, if Burnley have a manager, Burnley will become the champions'. Interestingly, mainly because the team was struggling, there was later criticism of Sudell's methods and growing calls for a different, less autocratic management model, based on committees with, for example, a sub-committee for team selection.[53]

Sudell, football and North–South tensions

Sudell's image and legacy have generally been associated with the success of Preston but he also played an important role in forcing the FA to legalise professionalism in 1885. This episode not only brought Sudell to national attention, it also revealed deep divisions within football and pointed to more general North–South tensions and stereotypes.

While culturally the North was perceived to be in direct competition with the South, it was not an overtly political tension. There was no movement for separatism, for example. Instead, as the North reaped the economic benefits of Empire, this drew it closer to the idea of Britain generally. Nevertheless, in linking the idea of the North and northernness to that of national culture more generally, Dave Russell has argued this has been largely constructed from a London perspective, and that 'the North' has been defined as an 'other', and 'ultimately, as inferior'. Unlike London and the South, the North has never been able to enjoy a broad-based cultural leadership, and that although the North has enjoyed 'some degree of agency it has been on terms dictated by the centre', namely the capital city.[54]

By the mid-1880s, Preston, under Sudell, was emerging as a dominant force. The issue of professionalism had been ignited by North End's expulsion from the FA Cup in 1884, bringing Sudell to the forefront of moves to legalise the payment of players.[55]

Later that year, 36 clubs from the North and the Midlands, led by Sudell, threatened to break away under the umbrella of a British Football Association. The FA in London took the threat seriously and reluctantly rubber-stamped professionalism the following year. At FA meetings, Sudell had led the call for its legalisation. He openly admitted that Preston North End were a team of professionals and pointed out that, 'if you refuse to legalise professionalism they will be amateurs from today – we shall all be amateurs, and you cannot prove otherwise'.[56]

Football, therefore, provided an opportunity for the North to assert itself over the South. However, this episode was also subject to much myth-making that portrayed the role of the Lancashire clubs in heroic dimensions. In addition, according to James Catton, Sudell emerges as a 'heroic figure, the pioneer and protagonist of the movement' who embodied Lancastrian honesty and self-respect.[57] Catton later places the struggle over professionalism in North–South terms. On the threat to form the British Football Association in 1884 over the issue, he states that 'The clubs were determined not to bow the knee to the southerners.'[58] In the penultimate FA meeting before legalisation, Catton suggests that Sudell took centre stage, 'The forces were arrayed – Lancashire and the North on the right side of the gallant Major [Sudell] and the southern and Midland organisations on his left.'[59] In a later reminiscence, Bentley paints a picture of Lancashire clubs 'in complete control: self-confident, practical and far too astute for the Southerners'. In reality, however, the dispute over professionalism was not a straight-forward North–South issue as some Lancashire clubs, Darwen and Blackburn Rovers for example, remained loyal to the FA.[60] Russell has suggested that it could have been more of an intra-middle-class conflict with the provincial, non-public school educated business and commercial classes uniting with the working classes in opposition to a public school elite.[61] (Mason has pointed out that there were public school boys on both sides.) Sudell, despite his educational background, belonged in the former group.[62]

North–South footballing rivalries were actually subtler and were based on a history of interdependence. London first played Sheffield in 1871, something that suggested a move towards a compromise and a merging of their different sets of rules. In addition, during the late 1870s and early 1880s a plethora of local football associations were formed but as Mason argues, the 'most significant fact to notice was that all these local associations looked to the FA itself and wished to affiliate with it'.[63] Although the Football League was formed in 1888 and dominated by northern and Midlands clubs until the 1930s, the FA Cup remained the premier national competition for many years to come.

Nevertheless, there were distinct North–South rivalries within football, which reflected those in sport more generally. Perhaps most symbolic was the victory of Blackburn Olympic over Old Etonians in the 1883 FA Cup; the first northern team to win the trophy. There were also representative games that reflected North–South differences. In 1879–80, the first North versus South game took place while in 1885, the Gentleman versus Players was first played. However, the regional connotations of this game were slightly blurred as Fred Dewhurst of Preston North End, who was an amateur, played for the Gentlemen team that was otherwise dominated by players from the South.[64] Sudell, both through his management of Preston North End and the eventual legalisation of professionalism, was not only at the centre of these North–South footballing tensions but he also personified a confident and assertive North. His role was further highlighted by the games Preston, pioneers of professionalism, played against the bastions of southern amateurism, the Corinthians. The second match between them took place in January 1885 at the Oval when the row over professionalism was at its height.[65] Catton suggests that it had an important bearing on the debate due to the respectable image that Preston gained from the fixture.

> There is no doubt whatever that the scientific and gentlemanly game which Preston played, impressed many influential personages with the important fact that even a paid player was not necessarily the highwayman of the football field without any trace of the chivalry which is said to have distinguished these knights of the road.[66]

To a certain extent the emphasis on the need to be seen as 'gentlemanly' and not just as 'highwaymen' suggests a northern inferiority complex and wanting to be judged against the standards of the footballing establishment.

Interestingly, this game produced a different reaction in Preston, or perhaps more accurately in the local papers, which emphasised, and exaggerated, North–South divisions. Instead of respectability, the *Football Field* promoted a populist tone in its report of the occasion.[67] It was Preston's first game in London and created a carnivalesque atmosphere as several hundred North End fans travelled to London. It was said that, 'There was almost as much pleasurable excitement in the "proud town" as if the premier club were about to contest a cup tie'. A large crowd in Preston later gathered outside the town's newspaper offices to get the result (Preston lost 3–2). Hill has argued that in future cup finals the narrative of the local press worked upon the theme of the 'invasion' of the metropolis by the North and employed oppositions of 'North' and 'South', and exaggerated cultural contrasts.[68] It was reported during the game, for example, that 'pious horror was heard in groans' by the 'swell' spectators when they reacted to a foul by a 'northerner'. There was also a thinly veiled reference to the on-going debate over professionalism and how the power within football was shifting northwards. It was noted that the crowd only numbered 2000, including those from Preston and it was commented that,

> this is the place where they profess to know so much about association football where the football parliament meets and where the final tie for the cup is played. Isn't it time for a revolution?[69]

Before the game, one Lancashire man was heard to remark, 'Now, then, North End'll lick 'em'. It suggested that he represented an 'everyman figure' who symbolised the relationship between provinces and metropolis'.[70] The report's final paragraph left nothing to suggestion. A Preston reporter was called a cad and 'he quietly replied by landing a stinging blow on the Cockney's optic, which nearly put up the shutters. Bravo, Frank'.

During the 1880s, there were regular digs at southern amateur teams by the northern press, particularly over the violent nature of their play. In two further games against the Corinthians over Easter in 1885, it was commented that 'the North Enders were more knocked about by the "gentleman amateurs" on Good Friday and Easter Monday than in any game during the season'. The report then further added, 'What do you think of that Mr Crump?' a clear reference to an arch opponent of professionalism.[71] This theme of southern amateurs roughing up the northern professionals arose again after Preston's defeat by West Bromwich Albion in the 1887 FA Cup semi-final. This loss was blamed on the treatment meted out to Preston by the Old Carthusians in the previous week's quarter-final. It was stated that the Walters (the brothers AM and PM) were the greatest sinners and that 'No doubt the charging is legitimate enough but it is dirty all the same.' The *Athletic News* further remarked that 'I should think our Cockney amateurs will keep a still tongue about the rough professionals.'[72] However, there was more than a touch of hypocrisy here as some of the Preston players were no shrinking violets themselves. One player, Sandy Robertson, was described as 'hard as nails', while Preston's amateur, Fred Dewhurst 'always played a hard vigorous, clever, gentlemanly game'.[73] Moreover, in a game against Blackburn Olympic, John Goodall struck an opponent and then showed dissent to the referee.[74]

Of course, it was not uncommon for southern newspapers and commentators themselves to perpetuate these divisions and stereotypes. N.L. Jackson, for example, was an evangelical of amateurism and was vexed by what he saw as a takeover of the FA by a 'North country clique'.[75] Following Blackburn Rovers' victory in the 1884 FA Cup, the *Pall Mall Gazette*, had described the Rovers fans as a 'Northern horde, hot-blooded, sharp of tongue, rough and ready, of uncouth garb, and strange oaths'. Writing in 1900 of Blackburn's triumphant homecoming in 1884, Catton declared that:

> The Lancashire people – the Northern horde – had the finest football team in the world in their midst, and what cared they for the criticism of London journalists as to the cut of their clothes and the roughness of their speech.[76]

Moreover, in Catton, Preston North End had someone who throughout his career would champion the claims of the Lilywhites as the best team ever to play the game.[77]

The rivalry between the Corinthians and Preston was also more complex than it appeared in the press. They played each other on numerous occasions in front of large crowds, and the Corinthians founder N.L. Jackson, like Sudell, was a football entrepreneur despite his amateur claims.[78] In addition, some players played for both clubs. Because he was an amateur, Fred Dewhurst turned out for the Corinthians on at least one occasion.[79] Moreover, the Corinthians goalkeeper, Dr Mills Roberts later joined Preston and was a member of the team that won the League. Despite the clear perpetuation of the perception of a North–South divide within the northern press, it did not prevent Preston answering the call of royalty to play against the Corinthians in the 1887 Jubilee Festival at the Oval in aid of the Imperial Institute. It was recognition of Preston's pre-eminence in the game. As a symbol of his reputation, Sudell led the team out on to the field. The occasion also allowed Sudell to meet and ingratiate himself with royalty as he sat next to the Prince of Wales, the future Edward VII.[80] The *Athletic News* typically perhaps was keen to over-emphasise Preston's benevolence, estimating that they lost £100 from playing at the festival instead of an arranged match against Bolton.[81]

From hero to zero

Within six years of winning the Double, William Sudell had almost disappeared from the public eye. The start of Sudell's downfall had really begun in 1893 when he lost control of the club. The competition in the football world had begun to catch up with the Invincibles and the running of the club as well as the mill became too much for him. This had also caused tensions within the club. In 1890, one player, Johnnie Graham, 'grossly insulted' Sudell after he was refused a transfer request.[82] For years, there had been mutterings of financial irregularities, and by then the club was bankrupt. Sudell proposed to float the club as a company. From here, with his health failing him, he gradually faded from the picture as far as Preston North End was concerned. But the worst was yet to come. In 1895, he was arrested and then convicted for embezzling funds from the mill and transferring them to the club. The trial caused a sensation in Preston and Sudell was sent to prison for three years.[83]

How did the newspapers receive Sudell's downfall? Details of the case appeared in newspapers in places as far away as Hampshire and London. However, the reports were sober and perhaps surprisingly when seen in the light of his crime and the prevailing powerful rhetoric of middle-class respectability, no overt moral outrage was expressed.[84] An editorial in the *Preston Herald* perhaps captured this restrained style of reporting while at the same time implying that Sudell had damaged his reputation as a member of Preston's social elite. 'We deeply regret that a man occupying such a position of trust and responsibility should have had such a terrible fall.'[85]

From football journalists, though, Sudell received some sympathy. An *Athletic News* editorial blamed 'Prestonians' for their lack of financial support for the club and linked it to the cause of Sudell's crime. He then asked readers to remember that Sudell was 'once one of the leaders in English football' and urge them not to kick him when he was down. The paper set up an appeal to raise money for Sudell's family.[86] Interestingly, Catton omitted any reference to Sudell's crime in his books, as did other publications like Gibson and Pickford's *Association Football and the Men Who Made It* (1906).

After the trial, there was little mention of Sudell until his death in South Africa in 1911.[87] His obituaries brushed over his crime and instead, they concentrated on his contribution to early professional football. *The Football Field* made no reference to it at all, only mentioning that he had sailed for South Africa some years previously.[88] Catton continued to doubt that Sudell had in fact committed any crime. 'Honest as the day, in my opinion and frank to a degree ... I respect him for the man I knew him to be, and I can never believe that he forfeited his honesty and self-respect.'[89]

There was no commemoration from the football establishment. This compared to the funeral of one of Sudell's contemporaries, Tom Watson. Representatives of the FA and the Football League had attended and over a hundred wreaths were laid at his grave.[90] Sudell received one wreath from the Western Province FA.[91] Moreover, there seems to have been no action taken by the club. By this time Preston had been formed into a company and perhaps the directors wanted to make a clean break with Sudell, and were not keen to readily invoke his memory due to the financial irregularities of the past. Although this could be interpreted as a snub to Sudell, there was in fact little commemoration or memorialisation within football during the early twentieth century. In comparison to current times, Dave Russell has noted that while football generally paid due respect to its dead, there was nothing distinctive about its public mourning in terms of frequency or style.[92] In addition, until Arsenal in the 1930s, the North dominated professional football both on and off the pitch. The Football League itself was a parochial and conservative northern organisation that did little to promote itself up to 1939.[93]

The resurrection of Sudell

By the early twenty-first century, Sudell had undergone something of a minor resurrection within the popular consciousness, at least in Preston. This was partly as a result of Arsenal emulating, and thus drawing attention to, Preston's 1888–89 feat of going through the league season undefeated in 2003–4. In 2008, a stand named after the Invincibles was unveiled at Deepdale.

To a certain extent, it reflected a vogue for memorialisation within society generally in the late twentieth century. Russell has argued that the death of Bill Shankly in 1981 and his subsequent memorial the following year in the shape of the 'Shankly Gates' marked 'the first of the new generation of permanent memorials' in football.[94] Since the 1990s there has been an acceleration of this process. While the hyper-commercialisation of football has brought with it new stadiums, there have been complaints of a lack of atmosphere inside them as well as criticisms that the game is selling out to financial greed. This has produced a sense of loss and nostalgia for so-called better times. In the face of criticism, football clubs have increasingly tried to maintain links with their past through the naming of stands after famous players for example. Nostalgia in football also seems to have been more prominent in northern towns and cities, like Preston, that have suffered from the post-war economic decline.

Nostalgia has also had implications for how football and its fans have used history. Johnes and Mason have argued that it is a 'highly selective and utilitarian employment of the past with little regard for chronologies or continuity'.[95] Histories of clubs have usually been posted on official club websites and have a reputation for being sanitised versions. This highlights the sensitivity of football clubs about their image as well as being selective about their history. While skeletons are generally kept in the cupboard, clubs histories are more likely to celebrate victories. On Preston's current website, Sudell's misdemeanours have been unsurprisingly glossed over, stating that the formation of the limited company in 1893 marked the end of the Sudell tenure, and rather incongruously that through Sudell, the name of the Invincibles was fully recognised.[96] Interestingly, the club's historian, David Hunt, claimed that the club's directors had not heard of Sudell until the 1990s.[97] In addition, Preston had already named two stands after former players: Tom Finney and Bill Shankly. Shankly's inclusion suggests that it was an example of reflective glory as despite being a long-serving Preston player, Shankly is better-known for his achievements as manager at Liverpool.

Conclusion

To state that William Sudell was a product of his time is to be lazy yet correct. If his rise took place in a northern context then so did his downfall. Here the press played an important part in framing his reputation and keeping his story 'in-house'. Nevertheless, he was successful in his main field – football management – at a time when the sport combined with notions of civic pride was taking on a national dimension. He was also the first manager to be seen to make a difference to a team. It set a template for the future but one that would not be used for a number of years to come. To a certain extent, he came to represent a confident industrial North, more assertive and not afraid to upset the South, and this was something that was largely conveyed by the northern press. Yet, it was really amongst the people of Preston rather than the North at large where his impact was greatest.

1   Arnold Bennett, *The Card* (London, 1984 ed.), p. 200.

2   Carl Niemeyer (ed.), *Thomas Carlyle: On Heroes, Hero-Worship and the Heroic in History* (Lincoln, Nebraska, 1966). He does not mention women.

3   Preston were also runners-up in the next three seasons. In the 10 years of Sudell's stewardship, Preston's record was: Played – 632; Won – 455; Drew – 75; Lost – 102; Goals For – 2194, Against – 739.

4   He also held other football posts at both regional and national levels. He was a representative of the Football Association Council and on the Lancashire Association Committee. Sudell was also the first treasurer of the Football League in 1888, and his work was rewarded with a life membership in 1894. He later sat on the council of the National Baseball League, which sounded grander than it was as it only contained four teams, each representing football clubs, including Preston, who all wanted to make some money over the summer.

5   J. Hill and J. Williams, 'Introduction' in J. Hill and J. Williams (eds), *Sport and Identity in the North of England* (Keele, 1996), p. 6.

6   R. Holt, 'Heroes of the north: sport and the shaping of regional identity', in Hill and Williams, *Sport and Identity*, p. 140. The other two are 'local hero' and those like Len Hutton who go on to be national figures.

7   Sudell's life and career have been referenced in a number of publications. The best and most detailed is David Hunt's *The History of Preston North End Football Club: The Power, The Politics and The People* (Preston, 2000). Others include Harry Berry and Geoffrey Allman, *One Hundred Years at Deepdale: 1881–1981* (Preston, 1982) and Simon Inglis, *League Football and the Men Who Made It* (London, 1988), pp. 28–30.

8   J. Hill, 'Anecdotal evidence: sport, the newspaper press, and history' in Murray G. Phillips (ed.), *Deconstructing Sport History: A Postmodern Analysis* (Albany, NY, 2006), pp. 120–1.

9   Ibid.

10 Bentley was a prominent Lancashire journalist who began writing for the *Bolton Cricket and Football Field* in 1884. In 1886 he became assistant editor of the Manchester based *Athletic News*, then the most popular football weekly in the country and the mouthpiece for the interests of northern football clubs. Catton began writing for the *Preston Herald* in 1875 and continued until 1883. He too wrote for the *Athletic News* and later became its long-serving editor (1900–24). Steve Tate, 'James Catton, "Tityrus" of *The Athletic News* (1860–1936)', *Sport in History*, 25, 1 (2005), pp.98–115.

11 *Athletic News*, 1 April 1889, p. 5.

12 Neil Carter, *The Football Manager: A History* (London, 2006), p. 46.

13 *Preston Herald*, 24 March 1888, p. 5.

14 *Football Field* (Bolton), 2 August 1890, p. 8. It had been postponed for a year due to the death of T.M. Shuttleworth.

15 In *The Card* there are number of references to Preston North End and the success the club enjoyed during Sudell's time.

16 Approximately £39,000 at 2007 prices.

17 Hunt, *Preston North End*, p. 46

18 J. Garrard and V. Parrott, 'Craft, professional and middle-class identity' in A. Kidd and D. Nicholls (eds), *The Making of the British Middle Class? Studies of Regional and Cultural Diversity since the Eighteenth Century* (Stroud, 1998), p. 149.

19 Tristram Hunt, *Building Jerusalem: The Rise and Fall of the Victorian City* (London, 2004), p. 118; Ross McKibbin, *Classes and Cultures: England 1918–1951* (Oxford, 1998), pp. 84–90.

20 See J. Stobart, 'Building an urban identity. Cultural space and civic boosterism in a "new" industrial town: Burslem 1761–1911', *Social History*, 29, 4 (2004), pp. 485–98; Hunt, *Building Jerusalem*; Kidd and Nicholls (eds), *British Middle Class?; Gender, Civic Culture and Consumerism: Middle-Class Identity in Britain 1800–1940* (Manchester, 1999).

21 *Preston Herald*, 24 March 1888, p. 5.

22 J. Tosh, 'What should historians do with masculinity? Reflections on nineteenth-century Britain', *History Workshop Journal*, 38, 1 (1994), pp. 179–202.

23 *Preston Guardian*, 29 March 1879, 2 April 1881.

24 Garrard and Parrott, 'Middle-class identity', p. 166.

25 Carter, *Football Manager*, p. 28.

26 *Preston Guardian*, 4 February 1888, p. 2. I am grateful to Victoria Roberts at the Harris Library, Preston, for this reference.

27 *Preston Guardian*, 1 February 1888, p. 4.

28 *Preston Chronicle*, 4 February 1888, p. 4.

29 Another candidate, R. Morton, also withdrew. This left the path clear for W.H. Woods to be elected. Interestingly, Woods attended the same meeting of Preston's Victuallers that Sudell had, on the day his withdrawal was announced. *Preston Guardian*, 4 February 1888, p. 2.

30 M. Taylor, *The Association Game: A History of British Football* (London, 2008), pp. 96–7.

31 Berry and Allman, *One Hundred Years*, p. 42.

32 Hunt, *Preston North End*, pp. 89–90. It was only in the inter-war years that average attendances topped 15,000, which might suggest that football then was not as popular as it has been perceived to have been.

33 Carter, *Football Manager*, Chapter 1.

34 *Football Field*, 30 January 1886, p. 5, 28 February 1887, p. 2, 9 February 1889, p. 2.

35 T. Mason, 'Football, sport of the north?' in Hill and Williams, *Sport and Identity*, p. 50.

36 Taylor, *The Association Game*, p. 9.

37 Holt, 'Heroes', p. 140

38 Dave Russell, *Looking North: Northern England and the National Imagination* (Manchester, 2004), p. 245.

39 *Evening News and Star* (Glasgow), 22 January 1887, p. 4.

40 *Preston Herald*, 24 March 1888, p. 5.

41 *Athletic News*, 4 September 1911, p. 4.

42 Hunt, *Preston North End*, p. 82.

43 Carter, *Football Manager*, pp. 37–8.

44   The term 'professor' may have had various meanings. Some felt that Scottish footballers played the game in a more 'scientific' way than English players. Amateurs though used the term ironically. Nick Ross moved to Everton for one season the year Preston won the Double in 1889 but returned to Preston the following year.

45   J. Catton, *The Real Football: A Sketch of the Development of the Association Game* (London, 1900), p. 152. This may have also been in conjunction with the captain, Nick Ross. In his autobiography, *Wickets and Goals* (London, 1926), p. 144, Catton claims that it was a Dr Gledhill who gave the instructions. Whoever was responsible, it still highlights how Sudell recognised the importance of tactics.

46   *Football Field*, 10 April 1886, p. 15.

47   Carter, *Football Manager*, p. 44.

48   *Football Field*, 3 December 1890, p. 3, 22 January 1887, p. 2.

49   A. Gibson and W. Pickford, *Association Football and the Men Who Made it*, vol. 2 (London, 1906), p. 160.

50   *Birmingham Gazette and Express*, 30 August 1911, p. 8. This was ironic in light of his connection with the town's Victuallers' Association.

51   *Athletic News*, 1 April 1889, p. 5.

52   *Birmingham Daily Mail*, 30 January 1893, p. 4.

53   Hunt, *Preston North End*, p. 90.

54   Russell, *North*, pp. 8–9.

55   Preston had been expelled from the competition in 1884 after the FA upheld a complaint from a London amateur side, Upton Park, that Preston had fielded a professional team.

56   Hunt, *Preston North End*, p. 58–9.

57   M. Taylor, 'Little Englanders: tradition, identity and professional football in Lancashire, 1880–1930' in S. Gehrmann (ed.), *Football and Regional Identity in Europe* (Münster, 1997), pp. 38–9.

58   Catton, *The Real Football*, p. 59. For a fuller account of this episode, see Tony Mason, *Association Football and English Society, 1863–1915* (Brighton, 1980), Chapter 3.

59   Catton, *The Real Football*, p. 61.

60   Taylor, 'Little Englanders', p. 40.

61   Dave Russell, *Football and the English: A Social History of Association Football in England, 1863–1995* (Preston, 1997), p. 27.

62   Tony Collins has argued that the split in rugby in 1895 was largely due to class while the importance of a North–South divide over the issue of broken time payments has been exaggerated. Tony Collins, *Rugby's Great Split: Class, Culture and the Origins of Rugby League Football* (London, 1998), p. xvi.

63   Mason, *Association Football*, p. 15.

64   *The Times*, 22 March 1886, p. 10.

65   They had first played against each other in Preston in December 1884. Preston won 3–1.

66   Catton, *The Real Football*, pp. 60–1.

67   *Football Field*, 24 January 1885, p. 11.

68 Hill, 'Anecdotal Evidence', p. 124.

69 *Football Field*, 24 January 1885, p. 11.

70 Hill, 'Anecdotal evidence', p. 125.

71 Charles Crump was President of the Birmingham FA 1875–1923 and an FA Councillor 1883–1923.

72 *Athletic News*, 8 March 1887, p. 1.

73 Gibson and Pickford, *Association Football*, p. 161; *Football Field*, 27 April 1895, p. 2.

74 *Football Field*, 30 January 1886, p. 5. The whole team required a police escort from the pitch as the fans threw snowballs at them.

75 N.L. Jackson, *Sporting Days and Sporting Ways* (London, 1932), p. 100.

76 Catton, *The Real Football*, p. 133, 131.

77 James Catton, *The Rise of the Leaguers from 1863–1897: A history of the Football League* (Manchester, 1897), p. 93; *The Real Football*, p. 150.

78 D. Porter, 'Revenge of the Crouch End Vampires: the AFA, the FA and English football's "Great Split", 1907–14', *Sport in History*, 26, 3, Dec. 2006, p. 411.

79 *The Times*, 24 December 1885, p. 7.

80 Hunt, *Preston North End*, p. 14. The Prince later agreed to be a patron of the Football Association. *The Times*, 14 March 1887, p. 7.

81 *Athletic News*, 15 March 1887, p. 1.

82 *Football Field*, 12 April 1890, p. 3.

83 Carter, *Football Manager*, p. 46.

84 M. Huggins, 'More sinful pleasures? Leisure, respectability and the male middle classes in Victorian England', *Journal of Social History*, 33, 3 (2000), pp. 586–7. From a modern perspective, the language used contained little hyperbole and reflected the verbosity of language used generally in the public domain. W.D. Rubinstein, *Capitalism, Culture, and Decline in Britain 1750–1990* (London, 1993), pp. 88–90.

85 *Preston Herald*, 13 April 1895, p. 4.

86 *Athletic News*, 15 April 1895, p. 1.

87 Perhaps ironically it was reported that he had committed suicide earlier that year on 9 May.

88 *Football Field*, 2 September 1911, p. 1.

89 Quoted in Inglis, *League Football*, p. 30.

90 Carter, *Football Manager*, p. 48.

91 *South Africa*, 2 September 1911, p. 535.

92 D. Russell, ' "We all agree, name the stand after Shankly": cultures of commemoration in late twentieth-century English football culture', *Sport in History*, vol. 26, 1 (2006), p. 3. One exception was the funeral of Herbert Chapman in 1934. Ibid.

93 Matthew Taylor, *The Leaguers: The Making of Professional Football in England, 1900–1939* (Liverpool, 2005), p. 281.

94 Russell, "We All Agree", p. 6.

95 M. Johnes and R. Mason, 'Soccer, public history and the National Football Museum', *Sport in History*, vol. 23, 1 (2003), p. 119.

96 http://www.pnefc.premiumtv.co.uk/page/History/0,,10362-1033965,00.html (accessed 21 September 2008).
97 Conversation with David Hunt, 23 January 2007.

CHAPTER 8

The Lives of Jackie Milburn: 'Footballer and Gentleman'

Richard Holt

Introduction

Jackie Milburn scored 200 goals in 398 games for Newcastle United between 1946 and 1957. His record survived for almost fifty years until another Geordie hero, Alan Shearer, finally overtook it in 2006.[1] Milburn's goals came in the post-war years during which Tyneside shook off the legacy of the Depression to enjoy a period of relative prosperity and full employment. Economic recovery and sporting revival went hand-in-hand as Newcastle United led by Milburn, their new centre forward, returned to the First Division in 1948 in front of record crowds. They won the FA Cup three times between 1951 and 1955. Milburn was one of only three players to play in all three Finals, scoring two outstanding goals in 1951 and a spectacular header in the first minute in the 1955 Final. He was a 'big game' player, with an immensely powerful shot and an exceptional turn of speed. He was a 'one club' player in a 'one club' city, a local, a miner, a fan as well as an iconic player in a club that loved its centre forwards. He brought pride back to a club which had languished and has never since recaptured its Milburn moment. 'Wor Jackie' –the possessive Geordie pronoun was unique to him – is arguably the most complete example of the professional footballer as a regional hero and symbol of community.

How did this happen? Unlike Matthews or Finney he was not a national figure with great achievements for his country. His England record was a modest 13 matches. But this had no bearing on his reputation on Tyneside. It may even have worked to his advantage in a place where club was more important than country. The fans in any case tended to believe their players were never given a fair chance by the FA selection committee. Success with Newcastle, not in the international arena, was what mattered. But even this is problematic. Before the First World War Newcastle had the best team in England but there is no Edwardian equivalent of Milburn. Achievement on the pitch is a necessary, but not a sufficient, condition of enduring public renown. What is most intriguing about Milburn is not so much his popularity as a player – that was self-explanatory – as his growing fame long after he had hung up his boots. To his own surprise, his legend grew. He could not understand why 'I have been more honoured after I finished my playing career' than during it.[2] Jackie's thought his career was 'unbelievable' – a word he repeated so often it became a catchphrase. He was baffled to find himself a symbol of something other than football. My subject here is the origin and creation of this myth.

Milburn and the North

Before unpicking the various strands and stages of the Milburn myth, however, there is the vexed question of 'the North' and its heroes. What kind of northern hero was Milburn? Did he even think of himself as northern? The 'North East' is a distinctive part of the North geographically and economically, and Tyneside, or the area identifying itself as a 'Geordie', is a special part of that region.[3] Milburn's world was certainly not 'the North' in general – like many Geordies he seemed quite indifferent to the 'North' in any wider sense. Leeds was as far away as Edinburgh. Milburn had both a sense of regional solidarity with the 'North East' – of the Wear and the Tees, alongside his particular passion for the world of the Northumberland coalfield and Tyneside. He had mixed feelings about living in the city itself. He eventually returned to end his days a few streets from the house where he had been born in Ashington, twelve miles north of the Tyne. He saw himself primarily as the son of a miner – a 'pit lad'.

This was a world where two ports and their coalfields struggled for regional dominance. It was not until the interwar years that the coalfield was properly linked to the city. Miners queued for buses to get to 'the match' and the Milburn legend has it that Jackie joined them, the player travelling to the match with the fans after a shift at the pit. The Newcastle–Sunderland derby was the sporting expression of this rivalry which was fierce but without rancour. There was a shared culture of labour, of unionism, Methodism and workingmen's clubs. Fans of one team would sometimes watch and even support the other against outside opposition. This had become unthinkable in the 1970s and 1980s when Milburn was reporting on matches. Jackie had a soft spot for Sunderland. He loathed Newcastle hooligans jeering the 'mackems' – a new word Milburn never used about Sunderland fans. He was 'Northumbrian' as well as 'Geordie', reflecting the overlapping identity of the area. Although he settled in the respectable Benton and Heaton areas of Newcastle for most of his working life, he moved back to Ashington in 1982, after having been burgled for the second time. Later in life he spent increasing amounts of time on the golf course at Morpeth or in his caravan on the coast at Seahouses. Milburn's affinity was not with Newcastle as a city but with the wider community of south and east Northumberland.[4]

All this helped in building a wider constituency for his reputation in the region. But it did not enhance his sense of being 'northern' in a general sense. What links Milburn to the north of England as a whole is not so much his sense of identity as the way in which his story was told. Whilst Jackie's was a Tyneside story, separate and removed like the place itself from the mainstream of northern culture, the narrative itself was deeply northern. The legend of 'Wor Jackie' was conceived in terms of the moral superiority of the North over the South. Geordies were presented as more 'real' than other people. There was an unspoken assumption of authenticity about northern life which was thought to be lacking elsewhere. It is this belief in the naturalness of the North, in the honesty and good nature of its people, their warmth and lack of affectation, which links Milburn's story to the wider narrative of the northern sporting hero.[5]

How was *this* version of a northern story told? There are six lives and various other biographical contributions. First there is his life as a player, beginning in 1950 in a series of ten articles in the *Newcastle Journal*.[6] This was followed by his ghosted autobiography, *Golden Goals*, published on his retirement from Newcastle United in 1957.[7] Next there is the post-playing career, which saw the publication of *Jackie Milburn's Newcastle United Scrapbook* in 1981, celebrating the post-war history of the club and his place in it.[8] This period saw a steady flow of material about him including magazine articles about his character, a civic testimonial, local radio broadcasts and a national television programme ('This is Your Life' in 1981). A musical, 'Wor Jackie', was completed shortly before his death followed by a regional television documentary. There have been three biographies since his death: John Gibson, *Wor Jackie: the Jackie Milburn Story*;[9] this was quickly followed by Mike Kirkup, *Jackie Milburn in Black and White: a biography*.[10] Finally, and most recently, there has been a new life by his son, Jack Milburn, *Jackie Milburn: a man of two halves*.[11] The memory of sporting heroes in the North as elsewhere tends naturally to fade with the passing of time. But the myth of 'Wor Jackie' has flourished in a remarkable, and arguably unique, fashion.

The player, 1943–57

The first two lives of Jackie Milburn appeared just at the moment when football biography and autobiography were taking off in the post-war years. Before then, as Woolridge has shown, sports autobiography as a genre was still in its infancy.[12] The 1950s was the decade that saw it flourish, with forty works published, most of which took the form of 'exemplary lives' concentrating on 'aspiration and improvement'. From this perspective, Milburn came into the game at just the right moment. Football was embedded in an urban industrial culture, which had finally found its voice in the Labour victory of 1945. It was time for the footballer as working-class hero to be given his due as a biographical subject. But, as Matthew Taylor has asked, what kind of 'subject'?[13] The tone of these ghosted works or 'as told to' lives rarely captures the 'real' qualities of the player as a person or of working-class culture more widely. Such works tended to be simple tales of obstacles overcome and opportunities taken; conflict, complexity or criticism of the club, the game or the country are avoided, and the overwhelming virtues of cheerfulness and respectability asserted in line with a reassuring vision of a shared national culture.

Milburn's story was first told in the *Newcastle Journal* in a series of ten full page articles running from November 1949 to January 1950 as 'My Life'. This form of autobiography in the local press seems to have been the most common one for footballers before the 1950s. Between January 1949 and April 1952 the *Newcastle Journal* ran articles about 23 different players in their 'Sportsmen Then and Now' series.[14] All of them were footballers but most were restricted to a single issue of the paper. Milburn was the first to be given a full series and was followed by Joe Harvey, the captain, Len Shackleton and Stan Seymour, the manager. Milburn's ten articles were signed by 'Jack' or 'Jackie' Milburn. Both forms of his name seem to have been used until the 1951 Cup Final victory when the openly affectionate 'Wor Jackie' was first used. Before then Milburn has been 'JET'. His initials (John Edward Thompson) made a neat link with the invention of the jet engine and his pace when on the wing, which sometimes sent him hurtling into the crowd by the corner flag. 'My Life' was the first 'autobiography', which set out many of the stories subsequently re-told and embellished by word of mouth or in print. The format was more or less the same from week to week. There was a full page article in the Saturday edition of the paper with a photograph of a pair of boots or a school team picture. These were signed by Milburn but clearly 'as told to' a journalist, confessing through his ghost-writer the articles had 'been no literary effort, of course. I'm a footballer, not a writer'.[15] His life story was shaped from the start by the press. This continued intermittently for forty years until the legend of the miner who was both an exemplary Geordie and a gentleman was complete.

The *Newcastle Journal*'s 'My Life' was the story of a fanatical schoolboy footballer kicking a ball around the back lanes, getting his first game for the school team, his trial for Newcastle and his early success with the club as they won promotion. It was a familiar narrative: the first instalment was full of stories of wearing out the toe caps of new shoes by kicking stones on the way to school or finding his first pair of boots on Christmas morning and dashing out in the dark to join other boys for a game in the back lane.[16] Then there was the kindly teacher at Hirst East elementary school, Mr. Denton, who taught him to shoot ('heel up, toes down').[17] Subsequent articles told the story up to his two trials for Newcastle, scoring six goals in the second half of the second trial, concluding with the 1947–8 season when Newcastle won promotion and Milburn moved from the right wing to centre forward.[18] He is described as a 'famous player'.[19] The words 'hero', 'star' or 'idol' were conspicuous by their absence.

This was 'the story of an ordinary little boy with a passion for football'.[20]

A trip to Newcastle was still a novelty. Jackie had never seen Newcastle United play until a wartime friendly six weeks before he signed, confessing 'the first First Division match I ever saw was Sunderland v Blackpool at Roker'.[21] This was a colliery story not a city narrative. Jackie was *not* born 'Newcastle daft'. He both achieved 'daftness' and had 'daftness' thrust upon him. None of his extended family, including the Charltons, played for Newcastle.

Hence the first 'Life' brought Milburn's personal history to the attention of Newcastle itself. But he was still seen as a pitman who played football rather than a symbol of the city. The day after his two goals in the 1951 Cup Final, he was photographed scouring the paper for the Ashington result. It was Ashington not Newcastle that laid on a civic reception in his honour. This was held at the Methodist Central Hall with admission for '640 members of the general public and the rest of the space reserved for the school choir, council officials and the Milburn family'.[22] 'Good owld Jackie' was the headline in the *Morpeth Herald*, which reflected favourably on his natural modesty, 'I never expected anything – well, I'm just a local lad'.[23] It is at this point that 'character' starts to become part of the story. A feature in *Charles Buchan's Football Monthly* called Milburn 'the idol of Tyneside' and 'obviously a nice fellow, quiet and chivalrous to opponents', a former colliery worker and 'a reluctant hero'.[24] He was one of the first footballers in the region to own a car and was asked to make a road safety recording, warning young drivers to take their chances on the pitch not at the wheel. He advertised breakfast cereal rather than beer. His wholesome image as 'the good man' took hold early in his career and stayed with him throughout his life.

Although his playing and personal status grew to cult proportions after the consecutive Cup Final victories of 1951 and 1952, the first full length life did not appear until his retirement from the club in 1957. According to the north-eastern football writer, Arthur Appleton, who knew Milburn well, *Golden Goals* was a rush job. Milburn spent a week talking on and off to a ghost writer with a secretary in attendance.[25] The book shows signs of the haste with which it was put together. It doesn't sound like Milburn. It has awkward, wooden passages and odd moments of moralising. 'Football was in fact our whole life outside the school room', to which Milburn is made to add, 'and I'm not sure it wasn't a better outlook than that possessed by many members of the present generation'.[26] He is set up as a role model by his 'ghost' writer, who intersperses the text with short homilies. 'I have always tried to do the right thing so that they [schoolboys] will never, because of any action of mine, be led off the right path'.[27] The book closes with Jackie's thoughts on stadiums. 'Amenities' would be improved by 'the remission of entertainment tax' and 'an increase in admission charges'.[28]

His attempt to 'talk posh' when asked to say a few words after the 1951 Cup Final was met with laughter and a voice shouting 'Taak tiv us in yor own language, Jackie'.[29] On that occasion he did, but not in *Golden Goals*, which conformed closely to the 'exemplary lives' model of other biographies. Len Shackleton was a 'dissident voice', admitting that he became a miner with Milburn 'to skive' and avoid national service.[30] *Golden Goals* simply noted 'Shack' was 'my assistant, and we became very close'.[31]

Milburn's son blamed 'the editor' for the stilted, pompous tone of *Golden Goals*, which was nevertheless the first book ever written by a Newcastle player and sold well.[32] It has revealing passages. For example, when Jackie is briefly sent as a servant boy to Surrey aged fourteen only to come scurrying back to Ashington; or the incident where his father gives him 'a hiding' after his school sports day to stop him getting a 'big head'. It was to this violent outburst that Jackie put down his 'life long inferiority complex'.[33] As Woolridge notes, *Golden Goals* 'is unsurpassed for its modesty and self-deprecation and its insistence on the ordinariness of the protagonist.'[34] He devotes a full chapter ('This is Me') to describing an average week: Laura's home cooking, his dislike of gardening, his experiments with tape recording, his preference for plain socks, watching television and reading thrillers, doing DIY, with Monday night for baby-sitting and Wednesday nights at 'the dogs' – a particular miner's passion.[35] The book ends on a note of cheerful stoicism – 'we professionals can't really grumble, can we?' – reminiscent of the working-class culture of Leeds in Richard Hoggart's *The Uses of Literacy*, which was first published in the same year as *Golden Goals*.[36]

The journalist

Milburn had intended to develop a small coach hire business on his retirement from Newcastle. Instead he went for three years as player-manager to Linfield, having been approached by the Belfast team after a friendly between the two clubs. The salary was better and he did not have to move to a First Division rival. In football terms, the move was a success but he began to get hate mail as a result of 'religious politics I knew nothing about'.[37] He then moved on to Yiewsley in west London before taking over from Alf Ramsay as manager of Ipswich in January 1963. These were difficult years. As a manager of Ipswich, he was not a success. The pressure was too much. He started drinking, became depressed and headed for home. The later lives of Milburn skim over this darker period to pick up the story on his return to Tyneside in 1964 to make a new start.

After a few casual jobs, the *News of the World*, Britain's biggest selling Sunday paper, shrewdly saw that anything signed by Milburn would sell. He was made a local football reporter – a job he held for twenty years. He was welcome around the football grounds of the North East, especially St. James's Park, sticking to simple match reports and preferring a private word with players or managers to asking questions at press conferences. He needed help from his fellow journalists. He got them to help him to write and they got to sit beside their hero. New recruits to the press box were greeted as friends. Brian McNally, who later became secretary of the North East Football Writers Association, was welcomed with 'Is this your first game, son?' and taken round to meet his new colleagues. McNally never forgot the kindness.[38]

The first fruits of Jackie's new career came in 1967 when Doug Wetherall of the *Daily Mail* organised a campaign to give Jackie a testimonial match ten years after his retirement. This proved a turning point. On the night of 10 May 1967 over 45,000 fans came to pay tribute to Milburn despite the pouring rain. Jackie was reunited with his old Cup Final team mates against the likes of Shackleton, Finney and Mortensen followed by a game against an international XI which included Bobby and Jack Charlton and Nobby Stiles from the 1966 World Cup-winning team and Ferenc Puskas of Real Madrid. Jackie made £8,200 that night – the biggest benefit up to that date at St. James's – but the boost to his image was far greater. The souvenir programme was widely sold and featured not only a host of playing tributes but also a prominent photograph of Jackie with his arm around Laura. The image of a happy couple was established in the public mind.[39]

Following the Testimonial, the *Evening Chronicle* immediately demanded 'Give magnetic Milburn a job, Newcastle'.[40] But Jackie already had a job and he wisely stuck to it, settling into a cosy routine of club gossip for his column, phoning in his short match reports and periodically turning down offers of work at the club. This was a good decision. He never had to take responsibility for the failures and could bask in the 'glory days'. This was done by accident rather than by design and from fear rather than wisdom. He was avoiding stress rather than managing his reputation. Milburn was not that clever. His simplicity was his story.

In 1978 June Hulbert interviewed him for *Northern Life*.[41] Hooliganism was at its height. He mixed some homespun wisdom about the police needing to be at double strength with nostalgia for the 1950s, for players who had modest wages and modest lives. Asked what was 'the greatest day of his life', he said it was the day he got married, rather than any of his Wembley finals. Hulbert then re-told the story, which had first appeared in *Golden Goals*, about how he met his wife, of love at first sight and a long happy marriage. In his fifties he was still 'long, lithe and good looking – there's a definite touch of the Gary Coopers about him'.[42] Male beauty was part of the Milburn myth. Women were attracted to him but there was no hint of scandal. He played golf *with* his wife. 'What we love is to get into our caravan and take off, probably for Scotland,' he told Hulbert, 'where you roll out of bed onto the first tee.'[43]

It was a vision of modest abundance, shared by so many of those who had grown up in the Depression and lived through the 'long boom'. He repeated these stories to Avril Deane for the women's section of the local paper a few years later. 'Idyllically happy after 38 years of marriage' was the strap line. Jackie still able to remember the first film they saw together ('Mrs Miniver') and Laura still had 'a silver dog he gave me on our first date'; 'he's a marvellous man. I knew when I met him we'd be together

... Jackie and me, we have this understanding ...'⁴⁴ Here was a football legend – a man's man – who loved spending time with his wife.

This breadth of appeal led him to be selected as one of nine Freemen of the City to be created on the occasion of its 900th anniversary in 1980. It was a formal acknowledgment of his special status not just as a player but a member of the community. Along with Cardinal Hume, he was the best known of the nine who were honoured. The council leader made much of Jackie's reaction on being told of it: 'What's a pit lad doing among that lot?'⁴⁵ It was this modesty, his roots in 'the heartland of Northumbria' and his place in the hearts of 'the legion of fans who still remember the great days' that set him apart.⁴⁶

His election as a Freeman set in train a new series of events, which transformed him into a civic and a national figure – a symbol of all that was best in Geordie life and culture. He had made good friends with several of his fellow journalists, especially John Gibson, the football writer of the *Newcastle Evening Chronicle*, who had watched him in awe from the Leazes end as a school kid. The two of them had 'shared a Press bench at St James's for seasons' and now worked together in the afterglow of his civic award to write *Jackie Milburn's Newcastle United Scrapbook*.

That Milburn did not feel he could compile a book of photographs and anecdotes by himself is revealing. He was really employed to be 'Jackie Milburn' and the sub-editors would shape his articles. It was John Gibson who gave him the idea and 'helped gather up the threads of my thoughts *and* memories and knit them together into a story of pride and love about "our Club".'⁴⁷ *Jackie Milburn's Scrapbook* is about Milburn the player *and* Milburn the fan. He mixes his own story with a supporter's appreciation of others, especially the centre forwards: Len White, Wyn Davies and Malcolm Macdonald ('Supermac'). Newcastle's victory in the Inter-City Fairs Cup in 1969 gets a good airing. 'Though my position was now in the Press box instead of out on the field, I still felt a part of it all.'⁴⁸

Milburn pays homage to the legends of the club that went before him establishing his sense of being part of a tradition greater than himself. Albert Stubbins was a particular favourite, 'a gentleman', the epitome of what a professional footballer should be, a man of 'dignity and humility'.⁴⁹ The *Scrapbook* has striking echoes of wartime patriotism with photographs of Jackie proudly shaking hands with Field Marshall Lord Montgomery at Portsmouth in 1949 and with Sir Winston Churchill before the Wembley final of 1952. Churchill, 'the greatest hero of my life', made an enormous impression by asking 'Are you going to grab the headlines again this year?'⁵⁰ He could scarcely believe the Prime Minister could have heard of him – and perhaps he had just been well-briefed – but to Milburn this meant everything. He was conventionally patriotic, perhaps especially so having missed military service in the war through working as a miner. His identity as an Englishman as well as a Geordie was clearly important to him.

According to Gibson, it was reading the *Scrapbook* which convinced a Thames Television researcher for 'This is Your Life' to select Milburn for the programme. Gibson along with Laura Milburn orchestrated the cast of Geordies and football celebrities for a half hour of 'pure nostalgia'.[51] Bobby and Jack Charlton, of course, but also Billy Wright, Tom Finney, Raich Carter and the nation's favourite German, Bert Trautmann, the heroic Manchester City goalkeeper who had been beaten in the first minute by Jackie's header in the 1955 Cup Final.

It was at this moment that the idea of Jackie as 'a gentleman' took hold. 'The public image of a nice guy isn't artificially created to promote a public figure', as Gibson wrote in a full page feature in the *Evening Chronicle*, 'he's simply a gentleman'.[52] This kind of tribute became increasingly common in the 1980s when Tyneside seemed anything but gentlemanly. His character as well his talent was underlined when he won the award of the region's top post-war player in 1987. This was repeated the following year when the Duke of Edinburgh presented Milburn with a Sports Council award for outstanding service to sport in the city. The Geordie gentleman was 'just amazed that people remember me'.[53]

Gentlemanliness had long been considered the defining characteristic of the English. Victorian Britain saw the emergence of a reformed gentlemanly culture, a code of honour, modesty and fair play closely associated with the idea of 'sportsmanship'. This gradually filtered down the social pyramid. Gentility 'is at the root of things, permeates the being and is a philosophy of life for all classes' noted a contributor to the *Times Literary Supplement* in 1908.[54] This notion gathered momentum between the wars. It is striking how often professional cricketers such as Hobbs and Woolley were referred to as 'gentlemen'.[55] Footballers lagged behind – Dixie Dean or Hughie Gallacher could hardly be called gentlemen – but gentlemanly ideals were steadily democratised. The idea of the gentleman was no longer tied to social class.[56]

Milburn's life story exemplifies this bigger idea. But it also complicates the 'northern sporting hero'. Historically northerners had been considered coarse and brutalised by their labour, at least amongst the southern middle classes. How could they be 'gentlemen'? This social definition of gentility, however, was changing as a more civilised vision of manhood was polished by wartime propaganda and hastened by the triumph of Labour in 1945. The working class came into the national consensus. Football stars, such as Stanley Matthews, were increasingly portrayed as role models for the nation: dedicated and modest, respecting opponents and referees and 'playing the game' on and off the field in the right spirit. Over the course of his life, Jackie came to be seen as fulfilling this role, combining a variant of northern popular culture with a wider sense of male virtue – the story of the Geordie as gentleman.

The afterlife

The extent to which Milburn fulfilled this vision became clear in the obituaries and the publications which followed his death in October 1988 from lung cancer at the age of 64 – he'd been a life long smoker, having a puff at half time was a part of the legend. Cardinal Hume had got to know him when they were both made Freemen of the City and had contacted the family during his final illness. Though not a Catholic, Milburn had touched the Cardinal deeply. 'He was not only a footballer, but a great gentleman, and a person who won instant respect. There was a quality of goodness about him which inspired others'.[57] 'Nobody was valued more dearly' was the *Mail on Sunday*'s verdict, 'on every corner his sleeve would be tugged and his hand shaken and Jackie would shrug and blush and mumble … "Very kind Newcastle people", he would say.'[58] David Lacey in the *Guardian* thought 'he was the best, certainly the best loved footballer that Newcastle United have produced'.[59] *The Times* carried a photograph of the cortège and the large crowds that lined the street outside the Cathedral, noting that 'in an area renowned for its appreciation of sporting personalities, it was a remarkable gesture for "Wor Jackie".'[60]

The local press had large photo spreads. In the *Northern Echo*, Doug Weatherall, who had orchestrated Milburn's testimonial, thought that 'his modesty was such that I don't think he really knew the joy he gave people'.[61] This stress on ordinariness, on the 'touchable hero' was echoed in the response to the 'Appeal' launched by the *Evening Chronicle* for a statue in his memory. Publishing a list of donations, it was striking how widely they were distributed across Durham and Northumberland. May Dowd of Jesmond wrote that 'it is wonderful that a good man can be given his place in history'.[62] The fund was boosted with reader offers such as 'a coffee mug with a picture of a man "loved by Geordies all over the world"' or video cassettes of the musical and the Tyne Tees television documentary.[63]

As the idea of Jackie 'the gentleman' took greater hold, so too did his association with the re-invented notion of Northumbria – a historic territory with a great history – uniting both the city and the county. Another contributor to the 'Appeal', a Geordie exile in London, called 'Jackie a real gentleman who brought great credit to his native Northumbria'.[64] The 'Wansbeck Writers Group', a coalfield collective, published poems on the statue that was duly erected in Northumberland Street in the heart of Newcastle.[65] This bronze statue by Susanna Robinson, which cost £35,000, was unveiled in November 1991 and shows Milburn with a ball at his feet about to unleash a shot. On the pedestal is the inscription 'Wor Jackie 1924–1988: Footballer and Gentleman'. The ball was stolen several times and the statue was re-erected closer to the ground in 1999 where passing fans now touch the boot for luck and in honour of his memory. Not to be outdone by Newcastle and to have a statue with a stronger physical resemblance as his family wished, a second work was commissioned by

Wansbeck District Council from John Mills, a nationally known sculptor, in 1995. The unveiling by his wife Laura led to a further round of tributes led by Jack Charlton. Remarkably, Tom Maley, a self-taught sculptor from Morpeth, made a third statue at his own expense, which was on exhibition at the Woodhorn Colliery Museum where Milburn had worked when it was an operating mine. It was then moved to a site outside St. James's Park in 1996 where it was damaged and removed by the sculptor pending a new casting in bronze.[67] A new work by Maley has been commissioned, placing Milburn alongside Alan Shearer. This will be erected outside the ground and keeps the Milburn legend alive by linking it to a man who is seen as sharing the moral values and local patriotism of 'Wor Jackie'. In terms of commemoration this is remarkable. Milburn has three statues – with a fourth to come – where greater players have only one and often no statue at all.

Mike Kirkup, an ex-miner and local writer, was the key figure in the later shaping of the legend and in keeping Milburn alive in the public memory. He had planned a musical on Milburn's life which he finished only weeks before Jackie's death. The family urged him to go ahead with it the following spring. 'Wor Jackie' won a £12,000 prize in the London Weekend Television 'Plays on Stage' competition and ran at the Newcastle Playhouse to full houses for three weeks, returning later for a further three-week run with cheap tickets sponsored by local businesses. This was followed by a Tyne Tees television documentary on Milburn's life. Kirkup's *Jackie Milburn in Black and White* appeared in 1990 – the same year that John Gibson brought out *Wor Jackie: The Jackie Milburn Story* – and was based on the long interviews carried out for the musical four months before Millburn's death. Kirkup and Gibson are different books united by a common affection for their hero. Gibson went for a short, straightforward account of the playing life, drawing on his long association with Milburn in the press box and their work together on the Scrapbook. Gibson is clear that Milburn's decision not to return as a player, coach or manager was critical to his heroic status. He was not cut out for management. 'It's a very different sort of pressure. It was not my sort,' he told Gibson.[68] There were limits to Milburn's abilities and aspirations. Even as a journalist, Gibson admitted, 'he was far too gentle; criticism came hard'.[69]

Kirkup's book is not the work of a football journalist, recalling great moments on the field. Instead it dwells more on the man in a warm and thoughtful homage to a hero by a writer immersed in the history of the coalfield. Kirkup went on to found and edit a local history magazine, 'A Creeful of Coals' in 1993, which still publishes essays, memoirs and photographs of colliery life. *Jackie Milburn in Black and White: A Biography* sets Jackie firmly in the context of colliery life and culture. It begins in Ashington in the maze of terraced streets to which Milburn returned later in life. Kirkup tries to track him down and is instantly pointed to the 'second house from the end' and catches Jackie in the front garden. The author, a little overwhelmed, is immediately sensitive to the subtleties of accent. 'The flatness of the vowels marked him instantly as being Northumbrian' – a composite regional accent, the voice of a man who came from the coalfield.[70] As usual, Milburn is touched and baffled that anyone wants to write about him – 'all I did was kick a bit of leather around a field' – but settles down to tell his story on regular Thursday sessions. This, as he explained, was 'wor lass's golf day' – golf was a late passion for them both and a mark of their modest social mobility.[71]

Kirkup's narrative is of 'character' and the coalfield culture that made it. Although the book is also a playing narrative, Kirkup's deeper interest is in Milburn the man and the miner. The book, which has an affectionate foreword by Jackie Charlton, ends with a series of tributes from a wide range of figures, mostly players and journalists, all of whom in one way or another had the same idea: what was special about Milburn was that he was not special; that he was ordinary, accessible and unspoiled in an age when star players were increasingly rich and remote. The final chapter of Kirkup's book closes on an unashamedly emotional note, celebrating the simple home life of the hero: 'My interview with Jackie Milburn – "player, talker, writer" – was nearing its completion as the front door opened and his wife Laura came smiling into view. After a few minutes of brief introductions he gave her the kind of look that bears witness to forty years of good marriage, and said "Champion! Haddaway put the kettle on".'[72]

Gibson and Kirkup were different kinds of biographer who shared a deep affection for their subject. Milburn's son, who broke a long silence to write about his father in 2003, was rather different. Being 'Jackie Junior' had not been easy. The son's memoir of the father is a mixture of praise, personal reminiscence and a certain degree of resentment. Growing up in the 1960s with a father who was out of step with a new generation added a new element. 'Our formative teenage years brought about family rifts that at the time seemed irreparable. Sometimes we just sloped around the home without speaking for days'.[73] This was the culmination of being moved constantly from school to school, his failure to live up to the football expectations of his father and friends, and taunting from boys at school. 'This nurtured a profound bitterness, one much deeper than any of my family knew … I became very withdrawn, with a rebellious mind.' To Jackie's disgust the house now echoed to the early Bob Dylan who replaced Frank Sinatra on the turntable. The battle between old parental values and the new generation began.[74] Jack Milburn's account is sub-titled *a man of two halves* and balances the playing and the private life, fleshing out the personality without denying the myth. This was a new slant on an old story and ends with an encomium – 'God bless you, Dad'.[75]

Conclusion

In the 1970s and 1980s Tyneside went into a spiral of economic and social decline. Football mirrored the fate of the city itself with failure on the pitch and hooliganism off it. When Jackie died in 1988, Tyneside was at its nadir. The crowds – running to tens of thousands – who milled around Newcastle Cathedral were mourning not only their favourite player but their favourite son. 'Wor Jackie' was a reminder of their football hey-day in the 1950s and of the pits and shipyards they had lost. As Archie MacPherson, the BBC's football correspondent, remarked, Milburn's life was about more than football: it was a moral tale of 'the rise of an honest young miner ... whose attitudes throughout seemed to represent all the finest features of a working class life in the north-east'.[76]

Tyneside had created its own version of a national ideal, of a working-class Geordie who was one of 'nature's gentlemen'. The image of the 'canny lad' was gradually overlaid with an ideal of popular gentility. As he approached Milburn's record of 200 goals in 2006, Alan Shearer paid tribute to Jackie's goal-scoring ability. But, he went on, 'from what I know what impresses me most is that he was a man of the people, and that is very, very important.'[77] Shearer was repeating what had become the Milburn mantra. In his concern for the man over the player, Shearer echoed Bobby Charlton, who grew up with Milburn as an 'uncle' (strictly-speaking a second cousin). He used the breaking of Milburn's record to re-emphasise how good a player Jackie had been, adding, 'a lot of people would say he was a better man than he was a footballer. He was a marvellous man.'[78]

Milburn's elevation into the ideal of Geordie manhood was a long process. It was the product of a unique combination of factors: his success and style in the big games; the lack of subsequent success outside the North East; his loyalty to the club; his warm, simple personality; the fierce identity of his public and the changing nature of Tyneside itself. These were the ingredients of his fame. Others have arguably done as much or more at other clubs. What made Milburn unique was his long-standing friendship with a group of local journalists, most of whom were also fans of the club. Milburn was not a media invention. For the record my interviews with his friends and relatives all confirmed the public image.[79] But he was nonetheless a product of the media, especially the local press. They kept him in the public eye and gradually re-shaped him as a Geordie 'gentleman'. To be a hero who is remembered within a particular culture requires a bedrock of achievement and a core of admirers who tend the flame. Milburn had both. His legend was both intensely local and diffusely national. He was a symbol of northern virtue just as Andy Capp epitomised northern vice – betting, boozing and womanising, even fighting on the football pitch. The cartoon stereotype was one way of representing the North East. The life of Jackie Milburn was another.

1   The full statistics are complicated by the fact that Milburn signed for Newcastle in 1943 and appeared 98 times scoring 38 goals before the official re-start of the Football League in the season 1946–7. Only the two goals he scored in the 1945–6 FA Cup competition count towards the official statistics. Shearer retired with a knee injury at the end of the 2005–6 season with a total of 206 goals for Newcastle in ten years.

2   *Newcastle Journal*, 10 October 1988; for a preliminary account of Milburn's 'afterlife', see my entry in the *Oxford Dictionary of National Biography* and in R. Holt, 'The Legend of Jackie Milburn and the life of Godfrey Brown', in J. Bale, M.K. Christianesen and G. Pfister (eds), *Writing Lives in Sport: Biographies, Life Histories and Methods* (Aarhus, 2004), pp. 157–70.

3   Robert Colls and Bill Lancaster (eds) *Geordies: Roots of Regionalism* (Edinburgh, 1992), provides a good introduction to the distinctiveness of the area; Robert Colls and Bill Lancaster (eds) *Newcastle upon Tyne: A Modern History* (Chichester, 2001) is the most up-to-date study of the city and can be supplemented by Robert Colls (ed.), *Northumbria: History and Identity 547–2000* (Chichester, 2007), especially Natasha Vall, 'Northumbria in north-east England during the twentieth century', pp. 277–92.

4   For a fuller discussion of the region, see R. Holt, 'Football and regional identity in the north of England', in S. Gehrmann (ed.), *Football and Regional Identity in Europe* (Munster, 1997), pp. 49–66.

5   J. Hill and J. Williams (eds), *Sport and Identity in the North of England* (Keele, 1996) stresses the variety of northern sporting identities.

6   *Newcastle Journal*, 4 November 1949 to 7 January 1950.

7   Jackie Milburn, *Golden Goals* (London, 1957).

8   Jackie Milburn, *Jackie Milburn's Newcastle United Scrapbook* (London, 1981).

9   John Gibson, *Wor Jackie: The Jackie Milburn Story* (Edinburgh, 1990).

10 Mike Kirkup, *Jackie Milburn in Black and White: A Biography* (London, 1991), p. ix.

11 Jack Milburn, *Jackie Milburn: Man of Two Halves* (Edinburgh, 2003).

12 Joyce Woolridge, 'These sporting lives: football autobiographies 1945–1980', *Sport In History* 28, 4 (2008), pp. 624–5.

13 Matthew Taylor, 'From source to subject: sport, history and biography', *Journal of Sport History*, 35, 3 (2009).

14 *The Newcastle Journal* 'Sportsmen then and now series' ran from Hughie Gallacher 8 January 1949 to Stan Seymour 21 April 1952.

15 *Newcastle Journal*, 7 January 1950.

16 Ibid., 5 November 1949.

17 Ibid., 12 November 1949.

18 Ibid., 7 January 1950.

19 Ibid., 5 November 1949.

20 Ibid., 5 November 1949.

21 Ibid., 12 November 1949.

22 *Morpeth Herald*, 4 May 1951.

23 *Morpeth Herald*, 11 May 1951.

24 *Charles Buchan's Football Monthly*, November 1951, p. 10.

25 Interview with the north-eastern sports journalist Arthur Appleton, 11 February 1997.
26 *Golden Goals*, p. 11.
27 Ibid., p. 73.
28 Ibid., p. 144.
29 Ibid., p. 143.
30 Woolridge, *Sport in History*, p. 631.
31 *Golden Goals*, p. 48.
32 Jack Milburn, *Jackie Milburn: A Man of Two Halves*, p. 119.
33 *Golden Goals*, p. 14.
34 Woolridge, *Sport in History*, pp. 632–3.
35 *Golden Goals*, 'This is me' pp. 73–8.
36 Ibid., p. 144; Richard Hoggart, *The Uses of Literacy* (Penguin ed. 1958).
37 Jack Milburn, *Jackie Milburn: A Man of Two Halves*, p.122; however, he later became a member of the Freemasons (Shiremoor Lodge No 9621), see John Webb, *Freemasonry and Sport* (Lewis Masonic, Surrey 1995), p. 29. I am grateful to Dr. Neil Carter for this reference.
38 *Newcastle Journal*, 10 October 1988.
39 *Jackie Milburn, Testimonial Match programme*, Wednesday 10 May 1967.
40 *Newcastle Evening Chronicle*, 11 May 1967.
41 June Hulbert meets Jackie Milburn, *Northern Life*, July 1978.
42 Ibid.
43 Ibid.
44 *Newcastle Journal*, 'Women's Journal' section, 17 February 1986.
45 *Newcastle upon Tyne, Council Minutes*, 1980, p. 377.
46 Ibid.
47 Jackie Milburn, *Scrapbook*, Acknowledgement, p. 4.
48 *Scrapbook*, p. 56.
49 Ibid., p. 13.
50 Ibid., p. 18.
51 Gibson, *Wor Jackie*, pp. 139–40.
52 *Newcastle Evening Chronicle*, 1 September 1981.
53 *Newcastle Journal*, 10 October 1988.
54 George Calderon's review of G.K. Chesterton, 'What's wrong with the world', *Times Literary Supplement*, 30 June 1908 cited in the TLS, 30 January 2009, p. 16.
55 For an extensive discussion see R. Holt, 'The batsman as gentleman: interwar cricket and the English hero' in G. Cubitt and A. Warren (eds), *Heroic Reputations and Exemplary Lives* (Manchester, 2000), pp. 225–41.
56 Sir Ernest Barker, *The Character of England* (Oxford, 1947) proposes this view.
57 Kirkup, *Jackie Milburn*, p. 172.
58 *Mail on Sunday*, 16 October 1988.
59 *Guardian*, 10 October 1988.

60   *The Times*, 14 October 1988.
61   *Northern Echo*, 14 October 1988.
62   *Evening Chronicle*, 16 October 1989.
63   Ibid., 8 December 1989.
64   Ibid., 16 December 1989.
65   Pamphlet entitled 'The Milburn Statue', The Wansbeck Writers Group, December 1991. Private publication in possession of the author.
66   *Newcastle Journal*, 28 September 1995.
67   Ibid., 14 December 1996.
68   Gibson, *Wor Jackie*, p. 128.
69   Ibid., p. 129.
70   Kirkup, *Jackie Milburn*, p. xi.
71   Ibid.
72   Ibid., p. 165.
73   Jack Milburn, *Jackie Milburn, A Man of Two Halves*, p. 177.
74   Ibid. p. 180.
75   Ibid. p. 239.
76   Kirkup, *Jackie Milburn*, cited on the back cover.
77   *Guardian*, 9 January 2006.
78   *The Sunday Times*, 4 December 2005.
79   These interviews were conducted in 1997 with Charlie Crowe, his team mate; Raymond Poxton, his school friend; Mike Kirkup; and his Milburn's sister, Jean Leitheid. Summaries in possession of the author.

CHAPTER 9

Champions of the Red Rose:
Three Lancashire Cricketing Heroes

Jack Williams

Those of us who enjoy talking about sport in the pub, on the way to a game or, if it is a cricket match, waiting for the rain to stop, know that selecting our sporting heroes can only be a matter of personal choice. But this personal element adds to the general enjoyment. What emphasis should be given to playing achievements and whether these are for club, region or country, fame or style is debateable. Sporting rivalries can cause one group's hero to be an anti-hero for others. The three cricketers of this chapter have been chosen because of the scale of their cricketing achievements since the Second World War and because their differing personas reveal much about the changing cultural contexts of cricket. It is recognised that others would argue that Cyril Washbrook and Michael Atherton merit more than passing references or that the stars of earlier periods such as the Tyldesley brothers, MacLaren, Duckworth and McDonald or even the writer Neville Cardus were the true heroes of Lancashire cricket.

Brian Statham – 'Gentleman George'

Brian Statham was known across the cricket world as George, a nickname he accepted early in his career because of the tradition among Lancashire players that the team needed to include one player called George. His contribution to the Lancashire County Cricket Club was immense. Between 1950 and 1968 he played in 430 first-class matches, the tenth highest number of all Lancashire players. Except for David Hughes, who played in six more matches and was a slow bowler, no bowler played more times for Lancashire. No one took more wickets for Lancashire than Statham and his total of wickets in all first-class cricket is higher than that of any other bowler who has played for the county. His bowling average of 15.12 runs conceded per wicket was bettered only by Alexander Watson who played for Lancashire from 1871 to 1893, when pitches were more helpful to bowlers. Statham's figures for Lancashire are all the more impressive because until Ken Higgs, who also played for England, joined Lancashire in 1958, he had no effective partner to share Lancashire's quick bowling. Given the physical demands of fast bowling, Statham must have expended more energy playing for Lancashire than any other player. Cyril Washbrook, Lancashire's captain from 1954 to 1959, described Statham as a captain's dream because he always bowled flat out and for as long as a captain asked.[1]

For many cricket followers Statham was among the greatest heroes of Lancashire cricket because of his achievements for England. He played in seventy Tests, more than any of his Lancashire predecessors, and took 252 wickets. For a time he held the record for taking most Test wickets. His fast bowling partnerships with Frank Tyson and Fred Trueman were among England's most effective. In 1954–5 he and Tyson had a key role in England's defeating Australia in Australia, the first time that England had won a series in Australia since the bodyline tour of 1932–3. From the 1953–4 tour of the West Indies until 1963 Statham was an automatic choice for England and was recalled for England in the final Test against South Africa in 1965 when he took five wickets for 40 runs in the first innings.

Statham was a very fast bowler though not usually so fast as Tyson or Trueman. He relied on movement off the pitch rather than swing but is usually regarded as the most accurate bowler of great pace. Len Hutton, England's captain in the early 1950s, said that he never saw a more accurate fast bowler than Statham.[2] Statham's temperament differed from that of other fast bowlers. He never exuded aggression or intimidation like Trueman or other fast bowlers since then. There are no reports of him sledging batsmen. He used the bouncer sparingly and even warned batsmen who tried to play him off the front foot that they were inviting a short-pitched delivery. In 1989 he said that he would have mutinied if a captain had asked him to bowl short. 'It's hardly cricket,' he said, 'when you pitch the ball in your half. I preferred to attack the stumps, make the batsman play. Bowling bouncers at tail-enders is sick and unrewarding.'[3] The least demonstrative of fast bowlers, he made no histrionic gestures when he just missed the stumps or a catch was dropped off his bowling. His easy-going and equable nature meant that few in cricket disliked him. Autobiographies and biographies of those who played cricket in the 1950s and 1960s hardly ever criticise him. In 1969 Neville Cardus commented that Statham was unusual for a fast bowler in having played around the world for twenty years and suffered so little animosity or abuse from opponents.[4] He never seems to have caused trouble in the teams he played for. He was, to use the hackneyed phrase, 'a nice man' and his bearing on the field conveyed this to spectators. Colin Schindler, the sports writer and Lancashire supporter, recalled when Statham died that he 'was our idol for all the right reasons that great sportsmen should become heroes ... he never posed with outrage as many of his contemporaries and all his successors now do, hands on hips, a volley of abuse aimed indiscriminately at batsmen, fielders, umpires and God … It pained us that Statham's action was deemed insufficiently classical as compared with that of Fred Trueman. To us it was an aesthetic delight, an awesome thing of beauty. Trueman's looked like the pumping pistons of a steam engine in comparison.'[5] The historian Eric Midwinter points out that Statham was 'always unruffled' and 'refused to be cowed by self-opinionated authority' but adds that Statham remained essentially an ordinary man and that his ordinariness reflected 'honesty of thought and purpose and its natural tendency to embrace companionability.'[6] Malcolm Lorimer, the Lancashire club's chaplain, has written that 'Brian's modesty was part of his genius…fame never separated Brian from his fellows, from the ordinary man in the street.'[7]

Statham, born and bred in Manchester, expressed pride in playing for Lancashire but in his three autobiographies he did not attribute his playing ability to being from Lancashire. This was very much in contrast to Trueman who argued that his aggressive fast bowling stemmed from being a Yorkshireman. In 1954 Trueman said that an aggressive approach was as vital for a fast bowler as swing and pace and that 'In Yorkshire they say "You don't build a fire-eater on lemonade and cream cakes." To be a fast bowler you've got to be a fire-eater.'[8] The cricket journalist and broadcaster Don Mosey, a friend of Trueman, described Trueman as 'first and foremost a *Yorkshire* bowler.'[9] Statham was a hero to followers of Lancashire cricket who took pride in him and had a sense that they could share in his achievements for the county and for England, but reports that he was exemplifying and shaping a Lancashire identity are rare. Probably no player was so loved by the supporters of Lancashire and while he may have personified qualities which they admired, it does not seem that they thought of him as a stereotypical Lancashire man.

Statham played when the social relations of cricket were being transformed. Until 1963 county cricketers were divided into amateurs and professionals. Traditionally the England and county teams had been captained by amateurs, many of whom had been educated at public schools and who in general were thought to be from the wealthier classes. After the Second World War most professionals had working-class origins but some had middle-class backgrounds and the most successful could aspire to a middle-class lifestyle. Statham's father was a dentist. In the 1940s and 1950s distinctions between amateurs and professionals weakened. Leicestershire in 1935, and only for one season, was the only county before 1939 to have a professional captain. By 1962 only five counties had not appointed a professional captain. In 1952 Len Hutton became England's first professional captain in the twentieth century. Cyril Washbrook in 1954 was Lancashire's first professional captain. Although the gulf between amateurs and professionals narrowed in the 1950s, much of it survived. Michael Marshall's conversations with cricketers about the amateur/professional divide show rising resentment among professionals over the privileged status of amateurs and particularly over amateurs who were 'shamateurs', nominally amateurs but who nevertheless received payment for playing. The England players Tom Graveney, Jim Laker and Fred Trueman, very different personalities, felt strongly about professionals being treated as second-class citizens in cricket.[10] Statham does not seem to have resented to a similar degree the privileges of amateurs which could perhaps reflect his easygoing nature or fatalism towards something about which he could do little.

In the 1950s and early 1960s traditional authority in society at large was challenged by the plays, films and novels associated with the Angry Young Men and the rise of satire. The Angry Young Men were never a united group but at this time most of them were on the political left though in later life John Osborne, John Braine and Kingsley Amis drifted very much to the right. Trueman, who made no secret of his support for the Conservative party, did not share the political views of the Angry Young Men in the 1950s but his rows with cricket authorities and perceptions of him as a rebel suggest parallels between him and the critics of traditional authority. The *Guardian* columnist Martin Kettle in 1993 recalled that 'the great thing about Freddie was that he was a rebel ... He had no respect for the public school officer class who dominated cricket in his era.'[11] In 1956 Statham wrote that 'Of course there is jealousy' between amateurs and professionals and suggested that all should be paid because 'Most amateurs, after all, are amateurs in name only' but he never became known as a fierce critic of amateur captaincy. He believed that a trade union for cricketers would 'promote grouses between employer and employee' and 'wouldn't be a good thing in cricket, where the peaceful, friendly atmosphere is so important.' He did not object to amateur captains being paid to be county secretaries because it kept 'first-rate men in the game'.[12] For some Statham may have been a hero because, being neither a firebrand nor a lickspittle, he symbolised a social harmony which transcended class divisions.

Statham was widely respected because he helped to keep alive the notion that cricket was infused with a high level of sportsmanship. From the late Victorian period apologists for cricket had argued that cricket encouraged selflessness, courage, conviviality and respect for others, qualities which were thought to express an English and Christian morality. Such beliefs survived the Second World War though in a weaker form. Part of the rationale for an amateur presence in first-class cricket, and especially for amateur captaincy, was that amateurs, because their livelihood was not dependent on cricket, could afford to play in a sportsmanlike manner. Although this view implied that financial gain could tempt professionals into sharp practice, professionals such as the Tyldesley brothers, who played for Lancashire before and after the First World War, Jack Hobbs and Herbert Sutcliffe were praised for their sportsmanship and dignity. Statham was often called 'Gentleman George'. Colin Cowdrey, who played as an amateur and as a prominent cricket administrator stressed the need for sportsmanship, said that if his son became a professional cricketer, he would want him to be like Brian Statham.[13] Statham's sportsmanship was usually seen as a facet of his innate good nature and, though probably a source of pride for Lancashire cricket followers, was not described as an especially Lancashire quality.

The first half of the 1960s was far from one of Lancashire's golden periods. After finishing second in the county championship in 1960, Lancashire was not in the top ten positions in any of the next seven seasons, the county's worst run in the championship to that time. Previously Lancashire had never finished outside the top ten in two consecutive seasons. Talented players including Alan Wharton, Bob Barber, Peter Marner and Geoff Clayton joined other counties. Three captains were sacked between 1960 and 1964. In September 1964 the committee advertised for a captain in *The Times*. As Lancashire's leading and most experienced player Statham could have been offended but there were no reports of any ill feeling on his part about this. Statham did tell the committee that he believed that he should be captain because the club was going through a precarious period and he knew that his reputation and record would command respect.[14] When a new committee was elected it made Statham captain. Brian Bearshaw's official history of Lancashire CCC says that Statham was a popular choice who led by example and nursed young players with a father's care. But Statham was not an outstanding success as captain. David Lloyd, a young player at the time, recalled that Statham's appointment was right on a short-term basis but that Statham led through 'his own peerless playing example rather than any inspirational skills in management or motivation'.[15] Peter Lever, another young Lancashire player, has said that when Jack Bond succeeded Statham as captain, it ended a decade of 'purgatory'.[16] During Statham's three years as captain Lancashire's position in the county championship rose from thirteenth to twelfth and then to eleventh, higher than in the previous two seasons, but the county was still far from a power in county cricket. Lancashire did not reach the final of the Gillette Cup, cricket's first limited overs competition which had begun in 1963. After retiring as a player Statham served on the Lancashire committee between 1969 and 1991 and was president of the club in 1997–8.

It would be wrong to see Statham as a plaster saint. Fred Trueman had the reputation of being a hell-raiser and a heavy drinker but those who knew him allege that he drank sparingly and came to resent being thought a heavy drinker. Statham seems to have drunk far more than Trueman. The sports columnist Ian Wooldridge described Statham as 'one of the last great spearhead bowlers to train on beer'.[17] After retiring from cricket Statham worked as a representative for a brewery, a position for which Malcolm Lorimer believes he was temperamentally unsuited, and this adversely affected his health. Although Statham's benefit in 1961 was the second highest of all players up to that time, and he was to have a smaller benefit in 1969, his final years were clouded with ill-health and financial difficulties, though he was never destitute.

In 1989 Fred Trueman organised a series of dinners to raise money for Statham which caused him great embarrassment but the response to these showed the respect in which he was held.[18]

Clive Lloyd

Clive Lloyd was the big star of Lancashire cricket in the 1970s and early 1980s. His record in Test cricket suggests that he was the best batsman who has played regularly for Lancashire since the Second World War. In 110 Tests for the West Indies he scored 7,515 runs, slightly behind Michael Atherton's 7,728 for England but Atherton had 37 more innings. Of Lancashire batsmen who have scored over 1,000 Test runs Lloyd's average of 46.67 is second only to the 59.23 of Eddie Paynter who played twenty times for England in the 1930s. Lloyd's nineteen Test centuries are more than those scored by any other Lancashire batsman. A very big man, Lloyd hit the ball with enormous power which made him exciting to watch. He once hit a ball 140 yards at The Oval and for the West Indies against Glamorgan in 1976 made the fastest individual score of 200 since 1903. In his early career he was among the best cover points in cricket and a more than useful medium-pace bowler.

Lloyd's playing achievements for Lancashire were equally impressive. He has the third best batting average for Lancashire and the best average in all first-class cricket of all Lancashire batsmen. Lloyd made a vital contribution to Lancashire becoming the great force in limited-overs cricket when this expanded with the start of the Sunday League in 1969 and the Benson and Hedges Cup in 1972. After lacklustre years in the County Championship, Lancashire won the Gillette Cup in 1970, 1971, 1972 and 1975 and lost the final in 1974. Lancashire won the Sunday League in 1969 and 1970 and failed to win it by a whisker in 1971. Enormous crowds watched Lancashire's limited-overs matches at Old Trafford. Although Lloyd did much to bring about Lancashire's rise in one-day cricket, much was also due to the inspirational captaincy of Jack Bond, a run-of-the-mill county player who brought the best out of others and persuaded them to enjoy playing. The enthusiastic play of wicket-keeper Farokh Engineer, who had joined Lancashire in 1968 and who played in 46 Tests for India, and the growing experience of home-grown players such as Peter Lever, David Hughes, David Lloyd and Jack Simmons were also important.

Born in Guyana, Lloyd was already a Test player when he joined Lancashire and was not a product of Lancashire cricket. No other overseas player who had already played Test cricket before joining Lancashire played for the county for so many seasons. Lloyd wrote in 1980 that 'it was clear to everyone in Lancashire, I was a Lancastrian through and through, and that meant a lot to me' and he called Lancashire 'my adopted and beloved home'.[19] While playing for Haslingden in the Lancashire League, he opted to join Lancashire even though Warwickshire offered better terms. Jack Bond recalls that Lloyd was a 'world-class player who'd come to Lancashire to give his all ... He took as much pride in his county as anyone in the side. And it was that which impressed a lot of the lads.'[20] David Lloyd says that 'Clive bought in to Lancashire completely' and that in Lancashire 'you shouldn't hear a bad word about him from anyone. If you do, they're bloody-well wrong.'

Lloyd was a major figure of world cricket in the 1970s and 1980s and certainly the biggest 'name' in global cricket to play for Lancashire at that time. Between 1974–75 and 1984–85 he captained the West Indies in seventy-four Tests, then an unprecedented figure. Of the eighteen Test series in which he captained the West Indies, sixteen were won, two drawn and two lost, a record which puts him among the most successful Test captains of all time. In the late 1970s and early 1980s the West Indies were the best team playing Test cricket. Between March 1980 and January 1985 they lost only one Test match. Under Lloyd's leadership the West Indies were equally successful in limited-overs cricket. Sixty-two of eighty-two one-day internationals were won and the West Indies won the first two world cups and lost the final of the third. Lloyd had very great fast bowlers and great batsmen in his West Indian sides but he gave them a more professional approach. He has said that he wanted to overturn the notion that West Indians were 'calypso cricketers', a 'phrase so patronising' which implied that West Indian players of immense natural ability were 'slap-happy, unthinking players who simply hoped for the best'. He wanted to show that 'we were strong, intelligent, professional people'. Viv Richards, the best batsman of Lloyd's team, said that Lloyd 'built us into a great team.'[22]

The respect of other West Indian players for Lloyd helped him to boost the power of players in cricket. Trevor McDonald has argued that the West Indies Cricket Board had often taken a highhanded line with its players but that Lloyd's decision to stand up to it over the Packer affair, which demonstrated the power of players, caused it to become more co-operative with players.[23] Had Lloyd not decided to join Kerry Packer's World Series Cricket, which led most of the other leading West Indian cricketers to follow his example, Packer's challenge to established cricket may have been less formidable. Many cricket followers saw World Series Cricket as a threat to Test cricket and thought that playing under floodlights in coloured clothing vulgarised the game. Some in Lancashire, though one cannot be sure of how many, perhaps shared this view. Lloyd found 'certain members at Old Trafford noticeably shunning me' and 'a distinct coldness instead of the usual northern warmth.'[24] As Lloyd's benefit occurred when he was contracted to play for Packer in the winter months, some Lancashire supporters asked why he needed more money.[25]

Lloyd's tactics as captain of the West Indies caused some to see him as an anti-hero. The West Indies' success was widely ascribed to four very fast bowlers who intimidated batsmen by persistently pitching the ball short so that it bounced around a batsman's upper body. Lloyd was accused of slowing over rates to keep bowlers fresh and to restrict scoring opportunities. Concentrating on fast bowling was condemned for driving spin bowling from Test cricket. In 1984 Robin Marlar, a former captain of Sussex, wrote that most of those on whose support England depended regarded the West Indian tactics as 'brutalising the game' and 'being boring to watch.'[26] John Woodcock, editor of *Wisden*, claimed that the West Indies were the worst offenders in the 'viciousness' of fast bowling which was changing 'the very nature of the game' by resorting 'ever more frequently to the thuggery of the bouncer.'[27] In 1985 the England opening batsman Graham Gooch wrote that tail-end batsmen who blocked balls against the West Indies would have bouncers bowled at them. In his view 'Most would freeze with terror, because they are not equipped to deal with it. If that is not intimidation, I don't what is.'[28] Lloyd described his team as furious with critics across the world who tried 'to degrade our excellence and our achievements. That is the real reason behind statements that we bowl too many bouncers…it's all being said by people who wish to deny us our rightful title as the best team around. It really makes me hopping mad.'[29] In his view those who could not play fast bowling should not have been playing Test cricket.[30] He thought that restricting how many bouncers which could be bowled in an over would lose the element of surprise and he saw 'no reason why we should change because we keep beating teams.'[31] Lloyd always maintained that if he had had spin bowlers who could have taken wickets regularly in Tests, he would have used them. In 2007 he recalled that he had not craved a pace attack but 'a *formidable* attack', one which would take twenty wickets. In any event, he used a slow bowler in all but two of the Tests when he captained the West Indies.[32]

Whether Lloyd's Test match tactics diminished his popularity in Lancashire is not clear. When he went out to bat in Test matches at Old Trafford he was cheered more loudly than other West Indian batsmen. Possibly many in Lancashire agreed with Graeme Fowler, the Lancashire and England batsman who opened the batting against the West Indian pace attack, when he pointed out that if England had had four fast bowlers, they would have used them.[33] On the other hand criticisms of Lloyd in England did not provoke a wave of public statements of support for him in Lancashire. There could have been pride that a Lancashire player had fashioned the most formidable side in international cricket mixed with disappointment that England was defeated so comprehensively. It may be that many had little difficulty in distinguishing between Lloyd the Lancashire county cricketer and Lloyd the West Indian Test captain.

Lloyd was part of the long-established cosmopolitanism of Lancashire cricket. The exact date for the beginning of the County Championship is debateable but around 1872–73 it was decided that a cricketer could not play for a county without being born there or having resided in it for two years. Relaxed over time, these rules were finally swept aside only for the 1968 season when each county was allowed to sign a player from overseas without a residential qualification. Because of the strength of league cricket in Lancashire and the employment of prominent cricketers as league club professionals, Lancashire had long been able to sign players who had not been born in Lancashire but had acquired residential qualifications for the county. Many of Lancashire's most illustrious cricketers before 1968, including the England players Johnny Briggs, Sydney Barnes, Arthur Mold, Cecil Parkin and Jack Ikin, were born outside Lancashire. In the Edwardian period the Australians Poidevin and Kermode played for Lancashire. In the 1920s the great Australian fast bowler Ted McDonald joined Lancashire after playing as the professional for Nelson in the Lancashire League. In 1949 another Australian, Ken Grieves, joined Lancashire from league cricket. This Lancashire practice can be seen as a continuation of the business ethos of nineteenth-century industrial Lancashire with its commitment to free markets and the right of labour to sell itself in the highest marketplace. But this interpretation can be pushed too far. The county club could have taken more advantage of the overseas talent on its doorstep. From the 1930s almost all leading West Indian cricketers played league cricket in Lancashire but until Sonny Ramadhin joined Lancashire in 1964, only Learie Constantine in the late 1930s seems to have been asked to play for Lancashire. Constantine did not join Lancashire because the Lancashire players thought that 'a black man taking the place of a white man in our side was anathema' and threatened not to play if Constantine were engaged.[34]

Lloyd was the first African-Caribbean to play for Lancashire. There were no widespread public objections in Lancashire to a black man playing for the county even though this coincided with race becoming a subject of national political debate. The first legislation to curb immigration was passed in 1961. Enoch Powell made his so-called 'rivers of blood' speech in 1968. Cricket and society at large were divided over whether the white South African team should tour England in 1970. The popularity of Lloyd and the Indian Engineer in Lancashire suggests a high degree of racial tolerance in Lancashire cricket although in the last three decades of the twentieth century ethnic discrimination was not absent from recreational cricket in Lancashire.[35] Lloyd has always been aware of racial prejudice. While accepting that his experiences have been 'overwhelmingly positive', he has wondered 'what other people think of you because of your colour.' He told his most recent biographer that slavery had robbed him of the culture of his West African ancestors and that he should have an African name.[36] Lloyd detected a racial edge in refusals to give the West Indies full credit for their playing achievements, saying this could be called 'all sorts of things, call it prejudice, call it racism, I don't know.'[37]

Instances of racist prejudice towards Lloyd in Lancashire were rare but not unknown. The Lancashire players had wanted Lloyd to succeed Jack Bond as the county captain in 1973 but the Lancashire chairman told them that he was not sure the club's committee would accept a black man as captain. David Lloyd, who succeeded Bond as captain, believes that Clive Lloyd was not appointed because his Test match commitments each winter would prevent him from being an ambassador for the club around the county.[38] Clive Lloyd captained Lancashire from 1981 to 1983 and again in 1986, seasons when his West Indian side was at the peak of its powers, but Lancashire achieved little under his leadership. Lancashire always finished in the bottom half of the County Championship and did not win any of the limited-overs competitions, although they reached the final of the NatWest Trophy in 1986. Lancashire players were adamant that Lloyd was a poor tactician.[39] In 1985 Mike Brearley, usually regarded as one of England's most astute captains, wrote that Lloyd's restraint and steadiness as captain had been important factors in the growing maturity of West Indian cricket but his 'lack of ideas when handling the ordinary Lancashire attack' had shown that he did not have 'a cricketing brain' though he said later that these comments were 'not… the main thrust of what I felt.'[40] Jack Bond and Peter Lever thought that Lloyd had difficulty recognising that ordinary players did not always share his serious approach and in appreciating that they could not do what he could do. David Lloyd, however, maintains that Clive Lloyd was a magnificent leader, an inspiration to his players and tactically aware but had 'a bloody awful side…if you ain't got the tools, you can't do it.'[41] Although many followers of Lancashire may have been disappointed that Lancashire did not do better under Lloyd's leadership, there were no complaints that Lancashire's lack of success resulted from having a black captain. Possibly Lloyd's popularity and esteem meant that those who may have held such opinions did not dare express them.

African-Caribbeans in England took great pride in the achievements of West Indian cricket under Lloyd's leadership. They attended in large numbers Tests against England in England and demonstrated their support in the noisier and more flamboyant style associated with watching cricket in the Caribbean. Yet despite Lloyd's popularity, very few of those who lived in Lancashire watched the county side regularly. Lloyd's playing achievements did not make the county club a multi-cultural institution. Similarly Indians living in Lancashire watched Indian touring sides but few went to Lancashire home matches when Farohk Engineer, who was also massively popular with Lancashire's white followers, was playing. Lloyd was a Lancashire hero among the white followers of Lancashire but for African-Caribbeans in Lancashire he was a West Indian hero.

Freddie Flintoff

Andrew Flintoff, usually known by his nickname Freddie, has been the great star of Lancashire cricket in the early twenty-first century. In 2003 the cricket journalist Mike Selvey wrote that Flintoff 'is the biggest crowd-pleaser to emerge here in England in two decades.'[42] Flintoff is one of the great all-rounders to have played for Lancashire and England, though Lancashire has produced few Lancashire-born all-rounders. Until the expansion of limited-overs cricket in the late 1960s reduced the number of three-day matches, the double of scoring 1,000 runs and taking 100 wickets was a measure of a cricketer's all-round abilities but Lancashire players took the double in only three seasons. Flintoff is the only Lancashire player to have scored more than 1,000 runs and taken over 100 wickets in Test matches for England although four of Lancashire's overseas players have done this for their home countries. Flintoff has often been compared with Ian Botham but Botham took only twenty-one Tests to score 1,000 runs and take 100 wickets for England. After playing in twenty-one Tests Flintoff had scored 643 runs and taken 33 wickets. Flintoff claims that because of his 'dodgy back' he had not been able to take seriously his bowling in Tests until 2001 but he can bowl very fast and makes the ball rear into the body of batsmen. By the end of March 2008 he had scored five Test match centuries and his fierce hitting could change the course of a match in a short time. He has scored more runs in limited-overs internationals for England than any other Lancashire player. Flintoff is a spectacular cricketer. His height and powerful physique give him a natural presence. It is almost impossible not to miss him in the field. As a batsman he hits the ball with great force and for great distances. In the calendar year 2004 he hit 46 sixes in Tests and one-day internationals. Flintoff's popularity in cricket is also connected with his affable and genial nature. Although failure in matches can leave him desolate, his enjoyment in playing cricket communicates itself to spectators.

Flintoff's heroic status in Lancashire rests on what he has done for England. Until the 1990s the esteem of other Lancashire heroes who played for England had rested on what they did for Lancashire and for England. Michael Atherton in the 1990s was perhaps the first Lancashire cricketer who was regarded primarily as an England player who also played for Lancashire. Flintoff has spent more time playing for England than for Lancashire. Before the 2008 season, he had played in seventy-three first-class matches for Lancashire and in sixty-six Test matches, but as Test matches are scheduled for one day longer than county championship matches, he must have spent more time playing in Tests than in the County Championship. He has played in 118 limited-overs matches for Lancashire but in 124 limited-overs internationals for England. Between 2002 and 2007 Lancashire played ninety-six county championship matches but Flintoff appeared in only thirteen. As international cricket provides a growing proportion of the income for cricket and in effect subsidises county cricket, the wellbeing of English cricket has become seen as being dependent on the England team being successful. Under the central contract system, introduced in 1999, the England and Wales Cricket Board pays players in the England squad and can withdraw them from county cricket in order to ensure that they are in prime condition for England games. Injuries over the past three seasons have also restricted Flintoff's appearances for Lancashire.

Flintoff's England career had a stuttering start. He was first selected for Lancashire and England on potential rather than performance. He played for Lancashire in the County Championship aged only seventeen in 1995 but scored only 7 and 0, took no wickets and dropped five catches. He played regularly in the Lancashire first team in 1997 but as Stephen Moss of the *Observer* noted, 'Flintoff blazed only intermittently for his county.'[43] In 1999 he made 143 against Essex Eagles in the National League, the highest score ever made by a Lancashire batsman since this competition began in 1969. The next season in a NatWest Trophy match he scored 135 not out which David Gower described as 'the most awesome innings we are ever going to see on a cricket field' but his overall play was less reliable, characterised by 'a once-or-twice-a-season extravaganza'.[44] When he first played in a Test match for England in 1997 he was only twenty, the youngest Lancashire player to play for England, and had played only fifteen county championship matches, but did little in the game. Only in 2004 did Flintoff add consistency to his play which allowed him to perform regularly at a level for England which fulfilled his potential. Flintoff's purple patch was the 2005 Test series against Australia when England won back the Ashes for the first time since 1989. *Wisden Cricketers' Almanack* rated him 'The Leading Cricketer in the World' for his 402 runs and 24 wickets against Australia and considered that he tipped the balance between the two sides. When England drew the final Test to make sure of winning the Ashes, the country was gripped with euphoria. For the first time an England Test team toured London in an open-topped bus. One hundred thousand people greeted them in Trafalgar Square.

Flintoff's heroic status is very much dependent on the 2005 Test series against Australia. In many ways Flintoff was what English cricket had been looking for, a superstar who could appeal to the public imagination like those of other sports. The 1990s and the beginning of the twenty-first century were dismal for English cricket. After drawing a Test series against Australia in 1986–87, England had lost seven successive Test series to Australia. England lost in the final of the cricket World Cup in 1992 but achieved little in the next three World Cups and had been particularly disappointing in that of 1999 which was played in England. The reform of cricket administration with the England and Wales Cricket Board replacing the Test and County Cricket Board in 1997 signalled that those within the game felt that cricket was in crisis. The gulf in public interest between cricket and football, whose Premiership had brought more money and new heights of media coverage, seemed to be widening. The counties' Twenty-20 Cup, launched in 2003, was encouraged in the hope that this shorter format of the sport would appeal to the young and perhaps attract more women.

Mike Marquesee described English cricket in the 1990s as an expression of an English national malaise, of a culture focused on the past and riddled with snobbery, class distinction and racism.[45] Yet in the early twentieth-first century Flintoff helped to give cricket an image with different, though sometimes paradoxical, cultural resonances. Flintoff's celebrity is based on the physical strength and aggressive masculinity which he displays on the cricket field but he has also been eager to be depicted as 'a new man', as one devoted to his wife and young children and who does not wish to hide the caring side to his nature. His autobiography published in 2006 includes one chapter entitled 'Family Man' and has seven large pictures of him with his children.[46] He freely admits that his wife did much to help him put his career on the right lines. Parallels suggest themselves with David Beckham, the megastar of English football. Over the past decade or so the wealth of sport stars has become a register of their status, a trend perhaps linked with the rise of Thatcherism and the belief that not maximising opportunities for commercial gain was moral weakness. Flintoff's earnings have never matched those of Beckham or other leading footballers but during the year ending in October 2006 he earned £3m from sponsorship and book deals. His contract with the ECB was reputedly worth £400,000. His six homes were valued at £6m.[47]

But Flintoff can also be seen as part of the 'laddism' of contemporary Britain with its emphasis on the night out of heavy drinking, curries and kebabs. His laddish lifestyle hindered his development as a cricketer. A night out in Manchester often began at 2 o'clock in the afternoon.[48] He has recalled that 'Things came a bit too quickly and I didn't do too well with it. I put weight on. My cricket wasn't great and I wasn't practising.' At one point he weighed more than the world heavyweight champion boxer Lennox Lewis. In 2000 the England management and his agents ordered Flintoff to lose weight.[49] The scale of the England team celebrations, in which Flintoff had the main role, when England won the Ashes in 2005 after drawing the final Test at The Oval, was treated as epic. The England team were reported to have ordered 240 cans of beer, 18 bottles of white wine, 12 bottles of red wine, 72 bottles of champagne and one bottle of brandy for their celebrations in the three hours after the end of the match. Through the night there was further drinking at a night club. More drink was available at the Lord Mayor's reception, on the open top bus tour of London, at the reception in 10 Downing Street and then at Lord's. The total cost of drink available for the England team was £34,000.[50] Flintoff admitted that he could not quarrel with the crowd in Trafalgar Square when it chanted 'You're pissed and you know you are!'[51] Ian Wooldridge wrote that the few moralists had complained about the England team's behaviour:

> 'had no idea of the difference between binge-drinking and a roaring celebratory knees-up after an astonishing triumph that had gripped both hemispheres. True, Freddie's eyes after 24 hours at it looked like slots at a bank pay-out and yes, he did stumble fractionally after another dawn refresher at the Mansion House. He even managed to get his hands on an afternoon beer at Number 10 … This wasn't some rabid city centre late on a Friday or a Saturday night. There was no public disruption, no vomiting in the street, no punch-up to require police attention and no drugs.'[52]

The laddish dimension to Flintoff's celebrity has links with the rise of the Barmy Army, the mainly young men with the money to follow England around that world and whose boisterous spectating with its repetitive chanting is far removed from the more refined and deferential forms of spectator conduct which were traditionally expected from England cricket supporters.[53]

After being seen as the great new hero of English cricket in 2005, Flintoff became an anti-hero when England toured Australia in 2006–7. Made captain because Michael Vaughan was injured, England lost all five Tests. Carrying the burden of captaincy and perhaps not fully recovered from an ankle injury, Flintoff did not match his achievements of 2005. At the Perth Test he went wicketless for the first time in 43 Tests. The *News of the World* had a headline Appalling Shameful Horrific England Shambles and *The Times* Scoreboard of surrender: England c Fear b Timidity ... 0. Worse was to follow. Whereas Flintoff's drinking was the stuff of legend in 2005, it led to his disgrace during the World Cup of 2007 in the West Indies. He was stripped of the vice-captaincy of the England team, who had not being playing well, after capsizing a pedal boat at 4 a.m. after an eight-hour binge and only thirty hours before England's next match.

There is no doubt that Flintoff has been one of English cricket's great heroes, perhaps a flawed hero, but a hero none the less. Some may argue that his appearances for Lancashire have been so few that he can scarcely be called a Lancashire cricketing star. But his general fame has exceeded that of his contemporaries in the Lancashire side and he always seems loyal to Lancashire. In 2005 he said that he loved playing for Lancashire and wished that he could have played more.[54] In his youth he chose to join Lancashire rather than Northamptonshire who had also arranged for him to study at Oakham School. He has written that 'I'd love to give something back to a county I've been with since nine years of age. They've been very good to me.'[55] He is proud of his roots in Preston and of being made a freeman of Preston in 2006. Followers of Lancashire have been proud of what he has done for England and probably see this as reflecting favourably on the county club though perhaps the club could have done more sooner to help Flintoff change his lifestyle. John Stanworth, the current director of Lancashire's academy, has recalled that 'we didn't have the right infrastructure to advise somebody with his potential. There was no father figure for him.'[56]

Cricket and Lancashire identity

Through their playing skills and status in cricket, Statham, Lloyd and Flintoff gave great pleasure and pride to followers of Lancashire cricket. They helped to focus a sense of Lancashire identity although it is difficult to detail the characteristics of such an identity or to measure its intensity and longevity. No doubt watching cricket boosted an awareness of a communal identity among those from different parts of what is the historic county of Lancashire but how far this was transferable to other

173

social settings is unclear. The achievements of Statham and Flintoff for England seem to have generated pride in what Lancashire was contributing to England and this could also be said for Lancashire's other successful England players. The achievements of Lloyd with the West Indies were welcomed by African-Caribbeans in Lancashire but seem not to have led many of them to identify with the Lancashire club. The very different personalities of Statham, Lloyd and Flintoff, and the differing periods in which they played, may have meant that they did not have an equal appeal to the same groups in Lancashire, while notions of what constituted 'Lancashireness' may have changed over time.

Sporting heroes, it has been argued, help their admirers to imagine who they are and perhaps what they would like to be. In Yorkshire, cricket certainly seems to have had this effect. Harold Wilson called Fred Trueman 'the greatest living Yorkshireman'. Stars of Yorkshire cricket such as Close, Illingworth, Trueman and Boycott all seem to have believed that how they played cricket was shaped by coming from Yorkshire and expressed Yorkshire character. Yet the playing successes of Statham, Lloyd and Flintoff, and other post-war stars of Lancashire cricket such as Washbrook and Atherton, were rarely described by them or others as having a distinctively Lancashire flavour or origin. It is hard to detect a common style of play, a typically Lancashire style and approach to cricket, among post-war players born in the county such as Winston Place, Harry Pilling, Jack Simmons, David Hughes, David Lloyd, Warren Hegg and Ian Austin who gave Lancashire sterling service without becoming stars of international cricket. Stars of the county club have been cricketers for Lancashire rather than Lancashire cricketers.

There are no obvious reasons why the heroes of Lancashire cricket have not been regarded as icons of a Lancashire identity on the same scale as their equivalents in Yorkshire. Yorkshire's greater playing success in the county championship before and after the Second World War may have strengthened beliefs about the county team expressing a county identity and although Lancashire has not won the county championship since 1950, it has had great success in limited-overs cricket. The Yorkshire club's tradition of spreading home matches across a variety of grounds in the county may have helped to foster a Yorkshire consciousness. Lancashire has always played the great majority of its home matches at Old Trafford. Lancashire and Yorkshire were both strongholds of league cricket but relations between the county club and the leading leagues and the county club were traditionally more cordial in Yorkshire than in Lancashire. The Lancashire League and the Central Lancashire League, the most prestigious leagues in Lancashire, have included clubs representing towns and have focused urban loyalties whereas the Bradford League and the Yorkshire Council have tended to have teams which represent localities within towns. Dave Russell and Stephen Wagg have shown that across the twentieth century it was imagined in Yorkshire that Yorkshire cricket expressed uniquely Yorkshire characteristics. In his analysis of cricket in the West Riding between 1820 and 1870,[57] Robert Light has stressed the cultural continuities of cricket in Yorkshire and has demonstrated how the popular culture of cricket in the West Riding, which included fierce competitiveness and acceptance of commercialism and professionalism, led to the county club becoming a focus for a Yorkshire identity.[58] Unfortunately there is no equally detailed examination of cricket in nineteenth-century Lancashire to establish whether, and how far, its cultural ramifications differed from those of Yorkshire.

The social and cultural contexts of other sports shed some light on why cricket has not been associated with a county identity to the same extent as in Yorkshire since the Second World War. Six Lancashire clubs, but only one Yorkshire club, have been association football's league champions since 1945 and perhaps football in Lancashire has expressed and reinforced town identities and rivalries which have eclipsed a county consciousness. In Lancashire and Yorkshire rugby league has encouraged town identities and a shared conviction of the North not being given due recognition by the South, but the sense of Yorkshireness associated with rugby league seems to be much stronger than a Lancashire identity. At rugby league matches supporters of teams from Yorkshire often chant 'Yorkshire! Yorkshire!' but followers of clubs from Lancashire do not chant 'Lancashire! Lancashire!'

The cosmopolitanism of Lancashire cricket can be seen as a further explanation of why Statham, Lloyd and Flintoff have not been thought of as expressing a distinctively Lancashire approach to cricket as do their equivalents in Yorkshire. From its origins the Lancashire club engaged cricketers from outside the county and the persistence of this practice gave Lancashire cricket a variety of styles and approaches to the game. In the second half of the nineteenth century recruiting players from outside the county may have reflected the county's industrial pre-eminence, the international dimension of its cotton trade and its free market ideology which stressed that the labourer should be able to sell his services wherever economic gains were greatest. Although Lancashire's industrial base was transformed in the twentieth century, recruiting players from outside the county had become standard practice for the Lancashire county club. Until the 1990s the Yorkshire club played only those born in Yorkshire, a policy which suggests that a Yorkshire consciousness was stronger than in Lancashire, though it may also have helped to create a Yorkshire consciousness, and may have been a result of Yorkshire having a more central role in pre-industrial England, when Lancashire was very much an economic and political backwater. But playing only Yorkshire-born players can also be interpreted as an inward-looking mentality. None of the overseas players who have played for Yorkshire since 1992 have matched the popularity of Lloyd or Engineer in Lancashire. The relative absence of a uniquely Lancashire approach to cricket and of uniformity among the heroes of Lancashire cricket reflects an outward-looking mindset which was both cause and effect of its cosmopolitanism.

1   Interview with Cyril Washbrook, 10 March 1992.

2   *Manchester Evening News*, 12 June 2000.

3   *Cricketer International*, July 1989.

4   *Wisden Cricketers' Almanack 1969* (London, 1969), p. 117.

5   *Guardian*, 17 June 2000.

6   Eric Midwinter, *Red Shirts and Roses: The Tale of Two Old Traffords* (Manchester, 2005), p. 165.

7   Malcolm G. Lorimer, ed., *Glory Lightly Worn: A Tribute to Brian Statham* (Manchester, 2001), p. 7.

8   *News Chronicle*, 29 July 1954.

9   Don Mosey, *We Don't Play Cricket It for Fun: A History of Yorkshire Cricket* (London, 1988), p. 130. For a discussion of the qualities associated with Yorkshire cricket since 1945 see Stephen Wagg, 'Muck or nettles: men, masculinity and myth in Yorkshire Cricket' in this volume.

10 Michael Marshall, *Gentlemen and Players: Conversations with Cricketers* (London, 1987).

11 *Guardian*, 22 June 1993.

12 Brian Statham, *Cricket Merry-Go-Round* (London, 1956), pp. 146, 167, 187.

13 *Lancashire County Cricket Yearbook 2001* (Manchester, 2001), p. 208.

14 David Lloyd and Alan Lee, *David Lloyd: The Autobiography* (London, 2000), p. 60.

15 Lloyd, *David Lloyd*, p. 60.

16 Simon Lister, *Supercat: The Authorised Biography of Clive Lloyd* (Bath, 2007), p. 60.

17 *Daily Mail*, 14 June 2000.

18 Interview with Malcolm Lorimer, 17 January 2000.

19 Clive Lloyd, *Living for Cricket* (London, 1980), pp. 28, 35.

20 Lister, *Supercat*, p. 63.

21 Lister, *Supercat*, p.175.

22 Lister, *Supercat*, pp. 21, 106.

23 Trevor McDonald, *Clive Lloyd: The Authorised Biography* (London, 1985), pp. 1–12.

24 Lloyd, *Living for Cricket*, p. 36.

25 Lister, *Supercat*, p. 119.

26 *Sunday Times*, 20 May 1984.

27 *Wisden Cricketers' Almanack 1984* (London, 1984), p. 50.

28 Graham Gooch and Alan Lee, *Out of the Wilderness* (London, 1985), p. 145.

29 McDonald, *Clive Lloyd*, p. 155.

30 McDonald, *Clive Lloyd*, pp. 85–6.

31 McDonald, *Clive Lloyd*, pp. 107–8, 110.

32 Lister, *Supercat*, pp. 102, 150.

33 Lister, *Supercat*, p. 148.

34 Brian Bearshaw, *From the Stretford End: The Official History of Lancashire County Cricket Club* (London, 1990), p. 271.

35 Jack Williams, 'Asians, cricket and ethnic relations in Northern England', *Sporting Traditions*, 16, 2 (2000); Jack Williams, *Cricket and Race* (Oxford, 2001), chapter 7.
36 Lister, *Supercat*, pp. 29–30.
37 Rob Steen, *Desmond Haynes: The Lion of Barbados* (London, 1993), p. 26.
38 Lister, *Supercat*, p. 82.
39 Atherton, *Opening Up*, p. 215.
40 Mike Brearley, *The Art of Captaincy* (London, 1985), p. 128; Lister, *Supercat*, p. 170.
41 Lister, *Supercat*, pp. 172–3.
42 Tanya Aldred, *Freddie Flintoff: England's Hero*, (London, 2005), p. 69.
43 *Observer*, 28 November 2004.
44 Stephen Moss, 'Ashes test awaits our "Freddy"', *Lancashire County Cricket Club Yearbook 2005* (Manchester, 2005), p. 24.
45 Mike Marqusee, *Anyone but England: Cricket and the National Malaise* (London, 1994).
46 Andrew Flintoff, *Freddie: My World* (London, 2006).
47 *Sunday Express*, 8 Oct. 2006.
48 Tim Ewbank, *Andrew Flintoff: The Biography* (London, 2006), p. 61.
49 Moss, 'Ashes test', pp. 20–2.
50 *Sun*, 14 Sept. 2005.
51 Andrew Flintoff, *Being Freddie: The Story So Far* (London: 2006), pp. 274–5.
52 *Daily Mail*, 17 September 2005.
53 Matthew Parry and Dominic Malcolm, 'England's Barmy Army: commercialization, masculinity and nationalism', *International Review for the Sociology of Sport*, 39, 1 (2004), p. 75.
54 Aldred, *Freddie Flintoff*, p. 69.
55 Andrew Flintoff with Patrick Murphy, *Andrew Flintoff: My Life in Pictures* (London, 2004), p. 204.
56 Moss, 'Ashes test', p. 22.
57 Dave Russell, 'Sport and identity: the case of Yorkshire County Cricket Club, 1890–1939', *20th Century British History*, 7, 2 (1996); Wagg, 'Muck or nettles'.
58 Robert F. Light, 'Cricket's forgotten past: a social and cultural history of the game in the West Riding of Yorkshire 1820–1870', De Montfort University Ph.D. thesis (2008).

CHAPTER 10

Ellery Hanley: Rugby League's Ice Dancer

Karl Spracklen

Introduction

In the 2009 series of the ITV television 'celeb-reality' programme *Dancing on Ice*, Ellery Hanley took on the role of the ungainly, ex-professional sportsman. Although Hanley failed to follow the transformational narrative from ugly duckling to graceful swan, his very presence on the programme signified his status as the most visible rugby league player of his generation (and the years subsequent to his retirement). In his status as a hero of rugby league, Hanley is both a reflection and a refraction of the game's northern, working-class heritage. He is a northerner from a working-class background in Yorkshire, and demonstrably proved his masculinity and his quiet, working-class toughness on the pitch. A feature article on Hanley in the March 2009 edition of *Yorkshire Life* ('The biggest and best selling county magazine in Yorkshire') demonstrates his elevation into the bourgeoisie of the North, alongside the likes of BBC Look North presenter Christa Ackroyd, interviewed in the same edition.[1] The magazine celebrates a certain image of Yorkshire: clean fields basking in sunlight, canal boats, neatly arranged flower displays in urban parks, adverts for designer lingerie for the leisured ladies of Harrogate and Knaresborough. In many ways, Hanley's presence in between these parochial, provincial and painfully suburban pleasantries is a mark of his ascendancy into northern acceptability. But Hanley's blackness, and his refusal as a player to talk to journalists, made his status as a northern sporting hero less assured than it might have been.

In this chapter, I will explore Hanley's career and status against the backdrop of northern-ness, and the northern English rugby league's white, working-class community. I will argue that the imagined status of the former, and the imaginary status of the latter, is something that Hanley – as a true icon – only managed to transcend once his career as a player was over.[2] Before I give an overview of Hanley's career, however, it is necessary to introduce and discuss the code of rugby league, and its critical relationship to the

North, northern-ness and northern men. This will allow Hanley to be better situated within this imaginary and imagined community of the game, and of the mythic north in which that game is the beginning and end of meaning.

Rugby league and northern men

> Rugby league was a game whose laws had been codified by workers in the forlorn north of England; miners and millworkers of Bradford and Wigan, Hull and Warrington, were invaded by that particular genius which concerns itself with the serious business of human games, and produced what was ... the supreme code, a cellular structure composed of thirteen players which mimicked art and war so exactly it became them.[3]

Inevitably, any research involves a process of self realisation, an exploration of the researcher, as well as the researched.[4] As a researcher and a fan I am inextricably bound to the culture of rugby league, and the people and places associated with it. I grew up looking at maps of the country, seeing the string of otherwise anonymous towns across the north of England where professional rugby league was played. To grow up knowing rugby league was to know that Hull was a divided city, that the Gallant Youths were Batley, that pies were synonymous with Wigan, and that the only Town worth talking about was Workington. Parts of the north of England where rugby league did not exist were not parts of my North.

It was invocations of a heroic struggle in the birth of the game of rugby league that first interested me in the sociology of sport.[5] As someone brought up in the culture of rugby league, I was exposed to the game's creation myths and morality plays from an early age. I knew it all, from the Split of 1895 referred to by Kenneally, to the machinations of anti-rugby league members of the Vichy government, who destroyed French rugby league in the war.[6] As I developed an academic interest in history, sociology and philosophy,[7] I realised the game of rugby league and the people it so often evoked in its own stories – as well as the images associated with the game – provided acres of intellectual space that had hardly been covered, with the notable exception of sociologists Dunning and Sheard and the historian Tony Collins.[8] The game of rugby league is working class, attached to its northern roots by history and parochial affiliation. When this attachment perseveres even though the locality that produced it has changed, there can arise a community that is associated with a set of symbols, shared meanings or imaginary sites.[9] I realised that what I was actually looking at, the community to which I belonged, was an imaginary community delineated by 'the game', a collection of tacit understandings shared by its members, and that the old, geographical locality represented by the team was only a contingent part of this imaginary community.[10] As my previous research into rugby league progressed, the idea that the people I spoke to used 'the game' to identify with this ghost of the past, this *idea* of what it meant to associate with a rugby league playing district, became very important, as values in 'the game' were conflated with the values of the working-class localities as *they remembered them*.[11]

This process resulted in what Benedict Anderson calls imagined communities, where historical invention has resulted in a cohesive structure for legitimising a sense of community in the present.[12] This was a process of reinvention of the past, inventing traditions that justified the values of the present.[13] As Eddie Waring put it:

> It's as North as hotpot and Yorkshire pudding. It's as tough as teak. It's rugby league – a man's game if ever there was one. Someone once said of rugby union, 'A game for ruffians played by gentlemen'... Gentlemen have played rugby league. Gentlemen still do. But the hard core of rugby league players, with their cauliflower ears, their broken noses, their busted and bruised bones, would rather be called, to use a three-letter word, MEN ... It's a down-to-earth game played by down-to-earth people. Good people. Solid people. To use that three-letter word again, MEN.[14]

For many years Eddie Waring was the voice of rugby league, an icon of the nation, whose particular West Riding pronunciation of the phrase 'and it's an up'n'under' when describing a high attacking kick (now called in more masculine terms 'the bomb') was mimicked by comedians everywhere. Eddie, the BBC's rugby league commentator, became a well known and much loved figure, with TV appearances on the 'Morecambe and Wise Show' and a job hosting 'It's A Knockout'. However, his fame seemed to eclipse the game of rugby league which he supposedly commentated on, and in the eyes of many rugby league fans Eddie was a northern caricature straight out of the Music Hall who did the image of rugby league no favours.[15] His image of 'the game' was inextricably linked with notions of masculinity, of community, of class, and of 'northern-ness'.[16]

On the issue of class it is clear from previous research that any attempt to make rigid definitions of social identity in rugby league based on economic data gives rise to insurmountable problems.[17] Class as a concept is best understood through the role of perceived consciousness[18] and language.[19] That is, class becomes a cultural marker that is contested and continually (re)defined by both theorists and the people who claim to live in a working-class habitus.[20] Class becomes, following Schutz, a way of making sense of everyday life, or as Fussell suggests, class becomes defined by perceived status and culture.[21] In rugby league, the game's symbolic boundaries and invented traditions are explicitly identified with a working class, hence the claim that rugby league is a working-class game. On the surface this claim is problematic – there are rugby league fans who would define themselves as middle class, there are working-class people at rugby union clubs, rugby league is a capitalist business, football also claims to be a working-class game, and so on. But when understood as a symbol it makes sense. The 'class-ness' of the imaginary community gives both traditionalists and expansionists another way of justifying their positions, with the former claiming southerners are too middle class for rugby league, and the latter arguing that working-classness can be shared globally in a pseudo-Marxist sense of solidarity: it also supports my contention that what is at stake is a tension over the interpretation of symbols and meaning, following the epistemological ideas of Latour, the later writing of Wittgenstein and the primacy of rhetoric theorised by Stanley Fish.[22]

So the code of rugby league uses historical discourses and cultural icons to define belonging and exclusion through imaginary communities. And it is in the symbolic boundaries and mutual knowledge of these imaginary communities, as well as the specific imaginary communities themselves, that rugby league differs from other sports. I suggest that these differences are so real for the people inside the imaginary communities, and that the boundaries are so normalised, that any attempt to merge the two codes of rugby, for example, would result in an uproar from union and league communities similar to that in 1995, in rugby league, over the formation of the Super League. While this would not stop any merger, it may result in the formation of a merged code at the elite, commercial level, and the retention of the two codes at a lower level. In brief, rugby league is perceived by the people inside it as working class, and in this country is inextricably associated with the north of England.

An analysis of the distribution of rugby league clubs (in this country – obviously this section does not apply to rugby league in other countries), both professional and amateur, shows that an overwhelming majority fall into the 'M62 Belt', with another large density of clubs along the west coast of Cumbria. So while rugby league has a regional bias towards the north of England, it is erroneous to say the north of England is rugby league's heartland. Rural areas, the North-East, Liverpool, Manchester, Stockport and (possibly) Sheffield are all areas where rugby league has not established itself. Nevertheless, there is a strong sense of 'northern-ness' among the players, supporters and administrators of rugby league. This perceived natural relationship between rugby league and the north of England is identified by traditionalists who see in the 'northern game' an expression of their distinctive fictive ethnicity and its attendant culture.[23] For example, in my initial research many of the respondents argued quite forcefully that rugby league was a 'northern game', shaped by northern men for northern men.[24] Others spoke of the relationship between this mythical 'northern-ness' and 'the game' through the way in which 'northern-ness', northern identity, was expressed in and through 'the game', in a way similar to the relationship between cricket and expressions of Yorkshire identity and character identified by Russell.[25] Another respondent explained about how 'the game' gave him – as an outsider – a template for the 'northern' form of life, how it 'showed me a way of living, admitted me into a world where I belonged … rugby league has this love affair with its people, its geography, you can't separate it from where it is, it is so involved.'[26]

Coming out of the fog at Bradford Northern

Ellery Hanley's childhood and upbringing is shrouded in mystery, as befits any mythological hero. He was born in Leeds, and it is at a club in Leeds where his rugby league career begins, but other matters are more difficult to clarify. Part of this mystery was cultivated by Hanley himself, who wanted to keep such things private, and who famously refused to talk about his early years in interviews with the press. That said, some facts did emerge in the 1980s about incidents of anti-social behaviour, and time spent in a young offenders' institution.[27] The subsequent tabloid speculation and allegations – playing on the stereotyped image of the wayward black youth – led to Hanley disengaging altogether with the rugby league media, and cultivated in him a need to be careful about revealing any information about his family and upbringing in Leeds. What mattered then, and what matters now, for Hanley, is the construction of a childhood of control, athletic prowess and discipline. In the article in *Yorkshire Life*, Hanley explains that 'I didn't have any heroes … but I had an instinct inside of me from a young age as a competitor. Being disciplined went back to when I was 13 and 14. I never drank alcohol, I never smoked. And that didn't happen because I wanted to be a sportsman, it happened naturally.'[28]

All the public information on official club websites and in Melling and Collins' study, states that Hanley signed professional terms with Bradford Northern in 1978, signing for the club from a junior amateur rugby league club called Corpus Christi. This club was one of many junior and open-age clubs that emerged in the 1970s following the formation of the British Amateur Rugby League Association in 1973. The club was based in the south-east of Leeds at the Corpus Christi Social Club, a working-men's club for Catholics associated with the nearby Corpus Christi church. The working-men's club drew its members from both the inner-city terraces of Harehills and the big council estates of Halton Moor and Belle Isle. In those big estates, the population in the 1970s was predominantly white, and remained so throughout the latter part of the twentieth century and beyond. Harehills, however, had always been more multiethnic and multicultural: a large Irish population being supplemented in the 1970s by black families moving down the road from Chapeltown, with a growing British Asian community nearer the city centre. The Irish Catholicism of the social club dictated a working-class whiteness to its members, then, but the sports teams that were based at the club attracted (and continue to attract) a more diverse range of participants.

Until the formation of BARLA, there was no structured, junior rugby league. Corpus Christi JARLC was formed to play in the rapidly changing junior leagues that followed the establishment of BARLA, and which were, in West Yorkshire, the precursors to the Yorkshire Juniors Amateur Rugby League. The club itself did not

182

survive very long, which was common for amateur rugby league teams throughout the 1970s and 1980s, as enthusiasts gave up or merged their clubs with ones with a more sustainable base. Many of Corpus Christi's volunteers and players merged with the open-age club Yew Tree (formed as a pub team) to become East Leeds, a club which still exists in the elite National Conference of BARLA, and which still has as its base a working-men's club. The Corpus Christi club, however, is still remembered by rugby league fans not only because of its connection with Hanley, but also for its association with the fearsome reputation of amateur rugby league teams from Leeds.

On the totalrl.com website, owned by the publishers of League Express and Rugby League World, there are two stories that exemplify this folk memory of Corpus Christi. The first story's narrator tells the tale of seeing Hanley in his playing days for Corpus Christi:

> My first game was to see one of my cousins in an amateur game during the seventies, my dad took me to see Redhill [from Castleford] play Corpus Christi [from Leeds]. I think it might have been a final or summat, as there were loads of people there. My cousin was lining up alongside Andy Goodway for Redhill, and playing opposite Ellery at pivot. Redhill won, and my cousin put Ellery in the shade that day, although I think Ellery might have had the better record at senior level.

> (Posted by Cas_Vegas_Merged, 6 October 2006, First RL Game Went To? Thread, The Rugby League Express Forum, totalrl.com)

In telling this story about his cousin, the narrator both brings Ellery Hanley to our level, but also reifies Hanley's subsequent career as a professional rugby league player. The story also confirms that Hanley, in his days at Corpus Christi, was already a play-maker and the key individual in the team (as he was at the height of his professional career); furthermore, Hanley's early pro career on the wing may be seen as another example of the stacking mentality towards black players, where white coaches and managers select black players in team games in positions where speed is important – and white players in positions of leadership and control.[29] The second story on the website mentions Corpus Christi in the context of a discussion about rough teams from Leeds:

> Another team from Leeds who a lot are writing about on this forum recently, is Queens they started of [sic] in the lower divisions of the Yorkshire League, players in that era for Queens, Andy Wilson, Derek Bridgeman, who played with a disability basically playing with one arm both these players went on to play for Sheffield Eagles, Bridgeman a very powerful player, Martin Richardson, a big prop called Freddie, Alf Weston ex Castleford forward. Queens in them days played on Scott Hall Road more than half the team

were coloured, and had a huge following. Very intimidating playing at Queens in those days. Also another tough place to go Belle Isle who played on the fields where Hunslet Parkside jnrs now play, you had to have your wits about you at 3.30pm when the Belle Isle pub kicked out & the bar crowd descended to the match. Just another piece of useless info another junior rugby team played on that same field called Corpus Christie [sic] in that team Ellery Hanley.

(Posted by Ralph2, 31 January 2008, Defunct Winners Thread, National Conference League Forum, totalrl.com)

The narrator of this story begins with old-fashioned comments about the ethnicity of the Queens players, as well as some expression of hegemonic masculinity through the sheer manliness of the player with one arm. Queens is one of the few clubs in amateur rugby league in the north of England (along with Queensbury in Bradford, and a couple of clubs in Huddersfield) that has an established tradition of black players, supporters and volunteers, though it has never been a club identified as only for black people like the cricket clubs identified in North-East Leeds by Ben Carrington.[30] The narrator moves from Queens to the council estate of Belle Isle, where the atmosphere is equally intimidating. But there is no mention of 'colour': the working-class crowd falling out of the Belle Isle pub will have been white, then as now. It is here that the narrator is reminded, seemingly in the act of composing the post, of the fact that Corpus Christi played on the same Belle Isle pitch. Again, the club is made notable because of the presence of Hanley – but what reception Hanley received as a black teenager from the patrons of the pub, rival teams from Yorkshire such as Redhill, or the supporters of his own team, is not known. What is known is that he stood out enough for his performances to be noted and remembered – and to be signed, as a seventeen-year old, in 1978, by Bradford Northern.

At that time, Bradford Northern was re-emerging as a top club following a decline and fall that had seen the original club collapse in 1964; there had been a rapid drop in attendances and only 324 spectators had turned up for a game against Barrow in the massive hole in the ground that is Odsal Stadium. The new club, formed in 1964, retained the name Bradford Northern – Northern was a reminder of the original club's formation in 1907, when the club called Bradford, a founding member of the Northern Rugby Union, converted to association football to become Bradford (Park Avenue) AFC.[31] The rugby supporters at the time rejected the switch to 'soccer', and founded Bradford (Northern Union) as a perpetual snub to the faddishness of association football, and to the middle-class rugby followers who had suggested that the club rejoin the Rugby Football Union.[32] Bradford Northern not only meant the Northern Union; it came to exemplify the northern quality of rugby league, its association with mills and the black-stained gritstone of Bradford's city centre. Odsal Stadium, high above the pollution of that city centre, hidden in a vast glacial hole that attracted fog and rain in unpredictable ways, epitomised the damp, cold, muddy conditions of rugby league in the era before the switch to summer and the Super League. Northern's supporters took the exposed conditions in a stoical manner, but for visitors Odsal remained a fearsome place to be – even a crowd of 10,000 barely filled its open terraces.

Hanley signed up to a club that had already won a Premiership trophy under the leadership of coach Peter Fox, a dour Yorkshire sporting hero from a famous rugby league family. Peter Fox had many idiosyncrasies as a coach, but he understood that British rugby league was a perfect alchemy of brutality and flair; he looked for players who could square up to the opposition in one moment, and make a sweeping pass-and-dash through the defence in the next. Ellery Hanley typified this contrast: he made his debut at Odsal against Rochdale Hornets on 26 November 1978, and scored the first of his 89 tries for Northern. At first, like so many black professional rugby players in the twentieth century, Hanley played on the wing,[33] but his ability to read and control the game helped him overcome any stereotypical stacking, and he started to appear in the centres, then, finally, at the pivotal stand-off position. By the early 1980s, Hanley was a regular fixture in the Northern first team, earning the nickname Mister Magic, and in 1984 he won his first cap for Great Britain against France, going on to be selected for an Ashes tour where he scored 12 tries. His pace and strength in his Northern years are highlighted in the collective memory of rugby league fans: Tony Collins refers to a length-of-field Hanley try in the 1983 Challenge Cup semi-final against Featherstone Rovers and describes it as 'embodying everything that he came to symbolise. It was based on strength and speed. It highlighted his self-confidence. But most of all it demonstrated his unquenchable determination to succeed'.[34] This try, coming as it did in a match shown on BBC television, introduced Hanley to a wider, *Grandstand*-watching audience across the country. The footage of the try was disseminated in VHS recordings through the 1980s and 1990s, and it has found a place on YouTube in a multi-clip tribute to Ellery Hanley's try-scoring and try-making abilities: a tribute that refers to him by his more famous nickname in rugby league, 'The Black Pearl'.

The Black Pearl

In the 1984–5 season, Ellery Hanley scored 57 tries for Bradford Northern in only thirty-seven appearances. His ability to score tries was matched by his professionalism and commitment to training, in an era of British rugby league where old-fashioned notions about natural talent were only just coming to be challenged by Australian methods of coaching and player development. Hanley was a model professional, an outsider in teams of hard men, boozers and overweight prop forwards. In the

Australianisation that followed the disastrous Ashes series of 1982, when the Australians won every single match against a British side, players and coaches who preferred the pull of pints to pulling weights were seen as liabilities at the top rugby league clubs. This was the beginning of the dominance of Australian coaches in the British game, and the beginning of the great rush to replace British players with younger, fitter, faster, yet stronger, more professional Australians. Hanley became a precious commodity, a British-born player who could compete with the Australians, and in 1985 he signed for Wigan for a transfer fee of £150,000 plus two players.

Wigan, across the Pennines in the historical county of Lancashire,[3] had been one of rugby league's most famous, and most successful, clubs, for much of the twentieth century. In 1980, however, the club was relegated for the first and only time in its history. Although Wigan regained a position in the old first division the following season, the drop led to a reorganisation of the club's board. Coming to power was a triumvirate of businessmen with a determination to adopt Australian methods on and off the pitch: Jack Robinson, Tom Rathbone and Maurice Lindsay. Under their leadership, with Lindsay increasingly the sole decision maker, Wigan's first-team became full-time professionals – a practice common in Australia but unheard of until then in the British game. Marketing and sponsorship deals raised spare cash, and this was used to pay players huge salaries: the incentives of full-time salaries compared to match-winning bonuses and expenses meant Wigan quickly attracted the attention of the best players (and, increasingly, their agents) in Britain, Australia and New Zealand. It was inevitable, then, that Wigan would be the club to entice Hanley away from Bradford: Lindsay made sure personally that Hanley signed the deal that took him over the hill along the M62 into the brave new world of Craven Park.

Under Maurice Lindsay, Wigan brought globalisation and the commodification of late modernity to rugby league. Denham has argued that Lindsay played a pivotal role in supporting the deal with News Corporation that led to the postmodern spectacle of the summer Super League. [36] As fan writer Harry Waller puts it, in the fanzine *The Greatest Game*:[37]

> Here at TGG Towers we're completely split down the middle about assessing Maurice's impact on rugby league. On the one hand, the dominance of Wigan, the selling-out to Rupert Murdoch, and the resultant lost years of international rugby league, mark Maurice out as a pariah. But on the other hand, the professionalisation of rugby union in the 1990s could have wiped out British rugby league completely as a professional sport if it wasn't for Maurice. He saw the threat to league from union, and the News Corp money came in just at the right time to keep rugby league alive. Our hesitation over whether he was a hero or a villain is no doubt repeated in every rugby league home in the country, though it would be a fair guess to suggest more people

think the latter, rather than the former. The long memories in Featherstone ... cast a shadow over Maurice's achievements.[38]

Hanley excelled in his six years at Wigan, though his try-scoring ability and leadership did not stop him from being put on the transfer list for disagreeing with the Wigan establishment over unspecified off-field issues. But even Lindsay knew getting rid of Hanley would be a stupid move, and when Wigan reached the semi-final of the Challenge Cup, coach New Zealander Graham Lowe recalled Hanley to the team. Hanley steered Wigan through to the final, and won the Lance Todd Trophy for the man-of-the-match in helping Wigan lift the Cup. At Wigan, Hanley established himself as the club captain and as a regular International for Great Britain, playing at stand-off and later, at loose forward; both these positions were decision-making roles in the game. He captained Great Britain in the 1988 Ashes series, leading the team to the first Test victory against Australia in ten years. He won numerous accolades, including twice being voted the British rugby league Man of Steel. That first Challenge Cup Final victory was followed by another three in a row for Hanley and for Wigan.

The late 1980s were a period in rugby league history when clubs from the Australian Rugby League, rich with earnings from sponsorship deals and gambling machines in their leagues clubs,[39] took advantage of relaxed rules on short-term contracts to buy in the best British rugby league players. As both the Australian Rugby League and the Rugby Football League played in winter, players could play all-year round, if their clubs were willing to release them, by moving from one part of the globe to another. Ellery Hanley was one of the players targeted by the Australians. In his first season down under he turned out for Balmain. It was his performance at Balmain, helping them to a Grand Final, and his heroics for Great Britain in the 1988 Ashes series, that led Australian journalists to call him the Black Pearl. This unsubtle compliment, of course, was double-edged. Hanley was a pearl of a player, of course, but pearls are not normally black. The nickname played on his exotic Otherness[40], as well as his unique athleticism and physicality. This casual racism by way of support was typical of the Australian rugby league community – Mal Meninga had been nicknamed 'Chicken George'[41] by that community – but whatever the meaning of the Black Pearl, the name stuck. When he returned to Australia to play for Wests in 1989, and when he played for Great Britain in later test matches, the Black Pearl was who he was. Eventually, the name was adopted in the British rugby league community, something many fans and journalists saw as unproblematic, like calling a lump of coal black. He was black, he was a pearl, therefore he was the black pearl: the simple logic obscured the racialisation of difference.

187

The outsider

The years between signing for Wigan and the end of the Ashes series in Australia in 1992 delineate Hanley's heroic status. He became the captain of his club and country. He became, along with Martin Offiah,[42] one of the most famous British rugby league players ever (the pair were certainly the most famous black rugby league players) – but unlike Offiah, the joke-cracking, sophisticated public-school boy from the south of England, Hanley was a proper northerner, someone nurtured in the grassroots of the game. And unlike Offiah, Hanley, at the height of his career, decided to stop giving interviews to journalists, whether they were from national newspapers or rugby league magazines. This reluctance to talk about his past was triggered, according to Collins, by tabloid stories in the mid-eighties about Hanley's criminal past.[43] His high profile as a black captain of a professional rugby league team, and later as a black captain of Great Britain, made Hanley a high-profile sports celebrity, the most visible rugby league player of his generation. For tabloid reporters looking for sex and sleaze stories, professional athletes were obvious targets. Hanley's evident mistrust of anyone inquiring into his past has already been noted – that mistrust led to a long silence in the rugby league press, which in turn led to rugby league journalists, administrators and fans questioning Hanley's commitment to the game and its values of working-class honesty and community. In my doctoral research in the early 1990s, in conversation in a pub I was told that certain black players like Ellery Hanley and Martin Offiah 'couldn't give a shit about rugby league, they're not bothered about tradition, they just want our cash.'[44] The use of the possessive 'our' is significant – even though both players mentioned had boosted rugby league's national profile, and had helped teams like Widnes, Wigan and Leeds (as well as the national side) to success, they were still not seen as 'ours', and as such dismissed as uncaring mercenaries (when in fact both players have expressed pride in rugby league as 'their' game). It seems that playing for money, as a living, is seen as morally inferior to playing rugby league for the love of 'the game', an attitude that paradoxically resonates with the sound of outraged defenders of rugby's amateurism such as the Rev. Frank Marshall of the 1890s.[45] Yet there is a clear case of double standards – white players, those who come from 'the game', are seen as role models when they sign big contracts, unlike the black players.

Hanley signed for his home-town club Leeds in September 1991, becoming both coach and captain, and alienating the Wigan fans who saw his move as an act of disloyalty and avarice. Hanley was linked at this time with the London Monarchs American Football Club, and was involved in their publicity, though ultimately he stayed with rugby league. In 1992, although he captained Great Britain in the Ashes series of that year, his performance was hampered by injuries. Leeds struggled to win any of the game's major competitions, losing the Challenge Cup final in 1994 to Wigan, whose try-scoring prodigy Martin Offiah humiliated Leeds with a length-of-the-field try that left Leeds full back Alan Tait red-faced and wilting in the heat of the afternoon. Losing to Wigan did not stop Hanley becoming coach of Great Britain – the first black Great Britain or England coach or manager in a professional team sport – though his tenure was brief and did not bring any lasting success. In 1995, Leeds again, under Hanley, faced Wigan at Wembley in the Challenge Cup, and again the Yorkshire club lost to their Lancashire rivals.

Despite his age, Hanley still managed to score 41 tries in his final season at Leeds; in the bidding war of the Super League era, Hanley was still seen as star commodity, and he found himself on an Australian Rugby League (the anti-Super League faction, or official faction, depending on whether you sided with Rupert Murdoch or not) contract and playing for Balmain Tigers. With Super League in contractual accord with the Rugby Football League in Europe, but engaged in struggle with the Australian Rugby League that culminated in a rival Australian Super League competition in 1997, Hanley found himself distanced from rugby league in Great Britain. Some of his supporters were now standard bearers for News Corporation, and any coaching career in the 'European' Super League seemed impossible. A return to the Great Britain coaching job was unlikely – but the truce between the two factions gave Hanley his chance to coach a Super League side. In 1999 he became the head coach of St Helens, and in his first season he took the club to a Super League Grand Final victory against his old club Bradford. His professionalism was recognised by his players, and by the Saints fans who continue to nominate him as one of the club's best coaches of the Super League era[46]. As before, however, his outsider status, and his refusal to compromise in his dealings with the press and officials, led to him disagreeing publicly in the 2000 season with some of the decisions made by the club's board of directors. It was only a matter of weeks before he was sacked by Saints – and with that, he dropped out of the game by taking up the offer of a coaching position in rugby union.

Returning hero at Doncaster: working-class icon and skating celebrity

In his absence, rugby league fans started to mythologise his abilities. A brief stint as coaching consultant at Castleford in 2004 did not turn into a permanent job, or yield a record of success. But his name became a regular sight on internet forums whenever a coach was sacked, and supporters started to speculate about who would replace that coach. Hanley started to appear in newspaper and magazine sports stories, but as a squash coach and a coaching consultant. It seemed that the trauma of Saint Helens in 2000 and Castleford in 2004 had been enough for Hanley, yet incredibly, in 2007, he was lured back to rugby league to coach National League Two side Doncaster Lakers in the 2008 season. Seemingly without effort, Hanley took the part-timers and veteran players at Doncaster all the way to the Grand Final, where they won promotion to National League One.

At the moment of success, Hanley made the decision to resign – again, under a cloud of speculation, this time over the financial situation of the club, or promises that had not been met, or some other, more enigmatic fall-out between Hanley and the men who employed him. Whatever the truth of the matter, the success at Doncaster followed by the resignation lifted Hanley's profile nationally and in the North: he was a working-class icon once again, northern sporting hero, and one with enough spare time to be able to concentrate on training for his new (albeit temporary) resurrection as a skating celebrity. Just months after leaving Doncaster, his appearance on *Dancing on Ice* was announced, and in the first episode it was revealed that he had been training for weeks to prepare himself for the twin ordeals of garnering the public vote and pleasing the panel of professional judges.

Hanley's iconic status as a northern sporting hero is, then, assured. But his unwillingness to compromise in some of his professional relationships, and in his dealings with the rugby league press and the wider sporting media, could have outweighed his playing record. Furthermore, his blackness always marked him out as an outsider in the closed community of rugby league in the north of England: like many other successful black players before him such as Billy Boston and Cec Thompson, he had to prove his worth as a northern man on and off the pitch, he had to be better than any of his white contemporaries just to have his blackness unremarked upon – and when he transgressed, he transgressed as a black man.[47] For Hanley, his negotiation into 'the game' was aided by his working-class background, and his athletic prowess, but his status as icon was never truly assured until his playing days were over, and the controversies of silence and Otherness were replaced by a nostalgia for his skills and ability.

The implication, then, is that 'the game' is inextricably linked to a sense of northern identity that is justified with recourse to the past, and which is expressed through the values seemingly inherent in 'the game' such as working-class honesty, 'pride', distinctiveness, manliness, toughness and physicality, equality of opportunity – 'a chance for any man to play according to his ability', and tension with southerners and the middle class. This sense of northern identity is seen as a source of strength for the traditionalists, for whom the relationship is natural and unassailable, and an articulation of their own sense of personal and social identity. Expansionists do not deny this 'northern-ness' an important role in defining and being defined by 'the game'. However, they feel it is the source of rugby league's failure to capture the imagination of populations outside the traditional heartland – as such, expansionist writers such as Phil Melling, Tony Collins and David Hadfield both recognise this relationship between 'the game' and 'northern-ness', and criticise and deconstruct the seemingly natural, normalised status of the relationship.[48]

Implicit throughout the construction of a northern identity is an understanding that the identity constructed is masculine: it is the northern man identified in the discourse of respondents and sources both in this chapter and previous writing. Given the way in which the imaginary communities of rugby league and other team sports produce, maintain, affirm and express masculine identity – particularly the hegemonic masculinity of western society – it is not too surprising to find his equivalent northerner present in the discourse surrounding 'northern-ness', particularly in rugby league and the invented traditions of 'the game'. It is this northern man that is the template for the fictive ethnicity of the population of the imaginary community, the cultural icon that defines belonging, that is supported by the invented traditions, and which shapes shared meanings, mutual knowledge and symbolic boundaries. Hence southerners are excluded from the definitions of proper belonging in 'the game' and women struggle to be accepted on equal terms to men if they take on roles other than the passive supporter or the wife/girlfriend. And black men like Hanley have their status as rugby-league playing northern role-models on a temporary basis, to be challenged if they themselves challenge the norms and values of the imaginary community of rugby league. Only now that Hanley's status is recognised beyond rugby league, and even beyond sport, can he be confident of his place in rugby league's history.

---

[1] C. Titley, 'The ice man cometh', *Yorkshire Life*, March, 2009, pp. 142–4. Christa, as a woman, is of course, subordinate on the programme to the much more famous anchorman Harry Gration, an ex-official of the Rugby Football League himself and a competitor for the title of most archetypal professional Yorkshireman alongside Dickie Bird, Richard Whiteley and, perhaps, Michael Parkinson.

[2] K. Spracklen, 'Black Pearls, Black Diamonds: Exploring Racial Identities in Rugby League', in B. Carrington and I. McDonald (eds), *'Race', Sport and British Society* (London, 2001), pp. 70–82.

[3] T. Kenneally, *A Family Madness* (Sevenoaks, 1985), pp. 31–2.

[4] P. Bourdieu, *In Other Words: Towards a Reflexive Sociology* (Cambridge, 1990); M. Ely, *Doing Qualitative Research: Circles within Circles* (London, 1991); W.F. Whyte, *Street Corner Society* (4th edn) (London, 1993).

[5] G. Moorhouse, *At The George* (Sevenoaks, 1989) and *A People's Game* (Sevenoaks, 1995); J. Vose, *Up t'Rovers* (Blackpool, 1992); I. Clayton and M. Steele, *When Push Comes to Shove* (Castleford, 1993); I. Clayton, *Merging on the Ridiculous* (Castleford, 1995).

[6] P. Dine, 'Money, identity and conflict: rugby league in France', *The Sports Historian*, 16 (1996), pp. 99–116; P. Dine, *French Rugby Football: A Cultural History* (Oxford, 2001); R. Fassolette, 'Rugby league football in France 1934–1954: the decisive years and their long-term consequences', *Sport in History*, 27, 3 (2007), pp. 380–98; K. Spracklen and C. Spracklen, 'Negotiations of being and becoming: minority ethnic rugby league

players in the Cathar country of France', *International Review for the Sociology of Sport*, 43, 2 (2008), pp. 201–18.

7   An interest that led to a PhD on rugby league and the north of England, and an academic life continuing that research.

8   E. Dunning and K. Sheard, *Barbarians, Gentlemen and Players* (Oxford, 1979); T. Collins, 'Noa Mutton, Noa Laaking: the origins of payment of play in rugby football, 1877–86', *The International Journal of the History of Sport*, 12, 1 (1995), pp. 33–50; 'Myth and reality in the 1895 split', *The Sports Historian*, 16 (1996), pp. 33–41; *Rugby's Great Split* (London, 1999) and *Rugby League in Twentieth Century Britain* (London, 2006).

9   A. Cohen, *The Symbolic Construction of Community* (London, 1985).

10 K. Spracklen, 'Playing the ball: constructing community and masculine identity in rugby league', unpublished PhD Thesis, Leeds Metropolitan University, 1996.

11 K. Spracklen, 'Playing the ball'; 'Black Pearls, Black Diamonds'; 'Re-inventing "the game": rugby league, 'race', gender and the growth of active sports in England', in J. Caudwell and P. Bramham (eds), *Sport, Active Leisure and Youth Cultures* (Eastbourne, 2005), pp. 153–67 and 'Negotiations of belonging: Habermasian stories of minority ethnic rugby league players in London and the South of England', *World Leisure Journal*, 49, 4 (2007), pp. 216–26; K. Spracklen and C. Spracklen, 'Negotiations of being and becoming', pp. 201–18; K. Spracklen, J. Long, J. and S. Timmins, 'Remembering, telling and reconstructing: oral histories of the northern working-class at leisure in rugby league', in B. Snape and H. Pussard (eds.) *Recording Leisure Lives: Histories, Archives and Memories of Leisure in 20th Century Britain* (Eastbourne, 2009), pp. 113–28.

12 B. Anderson, *Imagined Communities* (London, 1983).

13 K. Jenkins, *Rethinking History* (London, 1991); E. Hobsbawn and T Ranger (eds), *The Invention of Tradition* (Cambridge, 1983).

14 E. Waring, *Rugby League: The Great Ones* (London, 1969), flyleaf.

15 S. Kelner, *To Jerusalem and Back* (London, 1996), chapter one.

16 J. Williams, '"Up and under". Eddie Waring, television and the image of rugby league', *The Sports Historian*, 22, 1 (2002), pp. 115–37.

17 Spracklen, 'Playing the ball' and 'Black Pearls'.

18 H. Davis, *Beyond Class Images* (London, 1979).

19 P. Corfield, *Language, History and Class* (Oxford, 1991), G. Stedman Jones, *Languages of Class* (Cambridge, 1983).

20 P. Bourdieu, *Reproduction in Education, Society and Culture* (London, 1977).

21 A Schutz, *The Phenomenology of the Social World* (London, 1972); P. Fussell, *Class* (New York, 1983).

22 B. Latour, *The Pasteurization of France* (Cambridge, 1988); L. Wittgenstein, *Philosophical Investigations* (Oxford, 1968); S. Fish, *There's No Such Thing as Free Speech* (New York and Oxford, 1994).

23 Moorhouse, *At the George*; Clayton and Steele, *When Push comes to Shove*.

24 Spracklen, 'Playing the ball'.

25 D. Russell, 'Amateurs, professionals and the construction of social identity', *The Sports Historian*, 16 (1996), pp. 64–80.

26 Spracklen, 'Playing the ball', p. 240.

27 P. Melling and T. Collins, *The Glory of Their Times* (Skipton, 2004).

28 Titley, 'Ice man', p. 144.

29 J. Long, B. Carrington and K. Spracklen, '"Asians cannot wear turbans in the scrum": explorations of racist discourse within professional rugby league', *Leisure Studies*, 16, 4 (1997), pp. 249–60.

30 B. Carrington, 'Sport, masculinity and black cultural resistance', *Journal of Sport and Social Issues*, 22, 3 (1998), pp. 275–98.

31 Following another Bradford rugby club, Manningham, who became Bradford City.

32 Those rugby union supporters then proceeded to found a rugby union club, so that the original Bradford club's followers were divided across three football codes.

33 Long, Carrington and Spracklen, 'Asians cannot wear turbans'.

34 T. Collins, 'Ellery Hanley', in P. Melling and T. Collins (eds) *The Glory of Their Times* (Skipton, 2004), p. 178.

35 Technically, of course, Wigan is in Greater Manchester. But the pedant is reminded that the historical counties of England continue to exist as geographical entities, if not political ones.

36 D. Denham 'Global and local influences on rugby league', *Sociology of Sport*, 21, 3 (2004), pp. 206–19.

37 The rugby league equivalent of *When Saturday Comes*, and a fanzine that was once edited by the author of this chapter, as well as Tony Collins.

38 H. Waller, 'Maurice Lindsay: Nero or Caesar?', *The Greatest Game*, 54 (2008), p. 10.

39 What British readers might think of as social clubs, but on a vast, casino-sized scale.

40 S. Opotow,'Moral exclusion and injustice: an introduction', *Journal of Social Sciences*, 46, 1 (1990), pp. 1–20; Spracklen, 'Black Pearls'.

41 A black American slave character from the novel and TV drama series 'Roots'. Meninga is a member of Australia's indigenous community.

42 Offiah's iconic status is also recognised in the way he became, years after his retirement, a celebrity dancer on the BBC celeb-reality programme 'Strictly Come Dancing'.

43 Collins, 'Hanley', pp. 183–4.

44 Spracklen, 'Playing the ball', p. 249.

45 Dunning and Sheard, *Barbarians*; Collins, *Great Split*.

46 There are regular polls on the two biggest rugby league fan websites, totalrl.com and rlfans.com, and Hanley has been cited as one of the best coaches and one of best players in every one of them, whether they are polls about St Helens or about rugby league in general. Hanley is also in the RFL Hall of Fame, and is celebrated on the Australian fan website eraofthebiff.com.

47 C. Thompson, *Born on the Wrong Side* (Durham, 1995).

48 Melling and Collins, *Glory*; D. Hadfield, XIII Winters (London, 1994).

CHAPTER 11

John Conteh: More Kirby than Knightsbridge

John Sugden

Liverpool stands alongside Havana, Mexico City, New York and Detroit as one of boxing's premier breeding grounds. Hundreds of fighters such as Tommy Burke, Johnny Cooke, Billy Gannon, Hogan Bassey, Dick Tiger, Alan Rudkin, and of course, John Conteh, threw their first punches in one or more of the tough training gymnasia that pepper the city's working-class neighbourhoods.[1] In 2008 the city celebrated its status as Europe's Capital of Culture. In the build up to and unfolding of this portentous event the City's most famous celebrity sons and daughters were paraded as the embodiment of Liverpool's proud cultural heritage. Pop stars, poets, comedians, authors, playwrights, composers, artists and footballers were wheeled out to remind the world what prodigious talent the City had spawned in the postwar period. Missing from this roll of honour was John Conteh, arguably the best pound for pound professional boxer Britain has ever produced.

In more ways than one, Conteh was one of British sport's first superstars. In 1974 he beat Argentinean Jorge Ahmuda to become WBC Light-heavyweight Champion of the World and in the same year won the popular television competition 'Superstars', as well as being voted second in that year's BBC's prestigious 'Sports Personality of the Year' awards. A shade over six feet tall, Conteh was a muscular and handsome mixed-race light heavyweight. If George Best was the 'fifth Beatle' then John Conteh must have been the sixth and both men had the same incompatible characteristics: exceptional sporting talent, film star good looks and an insatiable appetite for the good life. One sportswriter perfectly captured Conteh's mix of Adonis and Hercules when he said of him, 'I'd love to borrow his body for the weekend. There are a couple of ladies I fancy and a couple of guys I detest.'[2] This perfectly encapsulates the reasons for Conteh's prodigious rise, calamitous down-fall and partial resurrection. The remainder of this chapter provides a detailed consideration of the personal, social and economic factors that framed and formed Liverpool's most famous boxer's turbulent career.

Those of us that either live in or come from the 'City of Culture' share a sense of pride that our home town should be singled out as a source of transnational creative energy and cultural dissemination. For some, however, there is an accompanying sense of uneasiness that our beloved town had been honoured in a way that suggests conventionality, conformity and incorporation into some pan-European urban establishment. More counter-culture than mainstream, Liverpool is anything but conventional and it does not feel particularly 'European' – despite a few token pavement cafes, bistros and cabinets full of European football trophies. Liverpool is a world city, a western-facing seaport which, in terms of cultural space and place, sits somewhere offshore between Dublin and New York. Its people – *Scousers* – have dialect which is more than a little of both. Liverpool is a brash, loud, hard and feisty city that wears its rich and long-standing African-immigrant heritage on its sleeve and John Conteh embodies all of this.

If you were given the task of designing a social, economic and cultural environment out of which to produce professional boxers you would be hard pressed to come up with anything better than Liverpool. More than any other sport, boxing thrives in the cracks between downtown poverty and uptown prosperity. While versions of *mano mano* combative events have been around since the beginnings of recorded history, the roots of the modern form of boxing are found in the booming cities of Regency England; that period after the Puritan government of Cromwell and before the new moralities and disciplines of the Victorian age imposed a more formal agenda for high and popular culture.[3] Sons and daughters of the wealthy and the powerful abandoned their country estates seeking diversion and entertainment in towns like London and Bristol while a displaced peasantry swelled these same urban spaces in search of work and shelter. The rough and ready pastimes of the desperate urban poor were perfectly suited to be exploited to feed the appetites of the sporting gentry or as Pierce Egan, a chronicler of the times and widely regarded as England's first sport journalist, called them the 'Fancy' – a gathering of *nouveaux riches* dilettantes whose staple activities were drinking, whoring and gambling. Alongside horse racing and cock fighting, boxing grew to be the sport of choice for the Fancy, not as participants, but as patrons, spectators and above all speculators. In this pre-dawn of industrialism there was no shortage of men who would take a chance in the ring: impoverished coal heavers; dockers; chair men (Sedan Chair carriers); demobbed soldiers and sailors; and even a few freed slaves. While much has changed in boxing since the Regency, the link that connects hardship and working-class urban poverty with the professional ring is as strong as ever.

Liverpool does not feature in the annals of boxing's bare knuckle pre-history. Until the late eighteenth century Liverpool was not much more than a small provincial coastal outpost. Slavery and textiles changed all of that.[4] Liverpool was one of the corners of the notorious 'triangular trade' via which ships full of tit tat and trinkets sailed to Africa's West Coast to trade for and fill their unkempt holds with bewildered kidnapped men, women and children destined for sale in the slave auctions of the West Indies and Mainland America. The proceeds from these auctions were then used to buy tons of cotton for use in the textile mills of East Lancashire where it would be turned to fabrics to help feed the boom in the first wave of capitalist mass consumer culture in Europe and further afield. Liverpool was the main conduit for this odious commerce and prospered to become the second city of Great Britain's burgeoning Victorian Empire. As Zack-Williams observes, 'the discovery of the New World and subsequent trade in human cargo transformed what was a small fishing port of little significance into a major seaport that has been described as the Gateway of the Empire'.[5]

In the nineteenth and early twentieth centuries, as emerging New World economies sought labour for their own commercial and industrial revolutions, Liverpool became a staging post for desperate migrants fleeing the famine, poverty and political persecution of their native countries. Waves of Irish, Italian, Polish, Scandinavian, German and Russian immigrants bound for New York and Boston mustered in Liverpool. Most sailed away but many stayed, adding to the City's exotic social mix. Slavery and migration gave way to mercantile trade as Liverpool grew to be the key western facing port, first of the Empire and then the Commonwealth. As a child in Liverpool in the 1950s and early 1960s I have vivid memories of travelling with my grandfather on the 'Dockers Umbrella', an overhead railway that connected dockyards from Seaforth in the North, past Queens, the Pier Head and Salthouse, to Garston in the City's South End. The bustling quaysides were crammed with exotically named cargo ships and ocean going passenger liners bearing the colourful funnels and liveries of Cunard, Blue Star, Empire, Elderdempster, Palm Line, and Pacific and Orient.

The sea has been a central influence in the City's distinctive culture, shaped on the one hand by the predilections of a wealthy merchant class, and on the other by the memories and memorabilia of a more transient gathering of migrants, sailors and stevedores. Where I grew up, there was hardly a family in any street that did not have at least one member who was connected to the sea. We listened to the tales of derring-do dads, uncles and cousins brought home from Sydney, Buenos Aires, Valparaiso, Calcutta and Africa's chillingly named Skeleton Coast. The exotic trinkets that spilled out of battered suit cases were eagerly awaited and absorbed along with the folk tales and sea shanties that were told and sung in parlours and pubs throughout the city.

Conteh's father hailed from Sierra Leone and was one of the thousands of foreign sailors to follow the tide into Liverpool, meet a local girl and never ship out. As Stephen Small illustrates, Liverpool's black population has a markedly different profile than that of most other British cities. To begin with it is the longest established, with many families being resident in the city for several generations and as such classifiable as 'indigenous'. Secondly, while there is a West Indian presence, the majority of Liverpool's black population hail originally from Africa's west coast. Finally, there is a much longer tradition of inter-racial marrying and Liverpool had, and to some extent still has, high indices of people of mixed race, usually the product of relationships between African men and English or Irish women.[6]

Conteh's father provides a close fit for this profile. He was an African Muslim and his mother was an Irish Catholic. John was born in Liverpool 8 (Toxteth) on 27 March 1951, the fourth eldest in a family of ten children, with seven brothers and two sisters. In the days before 'new towns' and urban gentrification, Toxteth betrayed most of the characteristics of a 'zone of transition' identified in the urban ecological model of city life developed by the Chicago School in early twentieth-century North America.[7] Sandwiched between the city centre, the docks and a belt of warehouses and factories, what a century earlier had been a neighbourhood of large townhouses for prosperous merchants and bankers, Toxteth was redeveloped as a warren of run-down apartments, bed-sits and tenements for accommodating the city's poor: a classic 'zone' and not most people's neighbourhood of choice as a foundation for a conventional journey to status and prosperity. It was, however, the perfect place to be born if you aspired to a career in the ring.

Eighteen months later, three miles away in another part of the city I would take my first breaths of air. Conteh and I were indirectly connected inasmuch as my father was a Detective Constable in the Liverpool City Police, based in C Division at the heart of which was Toxteth – or 'the Dingle' as it was better known in those days. My dad's accounts of the criminal and rough-house nature of life in Liverpool's South End were reinforced by the folkloric tales of the youth gangs with whom I hung out on the street corners of my own neighbourhood. We might take on 'the Old Swan' or 'the West Darby Road', but, feeding on racialised myths, we would steer well clear of 'the Dingle' and its exotic black and mixed-race gangsters – known locally and pejoratively as 'half castes'.

Liverpool is one of the first truly multi-cultural British cities, but while the city's culture was heavily influenced by contact with different racial and ethnic entities, Liverpool was no melting pot. Liverpool, with one of the first black populations of any significance, also initiated formal and informal processes and rituals of discrimination which today are recognised as institutionalised racism.[8] As the maritime economy slumped and the docks shut down, unemployment soared and while the whole of Liverpool struggled it was the city's black population that suffered most, particularly its youth. Poverty and misery foster resistance. This was graphically illustrated in July 1981 when fierce rioting erupted in Toxteth, the district where Liverpool's black and mixed-race urban poor were clustered leeward of the South End dockyards. As Zack-Williams observes, the Toxteth riots were the product of years of frustration born of 'the long term problems of racism in housing, education, health, and employment matched with a prevalent feeling of police brutality'.[9] As John Conteh said himself of this conflagration:

> The only thing that surprised me about that was that it took so many years for the resentment to manifest itself in unashamed civil disobedience. The reasons for this outburst have always been apparent in the backstreets of Liverpool for generations, yet no one ever really did anything about it.[10]

While this is where his social roots lay, young John would not stay in the South End for long. Conteh's father was a strict disciplinarian who demanded obedience and respect from his children – especially his sons. But he also wanted them to have the best opportunities and recognised the dangers and temptations that pervaded the tenements and streets of Liverpool's South End. Across Britain in the early 1960s an ambitious project of urban redevelopment and relocation was underway. In the language of the developers, the slums were torn down and the people of 'the zone' were enticed to move to brand new high-rise council estates and whole 'new towns' at the far periphery of the city. Put another way, long-established working-class communities had their hearts ripped out as their displaced inhabitants were transported to live in characterless grids of soulless, box-like houses and flats – albeit with hot and cold running water and indoor, flush lavatories.

Constructed on farmland north east of Liverpool, Kirkby was one such place. Rightly or wrongly Conteh Senior believed that Kirby would be a better place than Toxteth to bring up his children. His offspring did not share his view. They may have moved to a better house, but they were surrounded by strangers and unlike in the South End stood out as one of the few non-white families. As John recalls, 'when I was four years old, we changed our black ghetto for a white one'.[11] If anything the streets of Kirkby had more predators than those of South Liverpool, especially for the Conteh brothers whose mixed-race complexions made them easy targets for confrontation and conflict. It was for young John a Darwinian existence where the next confrontation was just around the corner. 'There was nothing sweet about those streets either. As a Kid in Kirkby it was only even money that you would get through the day without a barney [fight].'[12]

It was the realisation of this that led Conteh Senior – himself a proven street-fighter and former amateur boxer in Sierra Leone – to introduce John and his brother Robert to amateur boxing. It is a misconception that young working-class boxers are already the toughest kids, attracted to the gym to improve their already considerable street fighting skills. On the contrary, most join boxing clubs because they help them to avoid the rough and tumble of the streets, affording the opportunity to develop the atavistic skills and attitudes germane to youth cultures in inner-city neighbourhoods in a relatively safe and rewarding environment.[13] 'I never did relish the iron bar, the plank of wood, the half-a-knacker [half-brick] or the flick knife' recalls Conteh, going on to admit that he was 'physically afraid of street fighting'. When his father gave him the opportunity to take up amateur boxing as an 11-year-old, he recalls 'figuring out that it promised to be a whole lot safer than out on those mean streets'.[14]

Boxing might have been a temporary safe-haven for young John, but, contrary to his father's hopes, it would not keep him out of trouble. By the late 1960s, in my part of town, Kirkby was viewed not so much as a new town but as a new wild west. Fortunately, back then the absence of a cocktail of drug wars and gun culture meant the streets were physically dangerous but not deadly. Nevertheless 'the bizzies' (local slang for police) were omnipresent and frequent visitors to the Conteh household. Along with his brothers, John roamed with Kirkby's teenage street gangs and spent time in and out of reform schools for a series of petty misdemeanours. Then when he was fourteen he was caught breaking into a supermarket and sent to Westbank Approved School in Cheshire for a year, joining two of his younger siblings, Robert and Gerard, who were already there.

John respected his father and had deep affection for his mother as well as his brothers and sisters, but Approved School came as an orderly respite from the predatory environment that lay beyond the doors of his family home in Kirkby – including the local secondary school which appeared to him as little more than a concentrated extension of Kirkby's carnivorous teenage street culture. Run by nuns under the stewardship of a firm but fair Irish Headmaster, in Westbank, which was housed in a converted country manor in acres of grounds with excellent sports facilities, for the first time in his life young Conteh grew to like school. 'I loved life in Westbank,' reflected Conteh, 'so much so that, when I was released, I used to dream of running away from home again and breaking back in there.'[15] Under the influential guidance of P.E. teacher Leo Corcorin, it was in the gymnasium and on the sports field where Conteh excelled most. When years later Conteh went on to win the BBC's multi-event 'Superstars' celebrity contest, he would attribute this not just to years of boxing training but also to the eclectic grounding in sports that he enjoyed during his time at Westbank.

However, once released he was prone to intermittent periods on the dole or in low paid manual labour. While several of his contemporaries – including some of his brothers – drifted into lives of crime, Conteh senior continued to push his talented, but potentially wayward, son into the ring. This was the late 1960s when Liverpool was – and still is – a breeding ground for boxers and, underlining Kirkby's informal status as a 'school for hard knocks', some of the country's best amateur boxers, including Conteh, were nurtured in the town's boxing club under the critical eyes and punishing regime of Charles Atkinson and his assistant Tucker Hetherington. It was also the high point of Liverpool's reign as music capital of the western world with the Beatles and lesser 'Mersey Beat' bands and singers dominating the pop charts at home and abroad. At the same time at Anfield and across Stanley Park at Goodison, other locally born heroes were playing their way to fame and fortune with Liverpool and Everton, two of the country's most successful football clubs. None of this was lost on Conteh who dreamed of breaking free of a mundane and impoverished life to join the ranks of the city's rich and famous. Conteh had no educational qualifications and did not have musical talent. While he was a decent footballer, he was never good enough to make it as a professional. With only a basic education behind him and little in the way of entrepreneurial zest, other than crime, this left one only one route: boxing.

Conteh redoubled his efforts, both in the gym and on the various building sites where he worked as a hod carrier – an occupation that he deliberately took to help him develop fitness, stamina and strength. At every opportunity he also sneaked into the city's professional boxing gyms – a practice that was against ABA (Amateur Boxing Association) regulations – to train alongside and spar with experienced pro' fighters. His rigorous training regime began to pay off in 1970 when he won the ABA senior middle weight title, going on to win Gold in the Commonwealth Games in Edinburgh, beating Tanzanian Titus Samba in the middle weight final. The following year Conteh moved up a weight to light heavy and won his second ABA title.

Conteh's dexterity with hands and feet along with his athleticism and good looks were beginning to draw attention from professional promoters. At its grass roots, amateur boxing is wreathed in a worthy welfare rhetoric, positioning the sport as a harbinger of social reform: keeping potentially wayward young men 'off the streets' and helping to rehabilitate those who may have strayed.[16] While much of this is sincerely meant and in many cases true, it also helps to disguise the other main purpose of inner-city boxing clubs: identifying and recruiting 'hungry' young talent and developing and sifting it for graduation into the professional rings. Once this graduation takes place the language of welfare is replaced by that of the market place as the exploitation of an aspiring young fighter's body capital to generate wealth takes over. History tells us that in most cases this wealth generation is heavily biased towards managers, agents, promoters and sundry hangers-on rather than in favour of the boxers themselves and John Conteh's professional career provides an embodied case of this 'exploitation of disadvantage'.[17]

After his Commonwealth games triumph, Conteh's dream of fame and, particularly, fortune were stronger than ever. Rather than let him wait for the chance to compete in the 1972 Munich Olympics, there were plenty of boxing entrepreneurs lining up to help Conteh fulfil his dreams and when the first opportunity to turn professional was presented to him he took it. As Conteh himself admits, he was an easy touch. 'Lenny Martin rolled up outside our house in a shiny, new, chauffer-driven Rolls Royce. I liked his style. He had brought my mother a bunch of flowers. A bunch of flowers for my dear old mother and I'm anybody's!'[18] No matter that Martin did not even have a licence to be a boxing manager, he had turned up on Conteh's doorstep in a posh car and offered the young protégé £10,000 to sign on the dotted line. In

1971 this was a small fortune, especially in the experience of the Conteh family and John had little hesitation in agreeing to the deal. A sign of things to come in the history of Conteh's financial (mis)management, he only ever received half of this amount out of which he gave £3,000 to his mother.

Like so many of Liverpool's famous sons and daughters, Conteh was packed off to London to seek his fortune. There is a popular sea shanty called 'The Leaving of Liverpool' which is a romantic lament for all of the fortune-seeking seafarers who shipped out of Liverpool never to return. It offers a strong metaphor for the most gifted of Conteh's generation, for whom, given the city's rapid post-1960s economic decline, heartbreaking or not, leaving home was the only route to success. But there is a paradox here: those that leave and are successful not only rarely return, but are also viewed as 'lost' and even resented by those they have left behind. Liverpool's uneasy and often ambivalent relationship with The Beatles once they left best captures this tension, but it might also apply to Conteh. Once in London Martin put Conteh under the tutelage of George Francis, a former Covent Garden porter and ex-bare knuckle prize fighter who would not have looked out of place in a Henry Fielding novel. Conteh lived with Francis and his wife in a small council house in North London. George, who would become one of Conteh's greatest influences, was an old school trainer who believed in fitness first and technique second. Each morning would find Conteh putting in the miles around Hampstead Heath or pounding up and down Parliament Hill before spending hours training in Francis's Camden gym. Francis would go on to train a string of exceptional British fighters, including Frank Bruno. (Tragically, in 2002 Francis, aged 73, would be found hanging in his London home having taken his own life shortly after the loss of his wife and son through cancer.)

Conteh's first professional fight encapsulated the exploitative essence of the trade. It was an era when, unofficially, British boxing was controlled from London by a small number of wealthy Jewish promoters and match makers. Foremost of them was Jack Solomons, who set up the World Sporting Club, a parody of the gentlemen's sporting clubs of Regency England where besuited toffs would gather to be well fed and watered while gambling on the outcomes of pugilistic contests between virtually naked working-class gladiators. As Conteh recalled the scene of his professional debut, where, outside of the ring, the auditorium 'was bathed in soft light from giant, twinkling chandeliers, they [the punters] sipped wine, nibbled at petit fours and smoked large cigars'.[19] The only woman present was the model hired in to parade in a swimsuit in the breaks holding aloft a board indicating which round was coming next. When his turn came, Conteh made the girl redundant by knocking out his opponent, Okacha Boubekeur, an itinerant French-Algerian kitchen porter from Paris, with a left hook 56 seconds into the first round.

The boxing press told the young Liverpool boxer that he had been breathtaking, but Conteh knew better. As is the nature of the match-making game, Boubekeur had been deliberately selected so that the outset of Conteh's career – one that promised to lead to riches for him and those who stuck close – would get off to an unblemished start. So long as he got his fair share, Conteh was prepared to go along with the façade:

> Like any young hopeful, I wanted to believe it, but although I might have been wide eyed and innocent over the prospect of living in London, I was never that ingenuous about professional boxing. There were no illusions from me from the start. I knew that money not glory motivated the men who manipulated the sport from outside of the ropes. Therefore it followed that the people backing me were going to feed me as many easy ones they could reasonably hope to get away with. Boubekeur was one of them. Since I was in the business primarily for financial gain myself, I was not about to complain ... It was only later in my career, when they rolled up the heavy artillery and then tried to pay me peanuts for it, that I fell out with them.[20]

Conteh was on a fast track to stardom. In less than a year, from October 1971 to July 1972, John won all of his first eleven bouts, ten of them by knock out. Even though Conteh had won his amateur laurels at middle weight, in the opening contests of his career he fought as a heavyweight. John's natural fighting weight was light heavy – around twelve and a half stone. He could get away with this so long as he was matched against mediocre fighters, but he was always going to be outgunned if he was paired up with the top heavyweights of his generation which, with people like Joe Frasier, George Foreman and, of course, Muhammad Ali ruling the roost, is acknowledged as the heavy weight division's last golden era. Ali was an admirer of Conteh, having sparred with him in Las Vegas's Caesars Palace gym prior to the Liverpudlian's six-round knock out demolition of fourteen stone Terry Daniels. Despite this easy victory, according to Conteh it was Ali who persuaded George Francis that Conteh should drop down to light heavyweight, and who, in turn, persuaded Conteh that this would be his best chance of becoming a world champion.

This decision soon paid off as less than a month after his victory in Vegas, Conteh was back at the Wembley Arena to win the European light heavyweight crown, knocking out a brave, but bruised and battered German, Rudiger Schmidtke, in the twelfth round. Conteh may have moved down in weight but there was little doubt that he was moving up in class. His next opponent was the established British Boxing legend, Chris Finnigan, a middle weight gold medallist at the 1968 Mexico Olympics and holder of both the British and Commonwealth light heavy weight titles. Conteh's European belt was also on the line, making this contest a triple title clash with a purse of £34,000 to be split equally between the two opponents. It was a classic match up between Finnegan, the experienced southpaw counter puncher, and Conteh with his quick hands and feet and vicious left hook. Conteh won a unanimous points decision and those watching compared him favourably with the all-time great, Sugar Ray Robinson.

While successes in the ring were beginning to mount up, outside of it the small cracks that were to widen to blight his career were also beginning to appear. Post-swinging 60s London was still full of temptation for a handsome young fighter with money burning holes in his pockets. George Francis, who had old fashioned ideas about boxing, in which there was no room for booze and women, kept Conteh under close surveillance. Chaperoning was not so easy for Francis in Las Vegas where outside of his gaze Conteh managed to have a passionate liaison with Barbra Wilson, a beautiful, black sales assistant who according to Conteh, 'was as stunning to look at as the most expensive item in the high class souvenir shop in which she worked'.[21] Barbara was little more than another conquest and she would not be the last pretty woman to turn the young fighter's head.

Simultaneously as Conteh's stock rose the money was starting to flow in. Not all of it was going to Conteh of course as he had a variety of backers who all took more than their fair share of his earnings. What did come to him soon flowed out to his family. Given his humble beginnings it is natural that John would want to do as much as he could to share the fruits of his successes in the ring with his nearest and dearest. Only eighteen months into his professional career Conteh bought a large house for his family in Southport, 'a seaside spot that so many *scousers* fantasised about living in'.[22] He paid £25,000 for it and named it 'Champsville'. Conteh also put money in the bank for his mother and father to draw on for living expenses. At the same time Conteh was doing what he could to get the rest of his family involved in helping to 'manage' his career, while all around him a gaggle of trainers, managers, promoters and sundry hangers-on were competing to get a piece of Conteh Inc.

In 1973 Conteh made a triumphant return to Liverpool, completing an easy three-round victory over a hapless Fred Lewis in the city's iconic boxing venue, *The Stadium*. Reminiscent of his youthful dreams, Conteh received the kind of reception usually reserved for the Beatles or one of the city's triumphant football teams. This was an era that was yet to see the rise of the PR industry around the promotion and protection of sporting celebrities and it is hard to imagine how the former 'Scally' from Kirkby was expected to cope with his new-found stardom. As Jenkinson and Shaw describe it,

> Conteh was now enjoying the spotlight ... However, Lenny Martin had faded from his life and his management affairs were more and more being directed by his family. This was to have serious consequences later, but for now he had his eyes firmly set on a world title challenge.[23]

At the time the undisputed light heavyweight Wold Champion was the legendary American George Foster and Conteh's backers had tried their utmost to match the two. First Foster had to overcome the Argentinian challenger, George Ahumanda, which he proved incapable of. Watched by Conteh their fight in Albuquerque finished in a draw. Foster retained the WBC crown but because he failed to agree a date for a defence against Conteh, the number one contender, he was stripped of the title. Instead the Liverpudlian faced Ahumada in London on 1 October 1974, not even three years after he had thrown his first professional punch. As this extract from Boxing News illustrates, there was no doubt amongst the boxing *cognoscenti* that Conteh had come of age:

> Britain has a great world champion in Liverpool's 23 year old John Conteh, who gave a memorable boxing display to outpoint Argentine tough guy, George Ahumada over 15 memorable rounds at a packed Empire Pool, Wembley ... It was probably British boxing's greatest night since Randolph Turpin whipped Sugar Ray Robinson at Earls Court in July 1951 to win the world middle weight title. Conteh gave one of the best all round displays of fighting seen from a British boxer in the last 20 years.[24]

This should have been the beginning of a long and distinguished career at the top of his profession for the young fighter in peak physical condition. Instead, barely five years later, and after only twelve more professional fights, the 28-year-old Conteh left the ring for the last time a beaten and broken man. He saw it coming, saying, 'even at the height of the victory celebrations I shuddered as I felt the devil settle on my shoulders. Visions of the gutter accompanied the popping of the champagne corks ...'[25] While many of the problems which were to contribute to Conteh's downfall happened in the ring, most of the damage was done outside of it.

There is no evidence that Conteh ever read Karl Marx but he did seem to have a visceral grasp of one of Marxism's central tenets. From the beginning of his boxing career Conteh understood what most professional athletes never quite get: that without his labour the commercial enterprise that swirled around him amounted to nothing. In the aftermath of the Ahumada contest Conteh's management team – trainer George Francis, match-maker Micky Duff and promoter Harry Levene – lined up a series of fights which, in their view, would give the young champion more experience while at the same time boost all of their bank accounts. Conteh had other ideas both about who he should fight and how much his cut of the purse should be. 'Rightly or wrongly, my working class instincts told me that I was being exploited. I felt the top men in boxing were in the meat business and I was the meat in the middle of the sandwich.'[26]

Conteh sacked George Francis and refused to have any further dealings with Duff and Levene. Inside the ring Conteh was more than a match for anyone but outside of it the boxing establishment ran rings around him. Duff appealed to the BBBC (British Boxing Board of Control) who ruled in his favour, effectively barring Conteh from taking part in any promotions under their jurisdiction. In turn Conteh brought in a team of lawyers who, after a long series of legal battles managed to get the BBBC's decision overturned, but not before running up a crippling bill for the young champion. Adding insult to injury, Duff further appealed to the WBC (World Boxing Council) who ordered Conteh to pay him 35,000 dollars compensation. Conteh's stellar career had hardly begun and he found himself isolated and broke.

Conteh was determined to manage his own affairs. Things began quite promisingly when, aided and abetted by Don King, he was able to set up a £50,000 non-title bout with Willie Taylor, a tough brawler from Scranton, Pennsylvania. Things were going smoothly until the middle of the seventh round when Conteh connected a hard right with the top of Taylor's skull only to feel a sharp pain shoot up the length of his arm. Conteh managed to hang on and win the fight on points before being rushed to hospital to have his worse fears confirmed: he had broken his hand. While Conteh did not realise it at the time it would be this injury as much anything else which would eventually force him out of the ring.

Probably the most positive thing to happen to Conteh in his private life was a chance meeting at a promotional event in Earls Court with Veronica West who would become Conteh's wife and mother to his two children, James and Joanna. Despite a series of passing sexual indiscretions and a few more serious affairs – most notably with Stefanie, the daughter of Jake Lamotta – and Conteh's increasing dependence on alcohol and drugs, for the most part, Veronica stuck with him, over time proving herself to be Conteh's most lasting and stabilising influence. The same could not be said of most of Conteh's blood relatives. He bought a flat in Highgate, North London and from time to time, between spells in prison, one or more of his brothers would come to stay, ostensibly to help Conteh manage his affairs. Out of the spotlight, Conteh was just another lonely young northerner in London and he welcomed being surrounded by his siblings who in turn relished the opportunity to help John spend his money, experiencing the thrills and spills of the big city.

Conteh's appetites had been shaped by his days working on building sites in Liverpool where he had learned to work hard and play hard in equal measure. Then there had been a built-in discipline to this work/play balance: your disposable income – 'ale money' – was limited by and dependent upon working eight hours a day five or six days a week. Professional boxing had no such limits other than those either imposed by disciplinarian trainers and managers or in place through the sheer will power of the fighters themselves. Conteh had got rid of the former and displayed little appetite for the latter and as the 1970s progressed he became more familiar with the bright lights and fizz of the London jet set than the disciplined rhythms of the boxing gymnasium. Rather than protecting him from this, his brothers were leading the way. While he could not see it at the time, later, comparing himself with George Best, Conteh would come to understand how mistaken he had been to allow this state of affairs to continue:

> As I see it now the dilemma for fellows like George Best and me was that our families, friends and admirers could be our worst enemies. It was perfectly natural for those who loved us to want to bask in the reflected glory but the demands of being a celebrity meant being in the right places with the right people. Now, that might have been alright for show business personalities but for sportsmen, the right people were definitely the wrong people. The right people in the celebrity stakes are the ones who encourage you to take a drink, pull a bird, put yourself about in general. The right person from an athlete's point of view should be the trainer who wants to half kill you with fitness and pure thoughts and put you in bed like your mother did when you were a kid. Is it any wonder then that some of us manage to make such a terrible mess of our lives?[27]

And a mess Conteh's life was becoming. Up to and including his world title victory, in the first three years of his professional career Conteh had fought twenty-seven times, whereas in the final six years of his career he had eleven bouts only. This paucity of appearances was largely due to a combination of his broken hand and his bruising and losing battle with the British boxing establishment. Nevertheless there were some big paydays among the relatively few fights that he did manage to take on, including three successful defences of his WBC light heavyweight title against Lonnie Bennett, Avalro Lopez and Len Hutchins.

The downward tipping point in Conteh's career came when he refused to fight the WBC's mandatory light-heavy weight challenger, Miguel Cuello, and as a consequence was stripped of his title. Conteh wanted to fight Cuello on home soil, but the BBBC, who had bitter memories of their previous dealings with the Liverpudlian, refused to sanction the proposed live TV coverage. Without the fees from television a domestic contest was out of the question. The alternative offered was to take the fight to Monte Carlo, but stubborn until the end and still stewing over the BBBC's intervention, Conteh refused to fight anywhere other than in the UK, a decision that would cost him both his title and approximately half a million dollars. Instead Conteh stayed in his Highgate flat with his brothers Michael, Peter and Robert who were more than happy to help John drown his sorrows on the London pub and night club circuit.

Meanwhile the interminable legal wrangling among Conteh and a string of promoters and boxing organisations over who he should fight next, where and for how much, kept him away from a chance to win back his title and with it his reputation. When that chance eventually did come Conteh failed yet again to fulfil his potential. It was against the incumbent Yugoslavian champion, Mate Parlov in Belgrade in June 1978. Conteh claims he had been cheated out of his title through a combination of Parlov's cornermen using illegal substances to stem the bleeding from their man's cut eyebrows and biased judging. Nonetheless, lose he did in the aftermath of which he set out to drown his sorrows by throwing one of the biggest parties the Yugoslavian capital had seen in many a year. By this time, Conteh's father had returned to Sierra Leone, but apart from him every other member of the Conteh clan was in tow along with hundreds of fans from London and Liverpool. When the defeated champion came to check out of his hotel several days later he discovered that his bill was almost as big as his share of his losing battle with Parlov!

Conteh did manage to hang on to enough of his winnings to buy for £75,000 cash a large detached house in Bushey, Hertfordshire where he moved with Veronica who was pregnant with the couple's second child. Apart from his spell in Approved School, Conteh had never lived outside of the city and he found it very difficult to settle in this semi-rural idyll. He began to spend less time at home and more and more time in late-night drinking sessions in the West End where he was a regular in some of Soho's trendiest night spots. Conteh was finding it difficult to live without the euphoria that had come with his early career successes in the ring and in addition to lager and champagne, cocaine was added to his menu of mind-altering substances. Bouts of drinking and drug taking were interspersed with bit-part advertising appearances and a handful of non-title defences against has-beens, never-has-beens and never-will-bes. Even against such lesser opponents it was obvious that Conteh's lifestyle was having a debilitating affect on the ex-champion's fitness and form which was further undermined when he re-injured his fragile right hand after smashing his Rolls Royce in the West End in the early hours of one post-binge morning.

Conteh was to have two further and final shots at recovering his title, both against Mathew Saad Muhammad and both in the poor man's Las Vegas, Atlantic City. The first was an even and bruising contest with Conteh outboxing the champion who in turn bombarded the challenger with vicious right-hand blows, knocking him to the canvas twice in the final telling round. Conteh lost on points, but, with echoes of the Parlov encounter, after the fight it was proven that Muhammed's cornermen had used illegal substances to stem the bleeding from their man's badly cut eyebrows and the WBC had no choice but to order a rematch. It was in this fight that it became clear to one and all that Conteh's shenanigans outside of the ring had ruined his prospects in it for ever. Saad Muhammed was a Muslim who in the time that separated the two fights had kept to his strict alcohol-free diet and fitness regime. Conteh, on the other hand had, as usual, been living it up in the London club scene. He saw his own demise coming, 'I was a psychological wreck. I wasn't exactly in mint condition either. There was a time lapse of seven months between the two fights, but it felt like seven years. I was physically afraid this time. Obviously, I realised that I had ruined my body and dreaded that I would be knocked out for the first time in my life'; and so it came to pass as Muhammed smashed Conteh to the canvas no fewer than five times in the fourth round.[28] Literally and metaphorically, Conteh was out for the count.

Conteh was to fight one more time, appropriately back where it all began in Liverpool, against the relatively unknown James Dixon who was no match for Conteh, even in his debilitated condition. But by now Conteh's private life was completely out of control and he continued his downward spiral of depression and alcohol and drug abuse. He was in grave danger of following in the footsteps of another British world champion, Freddie Mills, who, unable to cope with life off the pinnacle, shot himself in his car outside the back of a London night club. Fortunately, Conteh still had Veronica and his wife and some of her husband's few remaining friends, persuaded him to check into a rehabilitation clinic in Chelsea where he was to spend five weeks drying out and undertaking addiction therapy. While the rehabilitation seemed to work, Conteh never did fight again. While in recovery it was discovered that he had a slight imperfection at the base of his skull and his boxing licence was withdrawn on medical grounds.

It is probably just as well. As with so many heroes of the ring, past and present, just as boxing had made Conteh so too it threatened to devour him completely, just as it had destroyed other former greats like Joe Louis, Leon Spinks and Mike Tyson. In the ring Conteh was a maestro, in total control within the boundaries of the canvas where he performed his artistry. Outside of it he was just another cocky, mixed-race kid from Liverpool, with too much money and not enough savvy, who lost control of just about everything. He took on the British boxing establishment like a one-man trade union and lost. In the process he made only a fraction of what his earning potential should have realised, but, aided and abetted by his brothers, it was still enough for him become addicted to a champagne and drug-fuelled social life that eventually was to destroy his capacity to do the one thing he could do well: box.

Boxing is a total institution which demands complete dedication and unyielding physical and emotional sacrifice. There is no room for anything else and if education and life-skills do not come with the fighter into the gymnasium, he is unlikely to pick them up as he pummels the heavy bag. Once he is done with the ring the only thing a boxer can usually become is an ex-boxer or make a comeback in the forlorn hope of redeeming his lost identity – something mercifully denied Conteh by injury – before fading into obscurity and often degradation. Conteh was spared the latter. His extended family must take their share of the blame for Conteh's precipitous decline, but his nearest family, Veronica and his two children, deserve most of the credit for his salvation, sticking by him during the worst of times and giving him the motivation to put his life back together piece by piece. John still lives with them in his Hertfordshire home. While Conteh is mostly remembered fondly and with respect in Liverpool's boxing fraternity, there is a view that he did not make the most of his rare talents. In retirement Conteh did a little TV work and made enough of a living on the after dinner speaking circuit to send both of his children to private schools. Now largely forgotten outside of boxing circles, Conteh is a member of one of England's finest golf clubs and occasionally caddies for his son James who plays off scratch. Maybe the cliché that 'you can take the man out of the ghetto but you can't take the ghetto out of the man' holds true for John Conteh, but the same will not be said of his son whom his father was able to proudly proclaim as 'more Knightsbridge than Kirkby'.[29]

1   Jim Jenkinson and Gary Shaw, *The Mersey Fighters. The Lives and Times of Liverpool's Boxing Heroes* (Preston, 2004).

2   Frank McGhee, *England's Boxing Heroes* (London, 1988), p. 60.

3   Kasia Boddy, *Boxing. A Cultural History* (London, 2008).

4   For a fuller understanding of the emergence of Liverpool as a mercantile and industrial city see John Belchem (ed.) *Liverpool 800* (Liverpool, 2006), especially chapters 1–4.

5   Alfred B. Zack-Williams, 'African diaspora conditioning: the case of Liverpool', *Journal of Black Studies*, 27,4 (1997), p. 529.

6   Stephen Small, 'Racialised relations in Liverpool: a contemporary anomaly', *New Community*, 17, 4 (1991), pp. 511–37. See also John Belchem and Donald M. MacRaild, 'Cosmopolitan Liverpool', in Belchem, *Liverpool 800*, pp. 375–91.

7   Robert Park and Edward Burgess (eds), *The City* (Chicago, 1925).

8   Diane Frost, 'Ambiguous identities: constructing and de-constructing black and white "Scouse" identity in twentieth-century Liverpool', in Neville Kirk (ed.), *Northern Identities* (Aldershot, 2000), pp. 195–217.

9   Zack-Williams, 'African Diaspora', p. 589.

10 John Conteh, *I, Conteh. An Autobiography* (London, 1982), p. 20.

11 Conteh, *I, Conteh*, p. 21.

12 Conteh, *I, Conteh*, p. 24.

13 John Sugden, *Boxing and Society. An International Analysis* (Manchester, 1996).

14 Conteh, *I, Conteh*, p. 24.

15 Conteh, *I, Conteh*, p. 25

16 Geoffrey Beattie, *On the Ropes, Boxing as a Way of Life* (London, 1996).

17 Sugden, *Boxing and Society*.

18 Conteh, *I, Conteh*, p. 36.

19 Conteh, *I, Conteh*, p. 39.

20 Conteh, *I, Conteh*, pp. 39–40.

21 Conteh, *I, Conteh*, p. 55.

22 Conteh, *I, Conteh*, p. 60.

23 Jenkinson and Shaw, *The Mersey Fighters*, p. 54.

24 Conteh, *I, Conteh*, p. 63.

25 Conteh, *I, Conteh*, p. 19.

26 Conteh, *I, Conteh*, p. 67.

27 Conteh, *I, Conteh*, p. 91.
28 Conteh, *I, Conteh*, p. 121.
29 Wayne Veysey, 'New Conteh Fights Back', *Evening Standard*, 7 July 2004.

CHAPTER 12

Wizards of the Wall: Wall of Death Riders as Northern Heroes in the 1930s

Vanessa Toulmin

Introduction

The inception of dirt track racing, or speedway, in the mid to late 1920s and the introduction of the Wall of Death attraction on British fairgrounds in 1928–9 created the persona of a new sporting hero, the daredevil motorcycle rider. Flourishing in the 1930s, the skill and exploits of these riders were first showcased within the sporting arena, via the sport of speedway racing which had grown in popularity throughout the decade. However, what is little realised is that many of these early stars of the speedway arena achieved greater fame and success as the earliest pioneers of the Wall of Death, the symbol of the 'hi-tech' modernist fairground.

Using the names and personas of First World War pilots and the stars of aviation, the former speedway riders borrowed the terminology and often the style and clothing of flying aces and became local celebrities in the regions where they performed, and, in some cases, figures of national and international renown. Moving from the highly commercialised world of professional dirt track riding to the futuristic and speed obsessed fairground environment, these early riders can be seen as a hybrid of the modern sportsman and the fairground circus performer and they slotted easily into the ever increasing celebrity-oriented world of the professional sportsman in the inter-war period. Based on the collections of two early riders that are held in the National Fairground Archive (NFA) at the University of Sheffield, this article will attempt to draw the links between speedway and Wall of Death riders in the late 1920s, early 1930s, and demonstrate how many became local pin-ups and working-class heroes in the north of England. I will also argue that both these forms of attraction, be it the speedway track or the fairground environment, provided an arena where the cult of the celebrity and the excitement of high-speed live performance was a natural

211

environment in which these riders flourished.

In contradistinction to most of the chapters in this collection, this study is concerned not so much with northern identity but with the exploration of a sport, or, in the case of Wall of Death riding, a sport-related activity, that has had little if any serious scholarly attention. However, the fact that it focuses on two northern-born and based riders is a reminder of how strongly rooted these elements of motor sport were within certain parts of the urban, working-class North. More crucially, the riders' biographies show the ease within which, at least in this specific environment that so skilfully blended sport and spectacle, the locally and/or regionally rooted hero could find themselves recast as standard bearers for an international, even placeless, cultural practice. Northern heroes could sometimes be heroes on a much wider canvas.

Spectator and sporting culture in the 1930s

Both sporting and leisure industries enjoyed huge commercial success in the interwar years. The working classes had benefited from changes in working hours, higher wages and also more resources and time to pursue leisure activities. Despite the recession which hit the north of England in particular, cinemas, music halls and spectator sports enjoyed a period of sustained attendance. Two new sports introduced in the 1920s which grew in popularity as a result of this increased interest in leisure and sporting pursuits were greyhound racing and speedway which in Manchester were catered for at the developing tracks at White City, Belle Vue, Audenshaw, Salford and Hardforth.[1] Although association football was the most popular and best attended sport in this period, local fluctuations, dependent on the success of the team, saw certain other sports retain some form of momentary dominance in terms of crowd attendance. For example, the new sport of speedway in Manchester gained from the drop in attendances at Old Trafford in the late 1920s and early 1930s whereas Manchester City in contrast was enjoying a boom period.[2] Prices of admission to boxing, racing, football, rugby, skating and the new sport of speedway showed little variation in entrance prices which were well within the means of working-class spectators. The demand for sport was buoyant and as Hargreaves writes:

> This was a golden age of football and cricket attendance ... new highly commercialised sport appeared in the 1920s, for example greyhound racing, speedway and Tourist Trophy motor cycle racing, which gained in popularity with working class people.[3]

Interest in sport in general and football in particular spread throughout the media with sporting publications enjoying a substantial increase in popularity in the interwar period. New titles servicing pre-existing and newly formed specialist sports came on the market with *Motor Cyclist Review* and *Speedway Gazette* catering for the motor cycle craze. Others centred on the dominant sports of football and cricket; for example, Amalgamated Press's *Football and Sports Favourite,*[4] a 2d weekly combining photographic features with gossip on teams and individual players, was launched in 1920. The newspapers and magazines gave the readers a strong sense of identification with their sporting heroes, as emphasised in the case of Football and Sports Favourite. Other new spectator sports also emerged at this time – in particular those associated with speed and high-risk activities. The 1930s was also the golden age of aviation when records appeared to be broken if not daily, at least weekly or monthly. The 1920s and 1930s saw the imagination of the British and American public captured by the magnificent men and women in their flying machines. Air displays and the cult of Charles Lindberg and his successful flight across the Atlantic in May 1927 created a craze for high-speed activities which were not readily accessible to the millions of spectators, and fans followed their pursuits via newsreel footage and newspapers. Aviators such as Charles Lindberg, Howard Hughes, Wiley Post, Amelia Earhart and Amy Johnson became household names. However, the emergence of speedway during this time also provided the working-class spectator with an accessible route to this high-risk glamour filled world of the daredevil hero. Speedway was a sport populated by local heroes riding a cheap and accessible new mode of transport, the motor bike. For a working-class spectatorship eager to experience first hand this quest for thrills and spills the speedway venues were nearby and affordable.

Speedway riders and the Wall of Death

The introduction of the Wall of Death fairground attraction and speedway racing both occurred in the late 1920s, with speedway as a sport first staged in December 1923 at the Maitland showground in Australia.[6] Interestingly, the dates of the appearance of speedway and the Wall of Death in the United Kingdom are within only a few months of each other.[7] For speedway, the meeting at High Beech in Epping Forest in 1928 appears to be the date agreed on for its introduction to the United Kingdom, with earlier examples disputed by specialists within the area.[8] In the case of the Wall of Death, the first report of this as a fairground attraction is in the *World's Fair* newspaper in 1929, although photographic evidence in the National Fairground Archive at the University of Sheffield Library reveals the presence of the wall at seaside resorts such as Scarborough, Ramsgate and Southend-on-Sea in 1928.[9] Also, the appearance of the Wall of Death at early speedway venues is becoming apparent through ongoing research; for instance, Clem Beckett, one of the greatest of all speedway riders, opened a Wall of Death at the newly formed Owlerton Stadium in Sheffield in 1929.[10] Historical research on the history of the sport in this period is particularly limited. What has been published on the development of speedway is generally based on the history of some of the original or premier clubs.[11] Wall of Death publications are similar, in that the recorded or documented history is mostly limited to individual riders or the production of nostalgic photographic collections. More importantly, other than in the riders' biographies, the links between the two activities are not stressed.[12]

Speedway appears to have started as a fully commercialised sporting activity with little evidence for amateur races in the late 1920s. Of the many new sports launched in this period, only greyhound racing equalled it in terms of spectator following and Jack Williams writes that by the 1930s:

> Crowds at the big events of the speedway calendar compared favourably with those of other sports and total spectator numbers were higher than those for county cricket and possibly either rugby code.[13]

Speedway tracks opened and flourished in major northern (and southern) cities. Two, White City and Belle Vue, opened in Manchester in 1928 and 1929 respectively, and Owlerton in Sheffield opened in 1929. A range of tracks in London were equally successful. Riders were attracted by the large crowds, which helped place them amongst the highest paid sportsmen in the 1930s, with well-known riders being paid appearance money as well as competing for cash prizes. It was not until 1938 that maximum payments were set by the Speedway Council. Speedway riders thus took their place among the new stars of sport and newspapers such as *Motor Cyclist Reviews, Speedway News* and *Speedway Gazette* catering for the fan base of this new, exciting sport.[14] Their popularity grew, and by 1930 the riders received the highest accolade in sporting material culture by appearing on cigarette cards published by Ogden under the series of 'Famous Dirt Track Riders'. Similarly J.A. Pattreioeux Ltd of Manchester produced a set of fifty under the title 'Dirt Track Riders'.[15]

In the early 1930s promoters introduced other attractions to speedway meetings in order to enhance them as a spectacle, with elephant parades, donkey races with well- known riders competing and stars of variety making guest appearances, all adding to the showbusiness element of the sport.[16] This kind of activity was frowned upon by the sporting authorities who were at pains to emphasise the sporting, as opposed to the entertainment, elements of the attraction. The riders competed under race names such as 'Speedy', 'Hurricane', 'Whirlwind', 'Bulldog', 'Cyclone' and so forth, all of which contributed to the atmosphere of thrills and velocity-induced excitement. As well as contracts that promised them a minimum of £10 a meeting, riders received payments for each individual race and a variety of individual and team prizes. So, with the sport flourishing, the fan base increasing, and the individual wages for star riders reputedly higher than those earned by the average First Division footballers, why in the early 1930s did many of the premier northern riders move from the arena of the speedway track to the latest novelty on the fairground, the Wall of Death?

The 1930s fairground and the Wall of Death

The appearance of the Wall of Death on the British fairground in 1928–9 came at an important time, as it marked the transition from steam-driven nineteenth-century attractions to the latest in white knuckle electric marvels. The clamour for new and modern sensations saw the advent of fast and exciting rides with many of the old roundabouts being superseded by the whip, the caterpillar rides and, of course, the Wall of Death. Relics of the bygone steam age were replaced by chair-o-planes from Germany and (in 1928) the dodgems; this was the age of electricity where rides were more streamlined, the artwork more deco and speed the attraction. The 1930s fairground was a place of speed and modernity:

> There is a craze for speed and the faster a machine can go, and the more sinking sensations it can produce in the pit of the stomach, the greater its popularity.[17]

The old sedate pace set by galloping horses and switchback roundabouts was no longer in vogue. The epitome of the new fast thrill ride of the 1930s was the moonrocket, a lighter, faster and electrically driven reflection of a modern age. The clean lines of modernity, reflecting a more dynamic streamlined effect, superseded the outdated displays of ornate carved work and grotesque figures.[18] Some of the most popular rides make their appearance on the fairgrounds for the first time in this period, including the Noah's Ark, the waltzer and, as we have seen, the Wall of Death. The Globe of Death, followed by the Wall of Death, arrived in the late 1920s and the impact of the daredevil riders who rode them was immediate. The 'death riders', as they became known, rode inside a wire mesh sphere (the Globe) or horizontally round a drum- or barrel-shaped wooden cylinder, 20 to 36 feet in diameter (the Wall). They were the new stars of the fairground shows, borrowing names from the Royal Air Force, wearing flying jackets and advertising themselves as the 'Wizards on the Wall'.

By the end of 1929 the wall was firmly established as a major entertainment attraction. Billy Butlin opened one of the earliest in Skegness in 1928–9 and other seaside resorts followed suit. Although Southend is seen by fairground historians as the site of the first documented report of the wall, with Tornado Smith and his partner, Margaret Dare, the exponents of this new attraction in June 1929, photographic evidence from other resorts and eye witness accounts show that walls existed in a wide variety of locations before this date.[19] What is clear is that by the end of 1929, major American companies were investing in the attraction and advertising for the best motorcycle riders in the country. The quest for speed and excitement on the early speedway tracks was mirrored by the technological innovations on the 1930s fairground and attracted some of the leading speedway riders to the new attraction of the Wall of Death. It was the money, travel and the possibility of trying one's skill in a new context that attracted two such pioneers of the track, William 'Billy' Bellhouse and Horace 'Skid' Skinner.

Wizards on the Wall

Billy Bellhouse and Skid Skinner were both associated with the Sheffield speedway track at Owlerton and appeared there in the 1929 season. Their link to Sheffield started with Clem Beckett, one of the three investors in the Owlerton stadium. Beckett, an Oldham-born racer, was both a pioneer rider on the speedway and one of the earliest proprietors of the wall in the United Kingdom. While both Bellhouse and Skinner had achieved local prominence on the speedway circuit, Billy was a lesser known figure than his younger stable-mate. Skid was a nationally respected rider and although he had travelled to Denmark with Beckett in 1930 and performed on the wall in front of the King and Queen of Sweden, he had returned and continued his speedway career. Billy in contrast was more a jobbing rider and one whose earnings never achieved the level of his more famous contemporaries.

Cyclone Billy

'Cyclone Billy' was the professional name of William Bellhouse, a Sheffield-born bike mechanic, who performed in the 1930s in the early days of both speedway and the Wall of Death. Apart from the archival material in the National Fairground Archive, very little is known about his career at Owlerton stadium, the major venue for early speedway racing in Sheffield. However, according to his family and material in the Bellhouse Collection, Billy was racing certainly by late 1928. Prior to his entry into speedway, he was a member of the Millhouses Motor Cycle Club and in 1927, joined the South Yorkshire Sports Stadium Speedway Racing Club. His status as a rider is corroborated by his membership card for the Northern Association of Track Riders (1929). In 1929 he appeared at the newly opened Owlerton stadium founded by the Provincial Dirt Tracks Ltd, a company which had been formed in March 1929, by Spencer 'Smoky' Stratton, Clem Beckett and Jimmy Hindle.[20] The first meeting attracted around 15,000 spectators and by the start of the 1929–30 season, with meetings still attracting crowds of up to 15,000, Billy Bellhouse had earned a certain notoriety in his local city as the following extract from a Sheffield newspaper for 1930 reveals:

> Billy Bellhouse was a Sheffield boy
> Who once threw cinders far
> Officials rubbed their hands with glee
> And thought 'Another Star'.[21]

However, after only two seasons at the Owlerton stadium, Billy left the speedway track and answered an advert which appeared in the Sheffield newspapers for an American Amusement Company, the 'Wizards on the Wall'.

Being experienced with most aspects of the motorbike from his days in Sheffield and an earlier career as a trick cyclist, the appeal of the new attraction was one that Billy could not resist, and in 1930 he sailed for Europe as part of the Wizards troupe.[22] For five years Billy and his fellow speedway rider Danny Carter travelled throughout the United Kingdom, South Africa and Europe, appearing as the star attractions at venues such as the Lunar Park in Bucharest in 1933, Kelvin Hall in Glasgow in 1931, Crystal Palace in London and the Cirque D'eu in Paris.[13] Between 1930 and 1935 Billy Bellhouse and the Wizards on the Wall opened in Romania, Spain, Holland, Algeria and Poland.[14] The company arranged the tour, handled the publicity, booked the venues and provided the American-style pilot costumes. Stage names were taken from First World War air aces and fake military titles incorporated into the publicity strengthened the link, with Billy becoming 'Lieutenant Bellhouse'. The arrival of this new attraction caused a sensation wherever they performed and new tricks were constantly incorporated into the act. The riders performed potentially neck breaking feats of daring and skill with Billy's trademark being his ability to drop down from the top of the wall to the bottom in less than a second. The trade name for this stunt was 'dipping and diving' and it became a main feature of subsequent Wall of Death performances. Other aspects of Billy's display included sitting on the handlebars and steering the bike with his legs, standing on the footboards, riding with no hands on the handlebars and, finally, ending the show sitting down on the footboard as the bike continued 'dipping and diving' up and down the wall. Jim Bellhouse recalls the gravity defying feats performed by his father:

> He used to tell me, he used to go up the wall and shoot back down again and throw his back end up. There used to be a safety wire round the top and the back wheel used to go up and hit the safety wire and then they'd dive down to the bottom of the wall again, you know, and up the other side.[25]

The acrobatic tricks performed by the Wizards would become the staple show for the generation of riders who succeeded Billy Bellhouse and his colleagues. Well-known stunts included being chased by a lioness round the wall, riding backwards, demonstrations of Go-Karting and the famous 'hell riders race', in which two or three riders would race around the wall at the same time. By 1933, such was his popularity that according to his son, his wage for a performance was 60 per cent of the takings and also a share of the tips that would be thrown into the ring during the show. The average takings for Billy's European tours are more difficult to estimate as they are recorded in the local currency. However, when one starts to compare and analyse the scribbled notes found in the back of Billy's diaries for both his Wall of Death takings and his speedway earnings, an interesting picture emerges.

Speedway takings 1929 season

18-5-1929   £1, 10s
20-5-1929   10s
19-6-1929   £3, 10s
20-6-1929   £3, 10s
24-7-1929   £6, 10s
12-8-1929   £1, 10s
19-8-1929   £2,10s
21-8-1929   £2, 10s

These are random dates taken from the diary and a fuller record can be found for each meeting but the details are revealing. In contrast to the highly advertised prize monies and wages publicised in the sporting press at the time, the average wage for speedway riders as opposed to the star attractions was not as lucrative as contemporary accounts would have us believe. The Wall of Death takings between 1930 and 1935 are, by contrast, quite astonishing. The full financial rewards are difficult to estimate for, despite the detailed listing of the wages and tips he earned on the wall, the records are recorded in the currency of the country where Billy was working. However, in the 1932 season when the Wall travelled to Poland, underneath the weekly columns of zlotys appear to be currency conversion records which reveal that he was earning around £75 a week on the wall with an additional £10 a week in tips. Before a full analysis can be attempted of course, the currency rates for each location must be demonstrated but just the simple notes in the takings books alone show a considerable boost in earnings for Billy when he exchanged the dirt track for the Wall of Death. A further factor for the attraction of the Wall over the speedway track is illustrated by the range of places and countries that Billy visited during his five years. In addition the Wall of Death riders were mobbed and greeted by thousands of fans wherever they went with female admirers (with the evidence of Billy's little black address book) being another attraction. The Bellhouse archive contains numerous newspaper clippings and reviews. So popular was the show in Poland that the local Poznan newspaper published a report in July 1932, on the English Wizards and their 'so called Wall of Death'.

'About this wall, fantastic stories are told and with great curiosity we go to see personally how much truth there is in the stories told.

When the journalist arrived at the venue he found a packed audience seated around the viewing platform at the top of the wall eagerly awaiting the start of the show:

The announcer enlightens the audience and explains that Lieutenant Billy Bellhouse will accomplish a break neck ride on the wall, performing acrobatics on his twin cylinder Indian motor cycle

The report continued to describe the action within the wall:

> Before we are able to grasp the situation, Lieutenant Billy strode across to his motorcycle, added some gas and in a moment was at the top of this vertical drum, riding around the top in circles and missing us only by inches. But that was not all, he rode and shot to the floor of the drum in less than a fraction of a second, was up again, and then up and down. Sometimes it seemed he would fly over the top cable. But always at the last moment he would dip over with a break neck swerve to the bottom of the wall.[26]

If economic factors and the quest for travel were the main reasons why Billy Bellhouse left the speedway circuit never to return, the decision by his fellow rider and contemporary in the Northern Riders Association, Skid Skinner to leave the world of speedway is not so clear.

Skid Skinner

In comparison with Bellhouse, more is known about the career of Horace 'Skid' Skinner and his time on the northern speedway circuit in the early 1930s. Born in Lincolnshire in 1910, his entry into speedway was through his interest in and passion for motorcycles and he soon became a regular on the White City track in Manchester, which opened in June 1928, and at Owlerton. White City was situated between Old Trafford football club and cricket grounds, and a quarter mile cinder track, with a capacity of 40,000 under cover, was constructed for the opening, with race meetings organised by the newly formed British Dirt Track Racing Association. The White City organisers soon realised that star performers increased the crowds and by the end of the 1928 season, attendances of between thirty and forty thousand became the norm, outstripping average attendance at the nearby football and cricket stadiums.[27] Famous riders included Arthur Franklyn, the local favourite, Clem Beckett (who would later die in the Spanish Civil War in 1937) and the young 20-year-old racer Horace 'Skid' Skinner.[28] In the two years that he competed at the White City track, Skid won the *Manchester Evening News* Cup, the track's 'Golden Helmet', the Corinthian Trophy and the Golden Sash and, by the end of 1928, he was one of the chief attractions at the track. His achievements were recognised by inclusion in J.A. Pattreioeux Ltd's set of cigarette cards, published in 1930.

In the scrapbooks compiled by his wife and fellow rider Alma Skinner, the career of Skid Skinner starts to emerge. Heavily featured in both the speedway and the local press in Manchester and Sheffield, the daredevil exploits of this young star of the track are covered in detail. By 1930, Skid's manager Francis L. Neep was producing a flyer listing his rider's achievements, including winning the Golden Helmet, Golden Gauntlet, Golden Sash, Golden Armlet and the Roy Bridgens Cup, all at the White City track. Victories at Liverpool and Sheffield are also listed, among them the

Yorkshire championship, alongside his international victories at Marseilles in France in 1933. Skid's portrait was often used to illustrate the up and coming stars of the track with one undated newspaper article describing him as a famous dirt track rider and another describing him as Sheffield's own speedway idol. He was also often featured in both the Sheffield and Manchester papers, with one claiming that there was 'no one more popular at White City or Owlerton' and noting that his 'daring riding can always be relied upon to provide thrills in plenty'. Many areas claimed him as a local hero, with Sheffield and Rotherham newspapers referring to him in despatches as the local rider but White City speedway never lost an opportunity to advertise him as their rider. This association between the rider and the local track is also seen in other advertisements and reports that appear in both the local press and the specialist papers at the time. Skid is referred to as the 'White City hero', the 'local rider', the 'Sheffield based star' and 'resident of Rotherham' in an attempt to localise his presence to the audience.[29] However, his prowess as a rider was not just local or restricted to the north of England.[30] Skid's pin-up and even national status was confirmed not just by his inclusion in the cigarette card series but also by his modelling contract for Burtons. Photographs from the consequent advertising campaign capture him wearing various casual sweaters and a smart raincoat.

The choice of a daredevil racing hero to be featured wearing Burton's clothes is interesting. Stephen Jones, writing on the relationship between the growth in sports goods manufacture and its relationship with spectator sports, comments that, in the pre-war years, spectators of sports were also keen participants: 'The growing consumer market in sports goods presumably had a symbiotic relationship with spectator sport.'[31] The relationship between leisure wear and sporting activities became more apparent during the 1930s as specialist outlets for sports grew rapidly during this time. For example, by 1929, Manchester had both a sports manufacturing sector and a retail industry that catered for a number of sports including football, cricket, boxing, golf and tennis. Whether the aim was to dress in clothing as worn by their sporting heroes or to purchase attire that enabled them to pursue sporting activities, the link between the sports spectator and the growing consumer industry became more apparent. The decision by Burtons to use Skid Skinner as a model in their catalogues and publicity in the early 1930s is interesting as it shows a level of recognition both in the expectations of the company, and also in the consumer, for this early speedway pioneer and Wall of Death rider. In addition, the manner in which Skid is dressed reflects an aping of dress normally associated with the English upper classes. In the same way that 'casuals' in modern football circles dress in yachting and sailing regalia (with labels such as Shark and Paul and Henry Lloyd favoured), the style of dress presented by the motor cyclists was similarly imitative. Alma Skinner, née Morley, wife of Skid Skinner and, as noted, a Wall of Death rider in her own right, revealed when interviewed that it was not only her riding name of 'Daredevil Alma Johnson' that was taken from

Amy Johnston. Alma continued the association by making her own clothes modelled on the latest styles as presented by the female aviators and the sporting attire favoured by the upper classes. The fact that Burton's used Skid Skinner in both their catalogues and poster campaigns does seem to imply a connection between the dress of the sportsman and the desire of the fans to dress like, or be associated with, him. Here we see the steady emergence of sport celebrity in the north of England, with a local speed hero photographed as a tailor's dummy and his image directed at a growing audience of working class admirer-consumers.

Skid appears to have left the speedway track for good by the mid-1930s although further research is needed in order to present a more detailed picture of his activities at the time. As Alma's scrapbook is largely undated, with only some inscriptions to act as a guide to dates, the cuttings for his speedway career seem to tail off by 1933. Throughout the mid-1930s Skid appears to have spent more time pursuing his career on the Wall of Death. The scrapbooks reveal a life of excitement and travel. The Wall of Death was a special attraction for the King and Queen of Sweden and Skid and his colleagues travelled throughout Germany, Holland and Europe. He was also the resident rider on many walls in Yorkshire. The showmen would use Skid's name extensively to advertise the show with flyers featuring his achievements; the headline 'Famous Skid Skinner one time idol of your local speedway', for example, formed part of the bills or posters appearing in Tinsley and Bolton-on-Dearne in the late 1930s.[32] By 1934, certainly the wall was his primary means of employment with Skid claiming that it was the difficulties and constant challenge of riding that maintained his interest. No detailed record of Skid's takings appear in the Alma Johnson scrapbooks but further research through the correspondence and business material in the collection could lead to a picture similar to that presented in the Bellhouse material. Skid as a speedway rider would have been one of the premier earners and it is probable that factors alongside or other than money would have been a factor for his crossover to the wall in this period

Conclusion

This brief overview of the relationship between the Wall of Death and speedway in the late 1920s, early 1930s is an attempt to begin examining both the impact of these riders as sporting heroes and their relationship to spectator culture at the time. The early riders welcomed the opportunity to test their skills either on the speedway track or on the Wall of Death. The element of danger and the risks involved for the riders were certainly factors in its popularity among the audience. Alma's scrapbooks are littered with obituaries for both speedway and Wall of Death riders and also with detailed descriptions of their near death defying exploits. When interviewed in 2005, she emphasised the freedom and excitement of life on the wall. 'It was the happiest time of my life, we had money, travel and crowds greeting us wherever we appeared.'[33]

The ability to travel, the independence from organisational bodies that were becoming more apparent in speedway and also the adulation and crowds the shows attracted, demonstrate how well the wall incorporated fan elements from show-business and popular entertainment. The skill level required in riding the wall is another factor that should be taken into account. When appearing in 1929 at the opening of the Owlerton stadium, the resident star Clem Beckett emphasises the risk elements of the sport and the wall:

> Beckett admits that riding around the wall is a much more dangerous and thrilling affair than even his hair-raising broadsiding on the cinders.[34]

Both Skid Skinner and Billy Bellhouse left the Wall of Death prior to the start of the Second World War. In the case of Billy Bellhouse, it was an accident on the more dangerous Globe of Death that ultimately ended his career and he retired to run a series of chip shops in Sheffield. As a result of the injuries sustained in his fall from the Globe, Cyclone Billy performed his last show in 1935. Although he attempted to seek compensation for his injuries, the contract signed by Billy in 1933 stipulated:

> That the director is not held responsible for any accident that may happen to his employees or for any sickness that the employees may suffer from during or resulting from their employee by the director.[35]

With Skid it was the outbreak of war that curtailed his career on the wall and a tragic hunting accident, in which he accidentally shot himself, resulted in his death in 1944.[36]

These daredevil riders either on the wall or on the dirt track can be seen as the working-class heroes in the age of speed. In addition to Bellhouse and Skinner, Tornado Smith, resident rider at Southend and one of the early pioneers of the wall, was a Suffolk hero and often featured in both local and national papers. One local Bloxford resident when interviewed recalled that Tornado was a hero to the young people:

> He bought a real sense of excitement to Boxford by his performances on the Wall of Death and he had a lot of admirers, of both sexes.[37]

If the aviators or pilots were the stars of the skies, the motorcyclists were the equivalent on the ground. When examined in this context, the choice of a speedway and Wall of Death rider in Burton's advertising campaign is also significant. Unlike the gentleman cricketers and other sporting heroes of the time who personified all that was good and English, the Wall of Death and speedway riders were by dress and lifestyle, rebellious and daring and embodied a more dangerous appeal to both men and women alike. The hazardous appeal of the motorbike and also the high level of mortality rates of the riders was also part of the attraction. It is no coincidence that the mode of dress and performance echoed the characterisation of the ace pilots from the First World War period and the daring exploits of those who appeared almost weekly to fly across the Atlantic or round the world in pursuit of fame and adventure. Additionally they were more accessible than the largely middle-class or upper-class aviation heroes who required vast sponsorship and funds in order to learn how to be a pilot and, even more crucially, to find the necessary resources to race. The bike in contrast was readily available to working-class men and women. The dress could be copied from magazines and with the Wall of Death, the riders could experience fame, travel and adulation far beyond the scope and dreams of the standard professional athlete be it in football or rugby at that time. These local riders, who through speedway were rooted in the areas where they rode, thus became more transitory figures, linked to a form of attraction that was constantly on the move. However, their identity both through advertisements and reports continued to be as the 'local boy' who through their skill and expertise on the speedway and the wall achieved regional and in the case of Skid, international acclaim.

---

[1] Stephen Jones, 'Working class sport in Manchester between the wars', in Richard Holt (ed.) *Sport and the Working Class in Modern Britain* (Manchester, 1990), pp. 67–83.

[2] Jones, 'Working class sport in Manchester', p. 70.

[3] John Hargreaves, *Sport Power and Culture: A Social and Historical Analysis of Popular Sport in Britain* (Cambridge, 1986), p. 86; see also Stephen G. Jones, *Sport, Politics and the Working Class: Organised Labour and Sport in Interwar Britain* (Manchester, 1988) and Tony Collins, *Rugby League in Twentieth Century Britain: A Social and Cultural History* (London, 2006).

[4] Dave Russell, *Football and the English, A Social History of Association Football in England, 1863– 1995* (Preston, 1997), p. 110.

[5] Ann Cooper, *On the Wing: Jessie Woods and the Flying Air Circuses* (Mount Freedom, New Jersey, 1993).

[6] Jack Williams, '"A wild orgy of speed": responses to Speedway in Britain before the Second World War', *The Sports Historian*, 19, 1 (1999), pp. 1–15.

[7] For history of the Wall of Death see Allan Ford and Nick Corble, *Riding the Wall of Death* (Stroud, 2006); see also Ken Fox, *Step Inside Now, Step Inside: My Life on the Wall of Death* (privately published by Ken Fox, 2008).

[8] Norman Jacobs, *Speedway in the South–East* (Stroud, 2003); Robert Bamford and J. Jarvis, *Homes of British Speedway* (Stroud, 2001, 2006 ed.); Brian Belton, *Hammerin' Round* (Stroud, 2003).

[9] See the Billy Bellhouse and Johnson/Skinner Collection at the National Fairground Archive at the University of Sheffield Library, http://www.nfa.dept.shef.ac.uk/holdings/index.html. For Bellhouse see NFA 0038 and for Johnson/Skinner see NFA 0046. All individual items will be listed with full archival references.

10   Undated newspaper article from Sheffield papers in the Alma Johnson scrapbooks, volumes 1–5, copies of which are held by the National Fairground Archive. The article states that very soon after the opening of the track a new attraction was found with Skid Skinner and Clem Beckett taking time on the Wall of Death that Clem had purchased soon after the opening in 1929.

11   See for example Trevor James and Barry Stephenson, *Speedway in Manchester, 1927–1945* (Stroud, 2003), Bamford and Jarvis, Homes and Belton, *Hammering Round*.

12   For riders' biographies see Peter Haining, *Tornado Smith, British Pioneer or the Wall of Death: The Story of Boxford's Famous Motorcycle Stuntsman* (Boxford: Boxford Community Council, 1998).

13   Jack Williams, 'A wild orgy', p. 2.

14   Ibid., pp. 5–6.

15   J.A. Pattreioeux Ltd of Manchester produced a set of fifty cards in 1929 and a further set of fifty-four in 1930. The 1929 set can be viewed on New York Public Library Digital Gallery on http://digitalgallery.nypl.org/nypldigital/ for both sets as can the later Ogden series.

16   Jack Williams, 'A wild orgy', p. 10.

17   *The Stalybridge Herald*, 29 July 1933.

18   Geoff Weedon and Richard Ward, *Fairground Art* (London, 1981) and Vanessa Toulmin, Pleasurelands (Hastings, 2004).

19   Neil Calladine, 'History of the Wall of Death, parts 1 and 2', in *Fairground Mercury*, 25, (Fairground Association of Great Britain, 2002), no. 2, pp. 8–13 and no. 3, pp. 7–10.

20   Bamford and Jarvis, *Homes of British Speedway*.

21   Undated cartoon for Billy Bellhouse, from the Billy Bellhouse Collection, 1930, NFA 178Z 15.7.

22   NFA 178Z15.32, business card for Bill Bellhouse, 'trick and fancy motorcyclist'.

23   See Billy Bellhouse NFA 178Z15.1–42 for ephemeral items including train tickets, visa applications, hotel brochures and other business related materials for travels between 1931and 1935.

24   See 178T5.7 Sciana Smierci, Wall of Death advertising bill for Billy Bellhouse, Poznan, Poland.

25   Jim Bellhouse interviewed by Vanessa Toulmin, January 1997 in his house in Sheffield.

26   Billy Bellhouse Collection NFA 178T5.1–5 for details of Poznan handbills and newspaper cuttings with translation.

27   For more details of White City and the early riders see James and Stephenson, *Speedway in Manchester*.

28   Ibid., pp. 176–192.

29   See Alma Skinner's scrapbooks for numerous articles, press cuttings and references for Skid's appearance and reports in the Manchester, Sheffield and Rotherham newspapers.

30   Various undated newspaper cuttings from the Alma Skinner scrapbooks, copies of which are held by the National Fairground Archive, University of Sheffield Library.

31   Jones, 'Working class sport in Manchester', p. 68.

32 Handbill for Skid Skinner, Alma Johnson, appearing 27–30 August, Tinsley Fairground, 1937, National Fairground Archive, Alma Johnson's scrapbooks, for Bolton-On-Dearne see *Top of the Bill: Ephemeral Collections in the National Fairground Archive*, an exhibition catalogue published in 2007, University of Sheffield, p. 5.

33 Alma Skinner, interviewed in her home in Rotherham by Vanessa Toulmin, 24 July 2005.

34 Taken from 'New Motor Cycle Sensation for Sheffield', undated Sheffield article in Alma Johnson scrapbook from 1929, NFA Alma Johnson Scrapbooks.

35 Contract for Billy Bellhouse, NFA 178F8, eight letters to Billy Bellhouse relating to business, legal and performing matters, c.1930–1950.

36 For details see obituaries in Alma Skinner scrapbooks for 1944.

37 Haining, *Tornado Smith*, p. 8.